Third Workshop on Economics and Natural Language Processing (ECONLP 2021)

Punta Cana, Dominican Republic and Online
11 November 2021

ISBN: 978-1-7138-9180-2

Printed from e-media with permission by:

Curran Associates, Inc.
57 Morehouse Lane
Red Hook, NY 12571

CURRAN ASSOCIATES INC. proceedings.com

Some format issues inherent in the e-media version may also appear in this print version.

Printed with permission by Curran Associates, Inc. (2024)

For permission requests, please contact the Association for Computational Linguistics at the address below.

Association for Computational Linguistics
209 N. Eighth Street
Stroudsburg, Pennsylvania 18360

Phone: 1-570-476-8006
Fax: 1-570-476-0860

acl@aclweb.org

Additional copies of this publication are available from:

Curran Associates, Inc.
57 Morehouse Lane
Red Hook, NY 12571 USA
Phone: 845-758-0400
Fax: 845-758-2633
Email: curran@proceedings.com
Web: www.proceedings.com

EMNLP 2021

ECONLP — Economics and Natural Language Processing

Proceedings of the Third Workshop on Economics and Natural Language Processing (ECONLP 2021)

November 11, 2021
Punta Cana, Dominican Republic and Online

Introduction

Welcome to ECONLP 2021! After launching the first Workshop on Economics and Natural Language Processing (ECONLP) at ACL 2018 in Melbourne, Australia and running the second one at EMNLP-IJCNLP 2019 in Hong Kong, China, the third ECONLP workshop is held at EMNLP 2021 in a hybrid manner, physically in Punta Cana, Dominican Republic, and virtually as an online event.

This workshop reflects the increasing relevance of natural language processing (NLP) for regional, national and international economy, both in terms of already operational language technology products and systems, as well as newly emerging methodologies and techniques as a response to new requirements at the disciplinary intersection of economics and NLP. The focus of the workshop is on the many ways how NLP supports and influences business relations and procedures, economic transactions, and the roles of human and computational actors involved in commercial activities (such as e-commerce).

The main topics ECONLP addresses include (definitely not excluding other areas of relevance for the broad workshop theme):

- NLP-based (stock) *market analytics*, e.g., prediction of economic performance indicators (trend prediction, performance forecasting, etc.), by analyzing verbal statements of enterprises, businesses, companies, and associated institutional, legal or administrative actors
- NLP-based *product analytics*, e.g., based on social and traditional mass media by monitoring, summarizing reviews, classifying and mining comments or complaint messages and other (non-) verbal types of customer reactions to products or services
- NLP-based *customer analytics*, e.g., client profiling, tracking product/company preferences, screening customer reviews or complaints, identifying high-influentials (peers) in economy-related communication networks
- NLP-based *organization/enterprise analytics*, e.g., tracing and pro-actively altering social images of organizational actors, risk prediction, fraud analysis, predictive analysis of annual business, sustainability and auditing reports
- NLP-based *analysis of macro-economic phenomena* in which national economies and the (inter)national banking system (IMF, Fed, PBoC, ECB) play an influential role
- Analysis of *market sentiments and emotions* as evident from consumers' and enterprises' verbal behavior traces and their communication strategies about products, services or market performance
- *Competitive intelligence* services based on NLP tooling
- Relationships and interactions between *quantitative (structured) economic data* (e.g., those available from sales databases and associated time series data, log data) and *qualitative (unstructured verbal) economic data* (press releases, newswire streams, social media contents, etc.)
- *Organizational information management* based on the content-based assembling, packaging and archiving of verbal communication streams in organizations/enterprises (emails, meeting minutes, business letters, internal reporting, etc.)
- *Credibility and trust models* for business agents involved in the economic process (e.g., as traders, sellers, advertisers) extracted from text/opinion mining their communication behavior (including historic or legacy data)

- *Deception or fake information recognition* related to economic objects (such as products, advertisements, etc.) or economic actors (such as industries, companies, etc.), including opinion spam targeting or emanating from economic actors and processes

- Verbally fluent *software agents* (chat bots for counseling, sales and marketing) as reliable actors in economic processes serving business interests, e.g., embodying models of persuasion, information biases, fair trading

- *Enterprise search engines* (e-commerce, e-marketing) involving NLP analytics

- *Consumer search engines*, market monitors, product/service recommender systems involving NLP analytics

- *Client-supplier interaction platforms* (e.g., portals, helps desks, newsgroups) and transaction support systems based on written or spoken natural language communication

- *Multi-media and multi-modality interaction platforms*, including written/spoken language channels, triggering or supporting economic processes

- Specialized modes of *information extraction and text mining* in economic domains, e.g., temporal event or transaction mining

- *Information aggregation* from economy-related single sources (e.g., review summaries, automatic threading)

- *Text generation* in economic domains, e.g., review generation, complaint response generation

- *Ontologies and knowledge graphs* for economics and adaptation of general-domain *lexicons* for economic NLP

- *Corpora and annotations policies* (guidelines, metadata schemata, etc.) for economics-related NLP

- *Economy-specific text genres* (business reports, sustainability reports, auditing documents, product reviews, economic newswire, business letters, law documents, etc.) and their usage for NLP

- Dedicated *software resources* for economic NLP (e.g., NER taggers, sublanguage parsers, pipelines or domain-adapted end-to-end systems for processing economic discourse)

Two types of papers were solicited for the ECONLP 2021 workshop:

- Long papers (8+1 pages) should describe solid results with strong experimental, empirical or theoretical/formal backing,

- Short papers (4+1 pages) should describe work in progress where interesting novel, yet still preliminary results have been worked out.

We received this year 16 submissions and based on a rigorous review process, we accepted 5 of them as long papers, 7 as short papers and rejected 4 submissions. Accordingly, the acceptance rate was 75%. The OC of ECONLP 2021 decided on such a proportionally high number of acceptances due to the exceptional quality of the papers under review. The acceptance/rejection ratio amounts to 3.0.

After three rounds, ECONLP has become ACL's anchor workshop for foundational and applied research at the intersection of Economics and Natural Language Processing. Submission numbers stabilize in the range of 15 to 20 papers, with acceptance ratios in the interval of 50 up to 75%.

Yet, ECONLP is only part of a series of workshops at the intersection of NLP, economics, and related scientific fields, such as artificial intelligence, machine learning, data science, knowledge discovery, Web science, and information retrieval. Two companion workshops are closely affiliated with other NLP conferences, namely this year's editions of

- *ECNLP 4 — 4th Workshop on e-Commerce and NLP @ ACL 2021* (with previous editions taking place at the Web Conference (WWW 2019 and 2020) and ACL 2020)
- *FNP 2021 — 3rd Financial Narrative Processing Workshop @ University of Lancaster, UK* (with previous editions taking place at COLING 2020, NoDaLiDa '19 (jointly with the MultiLing Financial Summarisation (FNP-FNS 2020) workshop), and LREC 2018)

But the theme of this workshop has attracted an even wider range of neighboring scientific communities, including NeurIPS, IJCAI, KDD, and SIGIR. Without aiming for completeness, the list below enumerates some recent events with a similar thematic scope:

- *FAIF 2020 — (1st) Workshop on Fair AI in Finance @ NeurIPS 2020*
- *FinNLP & FinSim & FinSDB 2020 — 2nd Workshop on Financial Technology and Natural Language Processing (FinNLP) with FinSim and FinSBD-2 Shared Task @ IJCAI-PRICAI 2020*
- *KDD-MLF 2021 — 4th Workshop on Machine Learning in Finance @ KDD 2021*
- *eCom 2021 — 5th ACM SIGIR Workshop on eCommerce @ SIGIR 2021*

These manifold acitivities are exciting to witness and, at the same time, indicate the added value of approaches complementing each other in this truly interdisciplinary field.

Finally, we want to thank all our collaborators. First of all, our colleagues who submitted their best work to this workshop. Their efforts are crucial for the development of this rapidly evolving field. Second, we are indebted to our PC members whose thorough, balanced and timely reviews were the basis for properly selecting the best-quality papers presented at this workshop. Last but not least, our sincere thanks go to our keynote speaker, Gerard Hoberg, from the Marshall School of Business, University of Southern California, Los Angeles, CA, USA, for his valuable contribution to this year's ECONLP. Finally, we hope the attendants of the workshop, whether physically or virtually present, will enjoy the presentations and discussions in Punta Cana or online.

The organizers of ECONLP 2021

Udo Hahn
Véronique Hoste
Amanda Stent

Organizers:

Udo Hahn	Friedrich-Schiller-Universität Jena, Jena, Germany (Chairman)
Véronique Hoste	Ghent University, Ghent, Belgium
Amanda Stent	Bloomberg, New York City, NY, USA

Program Committee:

Sven Buechel	Friedrich-Schiller-Universität Jena, Jena, Germany
David Carmel	Amazon, Haifa, Israel
Michael Chau	School of Business, University of Hong Kong, Hong Kong, China
Paulo Cortez	University of Minho, Guimarães, Portugal
Sanjiv Ranjan Das	Santa Clara University, Santa Clara, CA, USA
Brian Davis	School of Computing, Dublin City University, Dublin, Ireland
Luciano Del Corro	Goldman Sachs, Frankfurt/M., Germany
Lipika Dey	Tata Consultancy Services (TCS) Innovation Lab, New Delhi, India
Giuseppe Di Fabbrizio	VUI, Inc., Boston, MA, USA & Trento, Italy
Flavius Frasincar	Erasmus University, Rotterdam, Netherlands
Anjan Goswami	Adobe Inc., San Francisco, CA, USA
Petr Hájek	University of Pardubice, Pardubice, Czech Republic
Yulan He	University of Warwick, Coventry, UK
Qing Li	Southwestern University of Finance and Economics, Sichuan, Chengdu, China
Xiaodong Li	Hohai University, Nanjing, China
Pekka Malo	Aalto University, Aalto , Finland
Igor Mozetič	Jožef Stefan Institute, Ljubljana, Slovenia
Viktor Pekar	Aston University, Birmingham, UK
Nicolas Pröllochs	Universität Giessen, Giessen, Germany
Samuel Rönnqvist	University of Turku, Turku, Finland
Hiroki Sakaji	University of Tokyo, Tokyo, Japan
Kazuhiro Seki	University of Kobe, Kobe, Japan
Sameena Shah	JPMorgan Chase, New York, NY, USA
Kiyoaki Shirai	Japan Advanced Institute of Science and Technology (JAIST), Nomi, Japan
Heiner Stuckenschmidt	Universität Mannheim, Mannheim, Germany
Jacopo Tagliabue	Coveo Labs, New York City, NY, USA
Mengting Wan	Microsoft, Redmond, WA, USA
Frank Z. Xing	Nanyang Technological University (NTU), Singapore, Singapore
Wlodek W. Zadrozny	University of North Carolina at Charlotte, Charlotte, NC, USA
Zhu (Drew) Zhang	Iowa State University, Ames, IA, USA

Invited Speaker:

Gerard Hoberg	Marshall School of Business, University of Southern California, Los Angeles, CA, USA

Keynote talk: Using NLP to Model Product Market Boundaries, Market Structure, and Innovation

Gerard Hoberg
Marshall School of Business, University of Southern California, Los Angeles, CA, USA

Abstract

Research in financial economics utilizing natural language processing has modeled how U.S. companies compete across product markets, how they innovate, and how supply chains are organized. This presentation will summarize these models, how they have evolved to the present day, and new work in progress. A key technical foundation is that these concepts of market structure, which were developed by economic theorists, have relatedness and overlap as their very intellectual foundation. Hence NLP methods (new and old) that focus on textual relatedness make up an ideal toolkit for analyzing these economic concepts, which are also central to many applications aimed at understanding and predicting business success.

One of the most compelling properties of an NLP approach is that market structures can be updated and redrawn every year at low cost as textual corpora are updated. This observation indicates the use of NLP to measure innovation. This has led to many insights on how companies manage growth, whether and when they go public, and how they manage the risk of disruption. This work continues to evolve with a focus on innovation, disaggregating complex product portfolios, and to build NLP measures for private firms through their websites. Among other economic findings, this work reveals that U.S. companies are becoming increasingly complex and broad in their product offerings, a result that is not seen using standard numerical databases in the public domain. Work using these same methods has also been deployed in related settings such as modeling systemic risk.

Table of Contents

Conference Program

Thursday, November 11, 2021

09:00–09:20 *Opening Remarks and Status Report on Economics and NLP*
Udo Hahn

09:20–10:30 Session 1: Datasets for Economic NLP

9:20–9:50 *A Fine-Grained Annotated Corpus for Target-Based Opinion Analysis of Economic and Financial Narratives*
Jiahui Hu and Patrick Paroubek

9:50–10:10 *EDGAR-CORPUS: Billions of Tokens Make The World Go Round*
Lefteris Loukas, Manos Fergadiotis, Ion Androutsopoulos and Prodromos Malakasiotis

10:10–10:30 *The Global Banking Standards QA Dataset (GBS-QA)*
Kyunghwan Sohn, Sunjae Kwon and Jaesik Choi

10:30–11:00 Coffee Break

11:00–12:10 Session 2: Transformer-based Methodologies in Economic NLP

11:00–11:30 *Corporate Bankruptcy Prediction with BERT Model*
Alex Kim and Sangwon Yoon

11:30–11:50 *Is Domain Adaptation Worth Your Investment? Comparing BERT and FinBERT on Financial Tasks*
Bo Peng, Emmanuele Chersoni, Yu-Yin Hsu and Chu-Ren Huang

11:50–12:10 *From Stock Prediction to Financial Relevance: Repurposing Attention Weights to Assess News Relevance Without Manual Annotations*
Luciano Del Corro and Johannes Hoffart

12:10–12:45 Lunch Break

12:45–13:30 *Keynote: Using NLP to Model Product Market Boundaries, Market Structure, and Innovation*
Gerard Hoberg

13:30–14:30 Session 3: Applications in Economic NLP (1)

13:30–13:50 *Privacy enabled Financial Text Classification using Differential Privacy and Federated Learning*
Priyam Basu, Tiasa Singha Roy, Rakshit Naidu and Zumrut Muftuoglu

13:50–14:10 *Using Word Embedding to Reveal Monetary Policy Explanation Changes*
Akira Matsui, Xiang Ren and Emilio Ferrara

14:10–14:30 *To What Extent Can English-as-a-Second Language Learners Read Economic News Texts?*
Yo Ehara

14:30–14:45 Short Break

14:45–16:15 Session 4: Applications in Economic NLP (2)

14:45–15:15 *Effective Use of Graph Convolution Network and Contextual Sub-Tree for Commodity News Event Extraction*
Meisin Lee, Lay-Ki Soon and Eu-Gene Siew

15:15–15:45 *Cryptocurrency Day Trading and Framing Prediction in Microblog Discourse*
Anna Paula Pawlicka Maule and Kristen Johnson

15:45–16:15 *Extracting Economic Signals from Central Bank Speeches*
Maximilian Ahrens and Michael McMahon

Thursday, November 11, 2021 (continued)

16:15–16:45 Coffee Break

16:45–17:30 ***Discussion Round: Planning for an ECONLP Challenge Competition***

17:30–17:45 ***Concluding Remarks***

A Fine-Grained Annotated Corpus for Target-Based Opinion Analysis of Economic and Financial Narratives

Jiahui HU*§ and **Patrick Paroubek†§**
*Natixis CIB, Paris, France
†CNRS, France
§Paris-Saclay University, France
§LISN, Bât 507, Rue du Belvedère, 91400 Orsay, France
⋆jiahui.hu@student-cs.fr
†pap@limsi.fr

Abstract

In this paper about aspect-based sentiment analysis (ABSA), we present the first version of a fine-grained annotated corpus for target-based opinion analysis (TBOA) to analyze economic activities or financial markets. We have annotated, at an intra-sentential level, a corpus of sentences extracted from documents representative of financial analysts' most-read materials by considering how financial actors communicate about the evolution of event trends and analyze related publications (news, official communications, etc.). Since we focus on identifying the expressions of opinions related to the economy and financial markets, we annotated the sentences that contain at least one subjective expression about a domain-specific term. Candidate sentences for annotations were randomly chosen from texts of specialized press and professional information channels over a period ranging from 1986 to 2021.

Our annotation scheme relies on various linguistic markers like domain-specific vocabulary, syntactic structures, and rhetorical relations to explicitly describe the author's subjective stance. We investigated and evaluated the recourse to automatic pre-annotation with existing natural language processing technologies to alleviate the annotation workload. Our aim is to propose a corpus usable on the one hand as training material for the automatic detection of the opinions expressed on an extensive range of domain-specific aspects and on the other hand as a gold standard for evaluation TBOA.

In this paper, we present our pre-annotation models and evaluations of their performance, introduce our annotation scheme and report on the main characteristics of our corpus.

1 Introduction

Financial markets are places where the exchange and the processing of information are crucial in determining prices. Thus, the knowledge about the market participants' opinions is an essential driver of markets. Understanding how these opinions evolve is therefore valuable for financial participants and regulators.

The interaction of market participants determines market dynamics, and how market participants act is largely determined by their beliefs on the outlook. The importance of beliefs in shaping market dynamics reflects an element of a self-fulfilling prophecy: beliefs guide decisions that then validate the underlying belief. One of the classic models of this socio-psychological phenomenon is the Diamond and Dybvig's model (1983) about bank runs. The model demonstrates that even healthy banks can go bankrupt because of depositors' expectations about the behavior of others. If a large number of depositors expect the others to withdraw their funds, the only rational option for them is to be the first one to withdraw the money. If all the depositors decide to withdraw their money, the bank will go bankrupt despite of its initial financial health. In other words, unlike natural science, market dynamics are also determined by its participants' beliefs about the future. An investor buys or sells an asset based on his view about its expected future price. A recent study, for example, finds some evidence that investors' beliefs can be reflected in respondents' multi-asset allocation strategy (Giglio et al., 2021).

People's beliefs are formed as a result of changes in business activities, economic data, and financial outlook. Specialized press and communication of corporates are essential inputs in belief formation. Economists have been using sentiment indices obtained from surveys, such as the Purchasing Manager Index, to gauge the underlying economic activity. One limitation of sentiment indices is that information is restricted by the questionnaire design and update frequency. Consequently, these surveys provide an indication for the general direction of the economy but do not provide much additional

Proceedings of the Third Workshop on Economics and Natural Language Processing, pages 1–12
Punta Cana and online, November 11. ©2021 Association for Computational Linguistics

color in terms of "why" things are changing or what the underlying narrative is. One approach to get a better sense of the underlying factors is to analyze news articles. Numerous studies on news articles have been conducted in the past, though without using any algorithms ((Tetlock, 2007), (Baker et al., 2015)) or designing algorithms dependent on sentiment lexicons. For example, (Consoli et al., 2021) use the Loughran McDonald dictionary (Loughran and Mcdonald, 2011) to extract negative emotion from financial newspapers as explainable variable to predict sovereign debt spread. Thanks to recent progress in natural language understanding, it becomes possible to monitor economic narratives and opinions expressed in written texts. There are many approaches to address the problem, e.g., opinion classification (classifying opinions into positive, negative, and neutral) (Malo et al., 2013), topic modeling (probability models for discovering clusters based on the frequency of words in a collection of texts) (Azqueta-Gavaldon et al., 2020).

Although model accuracy of opinion categorization is crucial for its downstream economic and financial analysis tasks, performing fine-grained level target-based opinion analysis on texts written by domain experts is still a relatively unexploited field. In the literature about text mining applications in finance, one encounters most often dictionary-based or unsupervised learning approaches, and the performance of the language model is rarely discussed. One of the reasons for this state of affairs could be the lack of relevant annotated corpora.

To fill this gap, we introduce an annotated corpus that includes both information labeled by human and by algorithms. The corpus consists of texts from different reliable sources; its contents cover corporate news, macroeconomic statements, and comments relevant to financial markets. Each sentence in our corpus is annotated with the following information: (1) domain-specific concepts (2) span of words that potentially indicate the author's opinion (3) named entities (4) negative patterns. If the targets of opinion can be identified, we annotated the pair (target, polarity). In addition to these labels and relations, we also propose to consider specific rhetorical modes like domain experts do.

2 Related Works

Opinion analysis is the task of natural language understanding for classifying texts into positive, negative and neutral polarities. It sees increasing importance in the banking industry among regulators and financial participants. Most existing approaches of opinion analysis applied to economics and finance, however, attempt to detect the overall polarity of a sentence (Malo et al., 2013), or text (Cortis et al., 2017), leaving aside opinion targets.

A study on Twitter sentiment classification showed that 40% of errors resulted from the ignorance of target (Jiang et al., 2011). To the best of our knowledge, FiQA[1] task 1 is the first corpus that labels opinion polarities together with its targets from sentences of microblog and headlines. Nevertheless, its size is relatively small (1,313 samples), and it contains only relatively short sentences[2]. In the texts in which we are interested, sentences written by financial experts are likely to be more complex; as detailed in Table 12, the average sentence length from different texts sources is about 30 tokens, and the most extended sentence is 258.

As of the time of writing, among the analysis tasks, usually known as Aspect-Based Sentiment Analysis (ABSA) ((Pontiki et al., 2014), (Nazir et al., 2020)), there is only one economic news article related study on Target-Based Opinion Analysis (TBOA) (Barbaglia et al., 2020), which focuses on six macroeconomic aggregates. However, the dataset is not publicly available, and details regarding the statistics of this corpus are not specified.

We have created our corpus to respond to the need for TBOA corpus in economy and finance by incorporating argumentative and conditional opinions and opinions expressed inside a consequence or explicit speculation about the future. We are interested in combining two subtasks of ABSA (Pontiki et al., 2014): aspect term extraction (SB 1) and aspect term polarity (SB 2). This corpus aims to provides training and evaluation data to solve the following research problem:

Definition 1. Target-Based Opinion Analysis (TBOA)
Given a sentence of interest with n words **w**= $(w_1,...,w_n)$ and its corresponding word embedding **x**= $(\vec{x}_1,...,\vec{x}_n)$, the goal of TBOA is to predict **all targets** $\hat{t}$= $(\vec{t}_1,...,\vec{t}_m)$ which are communicated as central message and their **associated opinions** $\hat{y}$= $(\hat{y}_1,...,\hat{y}_m)$ **simultaneously**.

[1] https://sites.google.com/view/fiqa/home
[2] The longest sample in FiQA task 1 is composed of 31 words.

3 How we address author's stance

In this work, we are interested in sentences containing at least one expression of opinion about evolution in the economic and financial landscape[3], called subjective sentences. Their particularity is that writers use language to monitor and judge the flow of events or assess their impacts. Authors may:

(1) monitor changes by using language to describe in which direction an event or a concept evolves [a],
(2) express a judgment about these dynamics by clarifying their preference; furthermore their expectations can be diversely grounded in a mix of rationality and/or emotions,
(3) and assess the intensity of these dynamics.

[a] in the DOWN & LOW category, *plummet* and *decrease* convey the notion of scaling *rapid* and *median*, respectively.

Figure 1: Our focus on specific aspects of texts written by financial experts

3.1 Appraisal Theory

As theoretical grounding for our work, we have chosen appraisal theory (Martin and White, 2005) because it provides meaning-making elements to analyze any text that conveys positive or negative assessment, the text's corresponding intensity, and the author's involvement. It deals both with the evaluative language that construes the experience of the world (i.e., development of economy and business activities) and the language that opinion holders use to reveal their (personal) judgments to enact interpersonal relations in a communicative context. Thus, this framework is appropriate for analyzing beliefs that market participants form as a result of changes in the business and economic circumstances.

Under the appraisal framework, the evaluative language resources are divided into three semantic domains, namely

- Attitude: positive and negative assessments. It encompasses values by which a writer reveals his value by emotional response (called *affect*), institutionalized norms or ethics (called *judgment*), aesthetic and social valuation (called *appreciation*).
- Graduation: force and focus. It is composed of meanings by which propositions are strengthened (called *force*), and their boundaries are sharpened or blurred (called *focus*).
- Engagement: resources for positioning a writer's stance with respect to propositions conveyed by a text.

Inspired by the study about appraisal in opinion expressions (Asher et al., 2009), we make three axes to regroup opinion expressions that are relevant to opinions about changes of economic and financial activities:

- **Variation axis** which corresponds to (1) in Figure 1
- **Attitude axis**, i.e. (2) in Figure 1
- **Graduation axis**, i.e. (3) in Figure 1. It is complementary to *Variation axis* and *Attitude axis*. It can describe (a) the intensity, speed or quantity of changes, (b) whether the change happens suddenly or not, and (c) the measurement of quantity, extent, or proximity in time and space (e.g, small & large, a few& many, near & far)

3.2 Rhetorical Modes

Certain rhetorical modes are non-negligible linguistic phenomena in economic narratives, because they give hints to identify central messages in texts written by/for financial professionals. The presence of discourse techniques makes the opinions of some targets more relevant than others, and we only annotate (targets, opinions) which are perceived as central messages. For example, in the following argumentative sentence, author comments both on "*asset x*" and "*interest rates*". We restrict our annotation to the positive opinion toward the target "*asset x*", because the opinion about "*interest rates*" is the premise to support the author's stance on "*asset x*. The performance of the downstream task TBOA will be attenuated if the algorithm fails to distinguish the central message.

"*The asset x is going to be sought out, because I think interest rates ...*"

Argumentation

The author of any text can use a wide range of formulations and argumentative constructions to convince his audience to agree with his views. A common technique that Mario Draghi[4] used in his speeches from Q4 2011 to Q4 2013 is to establish shared premises to develop common ground with his audience, to persuade the world to believe

[3] We will use interchangeably *in the economic landscape* or *in the financial landscape* in the rest of this paper.

[4] President of European Central Bank from November 2011 to October 2019.

in the euro, and reassure that European Monetary Union will recover from the sovereign debt crisis (Jalo, 2021). Establishing shared premises is only a means to his goal: gaining adherence to his conclusion. Recent research in cognitive science defends the view that, in some circumstances, the purpose of reasoning is indifferent from assembling premises that support a conclusion favored by the author (Mercier and Sperber, 2011). The conclusion drawn by an investor may sometimes be more grounded in his desire to favor his own beliefs than in pure rationality.

Cause-effect relation

Similarly, the cause-effect relation represents 7% of the sentences in the speeches of central banks (see Table 10). A cause is an event precedent and contiguous to an effect (Richards, 1965). This succession order implies that the latter, i.e., new information, is more salient. Therefore we only extract opinions expressed inside the effect part of a causal relation.

Conditional Opinions

We also distinguish conditional opinions. In a conditional sentence, opinion expressions can be challenging to determine due to the condition clause (Narayanan et al., 2009). For example, in the sentence, *"If rents fail to keep pace with inflation, the requirement for higher yields will drive down real assets prices."*, the author is pessimistic about *"real asset prices"* under the stated hypothetical scenario, but does not express an opinion on *"rents"*. However, if we remove *"if"* in this sentence, the first clause becomes negative. It is crucial not to misinterpret the author's intent. To do so, we want to enable our algorithm to recognize conditional sentences. Therefore, in addition to annotating opinions inside the main clause, we label the span of words corresponding to the dependent clause.

Explicit speculations

Finally, it is common that an author indicates his level of conviction with respect to his attitudinal propositions. For example, in *"Within our mandate, the ECB is ready to do whatever it takes to preserve the euro. And believe me, it will be enough.*[5]*"*, Mario Draghi conveyed his strong conviction to save the euro; this strong degree of commitment plays an important role in appealing for adherence to his goal. Under the appraisal framework, the formulations related to the author's stance are grouped into the notion of *Engagement*. The two following example sentences[6] indicate respectively greater and lesser degrees of personal commitment from the author to defend his opinion. The level of commitment reflects the author's willingness to open up dialogic space for alternative viewpoints and his confidence in the stated attitudinal proposition.

- *The stock markets are in robust form.*
- *The stock markets are expected to be in a robust form.*

A low degree of belief is, in our standpoint, explicit speculation about the future. People are less inclined to make decisions based upon opinions with a low degree of conviction; thus, these opinions are less likely to be the main driver of market dynamics.

4 Methodology

Supervised learning approaches have showed their efficiency to predict target-oriented opinions in a similar task, i.e. SemEval-2014 Task 4 (Pontiki et al., 2014) which is a widely used benchmark for TBOA. However, to the best of our knowledge, no publicly available annotated corpus corresponds to our research problem. Therefore, we follow the standard scheme of corpus creation in natural language processing to create our corpus for TBOA specific to economy and finance.

The overall picture of our research is illustrated in Figure 2. It is mainly divided into three phases: Data Collection and Pre-annotation (i.e., machine-assisted annotation), Data Annotation, and Model Training. Only the first two phrases will be fully examined in this paper, especially our work in pre-annotation, which delivers satisfying accuracy and reduces laborious annotation workload. Future work will investigate appropriate neural network architecture to solve the task TBOA (see Definition 1) by using this corpus.

[5] source: ECB link

[6] These formulations were invented for demonstration.

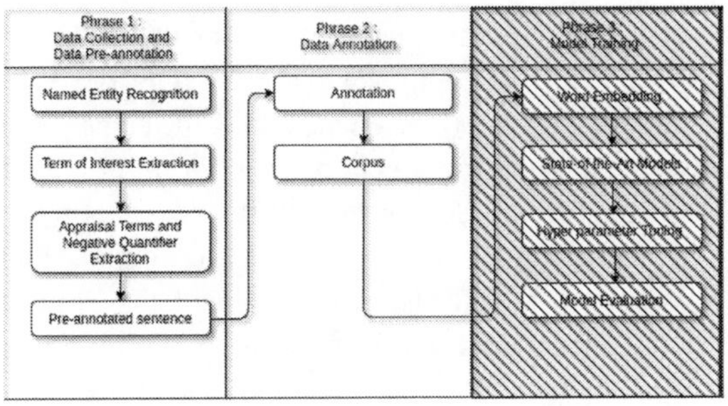

Figure 2: The structure of this study

Before discussing technical details, we want to specify why we use machine-assisted pre-annotations prior to applying manual annotations.

Motivations for adopting pre-annotation

Texts written by experts contain both factual and subjective sentences disproportionately. For our final task, i.e. TBOA, only subjective sentences with terminology terms in economics or finance are relevant candidates.

Definition 2 (Sentence of interest)**.** A sentence of interest is a sentence that includes at least one potential opinion indicator (i.e., appraisal terms) and one potential target (i.e.domain-specific terms, see 4.2.2).

Our pre-annotation experiments show that, except for earning call transcripts, sentences of interest are relatively rare compared to other types of sentences (see Table 6). This disproportionality will result in poor predictive performance on minority class (i.e., sentences of interest) in end-to-end leaning algorithms.

Furthermore, supervised learning models require a tremendous amount of labeled data to discover meaningful patterns in a dataset, even when disposing of a collection of sentences of interest. For a real-world application, creating a large dataset is costly and time-consuming. The primary motivation of automatically annotating certain information is to overcome these challenges by alleviating deep learning algorithm's difficulties in feature-finding and thus encouraging the algorithm to allocate more efforts in linking meaningful features to solve the assigned work. Side benefits are that these pre-annotations can ease the workload of the data annotator and can be represented in a structured way for data analysis from the first phase.

4.1 Data Collection

Our corpus is collected from a wide range of reputable sources of textual information which are complementary to each other, ranging from corporate finance to macroeconomics. While a company tends to attract investors by conveying positive news during earning calls, it usually adopts more prudential tones in the MD&A section of 10-K fillings (see below). News articles and Tweets provide outsider opinions on information communicated by central banks and corporates. Our raw dataset covers a period ranging from 1986 to 2021 (see Figure 5).

The size of raw data set of each data type is detailed in Table 1. Written texts of central banks are collected from their official websites[7]. Sentences of MD&A section (see further explanation below) are randomly selected from the dataset made available by (Ewens, 2019), and our 1,065 sentences of earning calls are randomly chosen from earning transcripts published between October 2017 and May 2021 by 8,912 public companies listed on NASDAQ, NYSE, NYSE MKT and TSX.

Central Banks	Earning Calls	MD&A	Tweets
22,259	1,065	4,793	2,628

Table 1 Number of sentences intended for pre-annotation

- **Central banks:**
  - ECB: Press conferences about ECB's monetary policy decision and speeches of ECB
  - FOMC: Meeting minutes of Federal Open Market Committee
- **MD&A**[8] (Ewens, 2019): Management Discussion and Analysis (item 7) is a mandatory and non-audited section of 10-K filings, an annual report that corporates submit to the U.S. Securities and Exchange Commission. MD&A represents the thoughts and opinions of the management of a public company[9] (called the C-suite) and provides a forecast of future operations. According to a survey of 140 sell-side analysts (Epstein and Palepu, 1999), the MD&A section is well-read and used.
- **Earning calls:** During earning call confer-

[7] source of ECB Speeches :link
source of ECB Press Conferences: link
source of FOMC minutes: link

[8] source of MD&A data: link

[9] A public company is a company whose shares are traded freely on a stock exchange.

ence, the C-suite, analysts, investors, and the media discuss the company's financial results and future plans. Participants can ask questions that may yield valuable information or ask for clarification on particular topics which were not addressed by the C-suite. They are considered as one of the key resources for investors. Financial analysts combine information obtained during the earning calls and from the MD&A section in fundamental analysis. A study on German companies finds some evidence that earning calls improve analysts' ability to forecast better future earnings of German companies (Bassemir et al., 2013).

- **News articles:** We use the Financial PhraseBank (FPB) dataset (Malo et al., 2013) as a composition of news article sentences. It is composed of 4,840 annotations at the sentence level. We randomly choose sentences from the corpus with 75% agreement (i.e. 3,453 sentences) among 5 - 8 annotators per sentence , and apply our annotations (see section 4.4.1). Note that we do not reuse any annotation of the FPB dataset and a small number of our polarity annotations differ from those of the original corpus.
- **Tweets[10]:** Social media messages of 19 domain experts.

4.2 Data pre-annotation pipeline

4.2.1 Named Entity Recognition

Named Entity Recognition (NER) is the task of detecting token-level instances of named entities from unstructured texts into pre-defined categories. Geographic locations (LOC), persons (PER), names of organizations or companies (ORG) are important hints for linking financial narratives to the corresponding entities. In *"Stock markets in [Europe$_{(B-LOC)}$] are expected to be in a robust form."*, the location [Europe$_{(B-LOC)}$] is an attribute of our term of interest *"Stock markets"* (see subsection 4.2.2). Its identification helps to target investors and analysts who follow the information flow of specific entities. It also enables joint analysis with structured numeric financial data organized by corporate name or geographic unit.

In order to choose an adapted model to label our dataset, we employ the CoNLL 2003 dataset (Tjong Kim Sang and De Meulder, 2003), one of the most famous corpora of NER, to evaluate different state-of-the-art models' performance for this task (see section 4.3). In additional to [LOC], [ORG], [PER] classes, [MISC] (miscellaneous) is the category of words derived from location (e.g., *Italian*), organization, person. Sentences of this dataset are taken from the Reuters Corpus[11], which is composed of Markets & Finance news of 90 categories[12]. 14,035 sentences were used for training, 3,250 for development and 3,453 for evaluation.

We have experimented with four NER systems, first three open-source libraries: SpaCy[13], Stanza (Qi et al., 2020)[14], and FLERT (Schweter and Akbik, 2020). In the FLERT model, firstly a transformer is fine-tuned on the NER task, and then the resulting features are provided to a BiLSTM-CRF (Huang et al., 2015) sequence labeling architecture. We also modeled a transformer with self-attention heads using BERT embeddings (Devlin et al., 2019) to predict named entities.

Model	[LOC]	[ORG]	[PER]	[MISC]	Time (min)
SpaCy	0.71	0.23	0.67	/	0.19
Stanza	0.92	0.74	0.89	0.85	7.55
BERT	0.93	0.87	**0.97**	**0.95**	8.07
FLERT	**0.98**	**0.88**	**0.97**	0.92	19.81

Table 2 F1-scores and computation time of the test set of CoNLL 2003 dataset

From Table 2, we conclude that classification precision is proportionate with computation cost. FLERT performs the best across all classes, its improvement on the class [LOC] with respect to BERT (the second-best model) are significant. Nonetheless, its computation costs is much higher than our BERT model. For this reason, we use the BERT model in our pipeline to automatically annotate named entities.

4.2.2 Term of Interest Extraction

The goal of terminology extraction is to locate relevant terms from unstructured texts. Terms of interest (TOI) are concepts in economics and finance in the form of their full name or abbreviation, including but not limited to:

- market-related terms: *FX, Forex markets, S&P 500 futures, traded commodities, etc.*
- accounting drivers: *free cash flow, ROA or return on assets, etc.*
- valuation divers: *EBITDA, EPS, NAV, etc.*
- macroeconomic aggregates: *growth rate, inflation, CPI, PMI, etc.*

[10]Obtained with Twitter API

[11]http://www.reuters.com/researchandstandards/

[12]for more details, see https://martin-thoma.com/nlp-reuters/

[13]Trained on *OntoNotes 5* dataset (18 classes) https://spacy.io/api/entityrecognizer

[14]https://stanfordnlp.github.io/stanza/ner.html

- risks factors: *VIX, volatility, CDS spread, etc.*
- others

To the best of our knowledge, there is no labeled dataset in economics & finance for terminology extraction. Therefore, we choose to identify these terms in an unsupervised manner: we firstly extract terminological candidates by identifying syntactically plausible noun phrases. Noun phrases that contain elements of a domain-specific thesaurus are labeled as terms of interest.

4.2.3 Appraisal Terms Extraction

The aim of appraisal terms extraction is to identify potential candidates in which an author expresses his opinion. More details about the composition of appraisal terms are provided in Table 13. Appraisal terms are pre-annotated with Algorithm 1.

Algorithm 1 key terms extractor

Input: sentence, predefined_list, tag
S' = spacy.nlp(sentence)
for $token$ in S'
    if $token$ is in predefined_list **then do**
        $res \leftarrow token$, start_char, end_char, tag
    end if
end for
return res

4.2.4 Negation

Negative quantifiers are assigned to an appraisal expression that inverses the appraiser's perception towards a target. Negative quantifiers are also pre-annotated with Algorithm 1. The list of negative patterns is detailed in Table 14.

4.3 Data Pre-annotation Evaluation Measures

To evaluate the performance of the chosen models for NER (i.e., BERT) and TOI, the annotator is asked to correct wrongly pre-annotated tags or add missing ones. The performance of pre-annotation our corpus is measured with F1-score:

$$F1 = \frac{2*precision*recall}{precision+recall}$$

At the time of writing, performance evaluation is calculated based on 2,297 sentences annotated by one annotator familiar with the domain terminology (one of the authors).

Evaluation of NER

NER is labeled with the IOB (inside, outside, beginning) format:

"[The$_O$] [European$_{(B-ORG)}$] [Commission$_{(I-ORG)}$] [said$_O$] [on$_O$] [Thursday$_O$] [it$_O$] [did$_O$] [agreed$_O$] [with$_O$] [German$_{(B-MISC)}$] [advice$_O$] [to$_O$] [consumers$_O$] [to$_O$] [shun$_O$] [British$_{(B-MISC)}$] [lamb$_O$] [until$_O$] [scientists$_O$] [determine$_O$] [whether$_O$] [mad$_O$] [cow$_O$] [disease$_O$] [can$_O$] [be$_O$] [transmitted$_O$] [to$_O$] [sheep$_O$]." .

The model performance is evaluated on entity-level with Seqeval[15] (Nakayama, 2018). We use its default mode compatible with *conlleval*, an evaluation system developed for the CoNLL-2000 shared task. The prediction of *[European Commission]* is considered as *True Positive* when the model return [B-ORG, I-ORG]. When the model makes a boundary error, for example [I-ORG, I-MISC], the entity is counted as two errors (false negative and false positive).

Class	Precision	Recall	F1-score	Nb entities
LOC	96%	99%	97%	336
ORG	96%	93%	95%	888
PER	85%	98%	91%	150
MISC	88%	72%	79%	412

Table 3 The performance of our corpus using the BERT model

The performance of [LOC] and [ORG] is slightly better on our corpus than on the test set of the CoNLL 2003 dataset. This is related to how machine-assisted annotation are validated for the evaluation of our corpus. The annotator corrects the label of NER if necessary. For our intended usage, we are more permissive to boundary variations. For example, under the CoNLL 2003 annotation guideline, *[Finnish KCI Konecranes]* should be labeled [B-MISC, B-ORG, I-ORG]. But the labels [B-ORG, I-ORG, I-ORG] given by the algorithm are accepted by the annotator, because the information valuable to our intended usage, i.e., company name, is identified correctly. The type of boundary variations which are not accepted in the CoNLL 2003 annotation guideline [16] but accepted in our corpus are listed below:

- articles: a, an, the
- honorifics: Mr., Ms., etc.
- *[MISC]* that precedes an organization

Evaluation of TOI

We consider the identification of TOI as a task of sequence labeling. Under the IOB format, the TOI *Forex market* can be tagged with ['B-TOI', 'I-TOI']. Its evaluation is computed with the Seqeval

[15]A python framework for sequence labeling evaluation. https://github.com/chakki-works/seqeval

[16]https://www.clips.uantwerpen.be/conll2003/ner/annotation.txt

(Nakayama, 2018).

Model	Precision	Recall	F1-score
our method	88%	90%	89%

Table 4 Model performance for identifying TOI in and out of the thesaurus

4.4 Annotation Process

After the pre-annotation phase, only sentences of interest are retained. The portion of sentences of interest varies from one type of data to another.

Type	CB	EC	MD&A	Tweets
Percentage of sentenced of interest	26%	63%	27%	15%
Randomly chosen sentences	22,259	1,065	4,793	2,628

Table 5 Percentage of sentences of interest from randomly chosen sentences

At the time of writing, we have annotated 2,297 sentences randomly selected from pre-annotated sentences of interest. The list of possible tags, labeled by algorithms and by human, can be found in Table 11. Our final corpus size is expected to be 4,000 sentences[17].

Type	CB	EC	News	MD&A	Tweets	Total
Expected Size	800	800	800	800	800	4,000
Percentage annotated	87.5%	83.9%	93.8%	12.5%	9.5%	57.4%

Table 6 Size (number of sentences) of the corpus

4.4.1 Data Annotation

Our corpus is annotated with INCEpTION (Klie et al., 2018), an open-source annotation platform. As exemplified in Figure 3, pre-annotated tag [TOI] stands for terms of interest and [APPRAISAL] for appraisal terms. The annotator is expected to **identify all targets towards which opinions are expressed, as well as their polarities**. Following the evaluation campaign DEFT 2018 (Paroubek et al., 2018), the annotator

(i) selects minimal information about the *Opinion & Emotion Expression* (i.e. *"dysfunctional"*, tagged [OEE]),

(ii) selects the most complete information about the target (i.e. *Sovereign bond market* in Figure 3) and attributes polarity (tagged [-] in Figure 3) to it,

(iii) then draws an unlabeled arc from [OEE] toward its corresponding target.

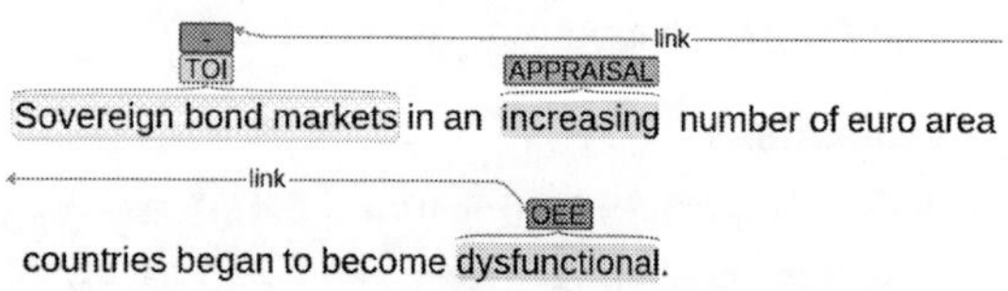

Figure 3: Example of a annotated sentence (explicit opinion)

While the opinion toward target *Sovereign bond market* displayed in Figure 3 is explicit, our corpus also contains implicit opinions based on knowledge of the world, such as Figure 4:

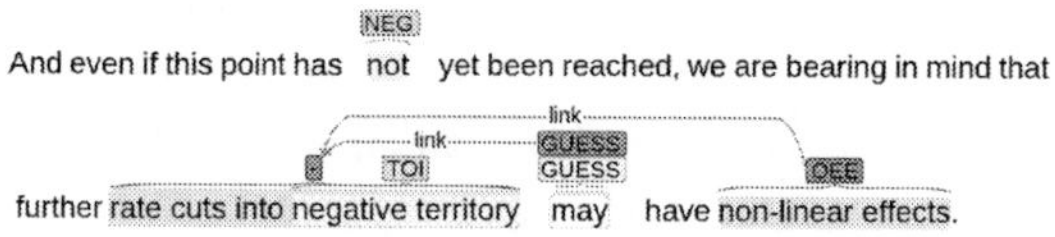

Figure 4: Example of a annotated sentence (implicit opinion)

We define four classes of polarities, namely positive, negative, noncommittal, and unknown; our corpus also contains sentences of interest for which no target can be identified. Polarities are attributed based on the following stance:

- the judgment related to the health of corporates and economic activities
- the judgment related to economic norms, which means *financial conditions* of an economy that contribute to financial stability (Arrigoni et al., 2020). The positive opinion of a target is associated with an easy access to finance. It means that economic agents (individuals, enterprises, or governments) can obtain adequate financial services, including credit, deposit, payment, insurance, and other risk management services.

As mentioned before, in the current stage the annotation was done by one of the authors.

4.4.2 Summary of the annotated corpus

At the time of writing, the annotated corpus contains 2,297 sentences labeled by human annotator.

Summary	CB	EC	News	MD&A	Tweets	Total
# sent. w. target(s)	433	438	540	61	50	1,522
# sent. w/o target	267	233	210	39	26	775
# sent.	700	671	750	100	76	2,297

Table 7 Statistics about annotated sentences with (w.) and without (w/o) target(s)

The following statistics were extracted from the 1,522 annotated *sentences w. target(s)*, called *subjective sentences* [18].

Aligned with our hypothesis, C-suites tend to convey positive information during earning calls, and central bankers are more likely to comment on both positive and negative sides of the economic environment (see Table 8). Targets of our corpus are composed of more tokens than the corpora of SemEval-2014 on Laptop and Restaurant Review (Pontiki et al., 2014) (see Table 9). When it comes to the usage of language, texts of central banks are more likely to express opinions with rhetorical modes, i.e. "argumentative opinions", "explicit

[17]We have not yet reached the desired size for this corpus; we plan to make the corpus available once kappa will have been measured and legal aspects have been assessed.

[18]Due to the small size of annotated sentences from MD&A and Tweets, we refrain from comments on their statistics.

expectations" and "opinions as consequences" (see bold-italic items in Table 10).

Polarity	CB	EC	News	MD&A	Tweets
Positive	45%	74%	68%	46%	45%
Negative	39%	17%	27%	50%	50%
Non-committal	16%	8%	5%	4%	4%
Unknown	0	1%	0	0	1%
Total opinions	710	706	626	102	74
Total nb sentences w. target(s)	433	438	540	61	50

Table 8 Statistics about polarities from subjective sentences

# tok.s	CB	EC	News	MD&A	Tweets	Laptop	Restau.
1	22%	31%	28%	23%	53%	62%	75%
2	38%	38%	49 %	31%	30%	29%	17%
≥3	40%	31%	23%	46%	17%	9%	8%
# targ.	710	706	626	102	74	2,966	4,728

Table 9 Statistics about number of tokens per target of our corpus v.s. the SemEval-2014 Task 4

Type	CB	EC	News	MD&A	Tweets
argumentative opin.	***5.76%***	4.35%	4.07%	6.56%	6%
conditional opin.	3.23%	1.14%	0%	3.28%	0%
explicit expect.	***7.16%***	2.51%	4.99%	6.56%	6%
opin. as conseq.	***6.93%***	0.91%	2.04%	11.48%	0%
Total	23.07%	8.91%	11.03%	27.87%	12%
#nb sent. w. target(s)	433	438	540	61	50

Table 10 Statistics about specific elements of our corpus

5 Conclusion

This paper defines an annotation scheme for identifying target-based opinions from sentences related to the economy and financial markets, by incorporating specific-domain use of language, namely formulations of argumentative and conditional opinions, opinions expressed in cause-effect relations, and opinions with a low level of commitment. The contribution of this paper can be summarized as follows:

1. Our annotation scheme considers rhetorical modes, which is, as far as we know, a novelty in opinion analysis applied to economic and financial narratives. It enables our corpus to describe faithfully how financial professionals communicate and analyze the evolution of events and changes in business data.
2. We designed a tailor-made pipeline by leveraging a set of techniques in Natural Language Processing (NLP) to pre-annotate informative features for identifying candidates relevant to TBOA and alleviating the workload of annotators. At this stage of our project, these pre-annotation models evaluation scores are significant enough to assume that most pertinent sentences are retained for TBOA.
3. Our manually annotated corpus responds to the need for high-quality training and evaluation data for the development of supervised learning algorithms in the research field of TBOA applied to economy and finance.

In the future, we want to develop neural models adapted to our corpus by incorporating fundamental approaches in NLP and domain-specific knowledge, in particular, we investigate the contribution of data augmentation approach to augment the size of our corpus.

Acknowledgment

We express our deepest thanks to Dr. Dirk Schumacher (Natixis Macroeconomic Research) for his valuable comments and support on this paper.

This work is supported by the grant CIFRE, a partnership between Natixis CIB Research and the LISN Laboratory (Interdisciplinary Laboratory of Digital Sciences).

References

Simone Arrigoni, Alina Bobasu, and Fabrizio Venditti. 2020. The simpler the better: measuring financial conditions for monetary policy and financial stability. Working Paper Series 2451, European Central Bank.

Nicholas Asher, Farah Benamara, and Yvette Yannick Mathieu. 2009. Appraisal of Opinion Expressions in Discourse. *LI*, 32(2):279–292.

Andres Azqueta-Gavaldon, Dominik Hirschbühl, Luca Onorante, and Lorena Saiz. 2020. Economic policy uncertainty in the euro area: an unsupervised machine learning approach. Working Paper Series 2359, European Central Bank.

Scott Baker, Nicholas Bloom, and Steven Davis. 2015. Measuring economic policy uncertainty. NBER Working Papers 21633, National Bureau of Economic Research, Inc.

Luca Barbaglia, Sergio Consoli, and Sebastiano Manzan. 2020. Forecasting with economic news. *Available at SSRN 3698121*.

Moritz Bassemir, Zoltan Novotny-Farkas, and Julian Pachta. 2013. The effect of conference calls on analysts' forecasts – german evidence. *European Accounting Review*, 22(1):151–183.

Sergio Consoli, Luca Tiozzo Pezzoli, and Elisa Tosetti. 2021. Emotions in macroeconomic news and their impact on the european bond market. *Journal of International Money and Finance*, 118:102472.

Keith Cortis, André Freitas, Tobias Daudert, Manuela Huerlimann, Manel Zarrouk, Siegfried Handschuh, and Brian Davis. 2017. SemEval-2017 task 5: Fine-grained sentiment analysis on financial microblogs and news. In *Proceedings of the 11th International Workshop on Semantic Evaluation (SemEval-2017)*, pages 519–535, Vancouver, Canada. Association for Computational Linguistics.

Jacob Devlin, Ming-Wei Chang, Kenton Lee, and Kristina Toutanova. 2019. BERT: Pre-training of deep bidirectional transformers for language understanding. In *Proceedings of the 2019 Conference of the North American Chapter of the Association for Computational Linguistics: Human Language Technologies, Volume 1 (Long and Short Papers)*, pages 4171–4186, Minneapolis, Minnesota. Association for Computational Linguistics.

Marc J. Epstein and Krishna G. Palepu. 1999. What financial analysts want.

Michael Ewens. 2019. Mda statements from public firms: 2002-2018.

Stefano Giglio, Matteo Maggiori, Johannes Stroebel, and Stephen Utkus. 2021. Five facts about beliefs and portfolios. *American Economic Review*, 111(5):1481–1522.

Zhiheng Huang, Wei Xu, and Kai Yu. 2015. Bidirectional LSTM-CRF models for sequence tagging. *CoRR*, abs/1508.01991.

Jyri Jalo. 2021. JyriJalo-MastersThesis. page 82.

Long Jiang, Mo Yu, Ming Zhou, Xiaohua Liu, and Tiejun Zhao. 2011. Target-dependent twitter sentiment classification. In *Proceedings of the 49th Annual Meeting of the Association for Computational Linguistics: Human Language Technologies - Volume 1*, HLT '11, page 151–160, USA. Association for Computational Linguistics.

Jan-Christoph Klie, Michael Bugert, Beto Boullosa, Richard Eckart de Castilho, and Iryna Gurevych. 2018. The inception platform: Machine-assisted and knowledge-oriented interactive annotation. In *Proceedings of the 27th International Conference on Computational Linguistics: System Demonstrations*, pages 5–9. Association for Computational Linguistics.

Tim Loughran and Bill Mcdonald. 2011. When Is a Liability Not a Liability? Textual Analysis, Dictionaries, and 10-Ks. *Journal of Finance*, 66(1):35–65.

Pekka Malo, Ankur Sinha, Pyry Takala, Pekka Korhonen, and Jyrki Wallenius. 2013. Good Debt or Bad Debt: Detecting Semantic Orientations in Economic Texts. *arXiv:1307.5336 [cs, q-fin]*. ArXiv: 1307.5336.

J. Martin and Peter White. 2005. *The Language of Evaluation: Appraisal in English*.

Hugo Mercier and Dan Sperber. 2011. Why do humans reason? arguments for an argumentative theory. *The Behavioral and brain sciences*, 34:57–74; discussion 74.

Hiroki Nakayama. 2018. seqeval: A python framework for sequence labeling evaluation. Software available from https://github.com/chakki-works/seqeval.

Ramanathan Narayanan, Bing Liu, and Alok Choudhary. 2009. Sentiment analysis of conditional sentences. In *Proceedings of the 2009 Conference on Empirical Methods in Natural Language Processing: Volume 1 - Volume 1*, EMNLP '09, page 180–189, USA. Association for Computational Linguistics.

Ambreen Nazir, Yuan Rao, Lianwei Wu, and Ling Sun. 2020. Issues and challenges of aspect-based sentiment analysis: A comprehensive survey. *IEEE Transactions on Affective Computing*, pages 1–1.

Patrick Paroubek, Cyril Grouin, Patrice Bellot, Vincent Claveau, Iris Eshkol-Taravella, Amel Fraisse, Agata Jackiewicz, Jihen Karoui, Laura Monceaux, and Juan-Manuel Torres-Moreno. 2018. DEFT2018 : Recherche d'information et analyse de sentiments dans des tweets concernant les transports en Île de France. In *DEFT 2018 - 14ème atelier Défi Fouille de Texte*, volume 2 of *Actes de la conférence Traitement Automatique des Langues, TALN 2018*, pages 1–11, Rennes, France.

Maria Pontiki, Dimitris Galanis, John Pavlopoulos, Harris Papageorgiou, Ion Androutsopoulos, and Suresh Manandhar. 2014. SemEval-2014 task 4: Aspect based sentiment analysis. In *Proceedings of the 8th International Workshop on Semantic Evaluation (SemEval 2014)*, pages 27–35, Dublin, Ireland. Association for Computational Linguistics.

Peng Qi, Yuhao Zhang, Yuhui Zhang, Jason Bolton, and Christopher D. Manning. 2020. Stanza: A Python natural language processing toolkit for many human languages. In *Proceedings of the 58th Annual Meeting of the Association for Computational Linguistics: System Demonstrations*.

Thomas J. Richards. 1965. Hume's two definitions of 'cause'. *The Philosophical Quarterly (1950-)*, 15(60):247–253.

Stefan Schweter and Alan Akbik. 2020. Flert: Document-level features for named entity recognition.

Paul C. Tetlock. 2007. Giving content to investor sentiment: The role of media in the stock market. *Journal of Finance*, 62(3):1139–1168.

Erik F. Tjong Kim Sang and Fien De Meulder. 2003. Introduction to the CoNLL-2003 Shared Task: Language-Independent Named Entity Recognition. In *Proceedings of the Seventh Conference on Natural Language Learning at HLT-NAACL 2003*, pages 142–147.

A Appendix

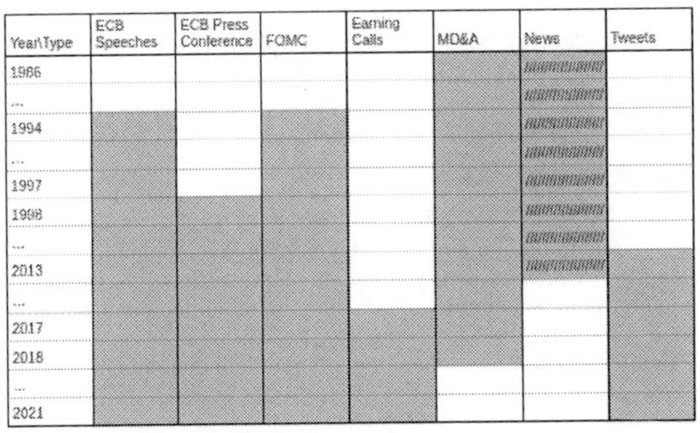

Figure 5: Shaded slashes of the column 'News' indicate that the time range of news sentences from the Financial PhraseBank dataset is incognito.

Labeled	Groups	Tags	Definition	Arrow
by algorithms	Named Entities	PERSON	people's name	None
		GEO	regions, countries	
		ORG	companies or institutions	
	Other Elements	NEGATION	absolute, partial or verbal negation	from [NEGATION] to its relevant [OEE]
		TOI	terms of interest in economics and finance	None
		APPRAISAL	opinion and emotion expressions	
by human	Opinion & Emotion Expressions	OEE	word of the span of words which indicated opinion holder's appraisal	from [OEE] toward its corresponding target
	Targets	-	target toward which a negative opinion is expressed	None
		+	target toward which a positive opinion is expressed	
		non-committal	target toward which opinion holder do not express their thoughts, attitude or intentions clearly.	
		unknown	annotators do not know which polarity to attribute for a particular concept/jargon, but **this tag should be used with caution**	
	Rhetorical Modes	RESULT	the span of words that declares: " something produces another thing as a result"; relation (cause, consequence) expressed by author	from [RESULT] to its relevant targets
		GUESS	explicit speculation about future	from [GUESS] to its relevant targets
		PREMISE	arguments used by opinion holder to support his opinion	None
		CONDITIONAL	expressed opinion are conditional on a specific clause	

Table 11 The list of possible tags labeled by algorithms and by human

Type	CB	EC	News	MD&A	Tweets	Laptop	Restaurant
min	6	8	6	13	10	3	7
max	77	80	53	258	27	83	79
mean	28.65	27.22	24.96	34.79	17.52	18.93	17.16
standard deviation	12.3	11.75	10.29	26.02	3.92	10.78	8.94

Table 12 The statistics about sentence length (i.e. number of tokens) by type of data source

Axis	Group	Definition	Example
Variation	UP/HIGH	gain in quantity or volume	rise, grow, upturn, recovery ...
	DOWN/LOW	loss in quantity or volume	escalate, downturn, plummet, ...
	STABLE	stable state	maintain, unchanged, hold, ...
	OTHERS	other expressions of variation	accumulation, surge ...
Attitude (rational)	APPRECIATE	recognition of value	good, well, sufficient ...
	NO_APPRECIATE	recognition of loss in value	inadequate, erosion, destructive..
	UNCERTAINTY	lack of visibility	risk, consolidation, speculative...
	ALARM	anxious awareness of undesirable outcome	pressure, tension, danger ...
	NON_SURPRISE	indicators to declare that observation are close to one's expectation.	in line with our expectation ...
	OTHERS	other expressions of attitude, such as multi-word expressions	surprise, surprisingly, surprised, ...
Attitude (emotional)	Over-confidence	intense feeling of excitement and strong desire to put ideas into practices	thrill, euphoria, greed,...
	FEAR	feeling of helpless, without any degree of control on the situation	anxiety, denial, panic...
	OTHERS	other expressions of over-pessimism or over-optimism, such as multi-word expressions	
Graduation	STRONG	high intensity	extremely, completely, rapid...
	WEAK	low intensity	gradually, slowly, steadily ...
	OTHERS	other expressions of intensity, strength and focus	

Table 13 Appraisal terms to monitor, judge the development an event or a concept, or to measure its impact.

	Words
Negative pattern	scarcely, scarce, fail, no more, nowhere, not, no, none, neither, little, deficiency, no longer, few, nowise, seldom, miscarry, in no manner, miscarry, nor, to no degree, hardly, zilch, nobody, cipher, by no means, lack, rarely, barely, nothing, deny, without, null, in no way, never, nada, cypher, naught, nix, zero, absence, nil, negate

Table 14 List of possible negative patterns

Type	CB	EC	News	MD&A	Tweets	Laptop	Restaurant
w. 1 target	61%	60%	86%	61%	60%	64%	51%
w. 2 targets	25%	26%	12 %	28%	32%	23%	29%
$\geq$ 3 targets	14%	14%	2%	11%	8%	13%	20%
Nb sentences w. target(s)	433	438	540	61	50	2,966	4,728

Table 15 Statistics about number of targets per sentence of our corpus v.s. the SemEval-2014 Task 4

EDGAR-CORPUS: Billions of Tokens Make The World Go Round

Lefteris Loukas[1,2], **Manos Fergadiotis**[1], **Ion Androutsopoulos**[1,2], **Prodromos Malakasiotis**[1]
[1]EY AI Centre of Excellence in Document Intelligence, NCSR "Demokritos"
[2]Department of Informatics, Athens University of Economics and Business, Greece

Abstract

We release EDGAR-CORPUS, a novel corpus comprising annual reports from all the publicly traded companies in the US spanning a period of more than 25 years. To the best of our knowledge, EDGAR-CORPUS is the largest financial NLP corpus available to date. All the reports are downloaded, split into their corresponding items (sections), and provided in a clean, easy-to-use JSON format. We use EDGAR-CORPUS to train and release EDGAR-W2V, which are WORD2VEC embeddings for the financial domain. We employ these embeddings in a battery of financial NLP tasks and showcase their superiority over generic GloVe embeddings and other existing financial word embeddings. We also open-source EDGAR-CRAWLER, a toolkit that facilitates downloading and extracting future annual reports.

1 Introduction

Natural Language Processing (NLP) for economics and finance is a rapidly developing research area (Hahn et al., 2018, 2019; Chen et al., 2020; El-Haj et al., 2020). While financial data are usually reported in tables, much valuable information also lies in text. A prominent source of such textual data is the Electronic Data Gathering, Analysis, and Retrieval system (EDGAR) from the US Securities and Exchange (SEC) website that hosts filings of publicly traded companies.[1] In order to maintain transparency and regulate exchanges, SEC requires all public companies to periodically upload various reports, describing their financial status, as well as important events like acquisitions and bankruptcy.

Financial documents from EDGAR have been useful in a variety of tasks such as stock price prediction (Lee et al., 2014), risk analysis (Kogan et al., 2009), financial distress prediction (Gandhi et al., 2019), and merger participants identification (Katsafados et al., 2021). However, there has not been an open-source, efficient tool to retrieve textual information from EDGAR. Researchers interested in economics and NLP often rely on heavily-paid subscription services or try to build web crawlers from scratch, often unsuccessfully. In the latter case, there are many technical challenges, especially when aiming to retrieve the annual reports of a specific firm for particular years or to extract the most relevant item sections from documents that may contain hundreds of pages. Thus, developing a web-crawling toolkit for EDGAR as well as releasing a large financial corpus in a clean, easy-to-use form would foster research in financial NLP.

Corpora	Filings	Tokens	Companies	Years
Händschke et al. (2018)	Various	242M	270	2000-2015
Daudert and Ahmadi (2019)	Various	188M	60	1995-2018
Lee et al. (2014)	8-K	27.9M	500	2002-2012
Kogan et al. (2009)	10-K	247.7M	10,492	1996-2006
Tsai et al. (2016)	10-K	359M	7,341	1996-2013
EDGAR-CORPUS (ours)	10-K	**6.5B**	**38,009**	**1993-2020**

Table 1: Financial corpora derived from SEC (lower part) and other sources (upper part).

In this paper, we release EDGAR-CORPUS, a novel financial corpus containing all the US annual reports (10-K filings) from 1993 to 2020.[2] Each report is provided in an easy-to-use JSON format containing all 20 sections and subsections (items) of a SEC annual report; different items provide useful information for different tasks in financial NLP. To the best of our knowledge, EDGAR-CORPUS is the largest publicly available financial corpus (Table 1). In addition, we use EDGAR-CORPUS to train and release WORD2VEC embeddings, dubbed EDGAR-W2V. We experimentally show that the new embeddings are more useful for financial NLP tasks than generic GloVe embeddings (Pennington et al., 2014) and other previously released financial WORD2VEC embeddings (Tsai et al., 2016).

Correspondence: eleftherios.loukas@ey.com, eleftheriosloukas@aueb.gr

[1]See https://www.sec.gov/edgar/searchedgar/companysearch.html for more information.

[2]EDGAR-CORPUS is available at: https://zenodo.org/record/5528490

Proceedings of the Third Workshop on Economics and Natural Language Processing, pages 13–18
Punta Cana and online, November 11.

Finally, to further facilitate future research in financial NLP, we open-source EDGAR-CRAWLER, the Python toolkit we developed to download and extract the text from the annual reports of publicly traded companies available at EDGAR.[3]

2 Related Work

There are few textual financial resources in the NLP literature. Händschke et al. (2018) published JOCo, a corpus of non-SEC annual and social responsibility reports for the top 270 US, UK, and German companies. Daudert and Ahmadi (2019) released CoFiF, the first financial corpus in the French language, comprising annual, semestrial, trimestrial, and reference business documents.

While some previous work has published document collections from EDGAR, those collections come with certain limitations. Kogan et al. (2009) published a collection of the Management's Discussion and Analysis Sections (Item 7) for all SEC company annual reports from 1996 to 2006. Tsai et al. (2016) updated that collection to include reports up to 2013 while also providing WORD2VEC embeddings. Finally, Lee et al. (2014) released a collection of 8-K reports from EDGAR, which announce significant firm events such as acquisitions or director resignations, from 2002 until 2012.

Compared to previous work, EDGAR-CORPUS contains all 20 items of the annual reports from all publicly traded companies in the US, covering a time period from 1993 to 2020. We believe that releasing the whole annual reports (with all 20 items) will facilitate several research directions in financial NLP (Loughran and McDonald, 2016). Also, EDGAR-CORPUS is much larger than previously published financial corpora in terms of tokens, number of companies, and year range (Table 1).

3 Creating EDGAR-CORPUS

3.1 Data and toolkit

Publicly-listed companies are required to submit 10-K filings (annual reports) every year. Each 10-K filing is a complete description of the company's economic activity during the corresponding fiscal year. Such reports also provide a full outline of risks, liabilities, corporate agreements, and operations. Furthermore, the documents provide an extensive analysis of the relevant sector industry and the marketplace as a whole.

	Item	Section Name
Part I	Item 1	Business
	Item 1A	Risk Factors
	Item 1B	Unresolved Staff Comments
	Item 2	Properties
	Item 3	Legal Proceedings
	Item 4	Mine Safety Disclosures
Part II	Item 5	Market
	Item 6	Consolidated Financial Data
	Item 7	Management's Discussion and Analysis
	Item 7A	Quantitative and Qualitative Disclosures about Market Risks
	Item 8	Financial Statements
	Item 9	Changes in and Disagreements With Accountants
	Item 9A	Controls and Procedures
	Item 9B	Other Information
Part III	Item 10	Directors, Executive Officers and Corporate Governance
	Item 11	Executive Compensation
	Item 12	Security Ownership of Certain Beneficial Owners
	Item 13	Certain Relationships and Related Transactions
	Item 14	Principal Accounting Fees and Services
Part IV	Item 15	Exhibits and Financial Statement Schedules Signatures

Table 2: The 20 different items of a 10-K report.

A 10-K report is organized in 4 parts and 20 different items (Table 2). Extracting specific items from documents with hundreds of pages usually requires manual work, which is time- and resource-intensive. To promote research in all possible directions, we extracted all available items using an extensive pre-processing and extraction pipeline.

In more detail, we developed EDGAR-CRAWLER, which we used to download the 10-K reports of all publicly traded companies in the US between the years 1993 and 2020. We then removed all tables to keep only the textual data, which were HTML-stripped,[4] cleaned and split into the different items by using regular expressions. The resulting dataset is EDGAR-CORPUS.

While there exist toolkits to download annual filings from EDGAR, they do not support the extraction of specific item sections.[5] This is particularly important since researchers often rely on certain items in their experimental setup. For example, Goel and Gangolly (2012), Purda and Skillicorn (2015), and Goel and Uzuner (2016) perform textual analysis on Item 7 to detect corporate fraud. Katsafados et al. (2020) combine Item 7 and Item

[3] EDGAR-CRAWLER is available at: `https://github.com/nlpaueb/edgar-crawler`

[4] We use Beautiful Soup (`https://beautiful-soup-4.readthedocs.io/en/latest`).

[5] For example, sec-edgar can download complete HTML reports (with images and tables), but it does not produce clean item-specific text.

1A to detect Initial Public Offering (IPO) underpricing, while Moriarty et al. (2019) combine Item 1 with Item 7 to predict mergers and acquisitions.

Apart from EDGAR-CORPUS, we also release EDGAR-CRAWLER, the toolkit we developed to create EDGAR-CORPUS, to facilitate future research based on textual data from EDGAR. EDGAR-CRAWLER consists of two Python modules that support its main functions:

edgar_crawler.py is used to download 10-K reports in batch or for specific companies that are of interest to the user.

extract_items.py extracts the text of all or particular items from 10-K reports. Each item's text becomes a separate JSON key-value pair (Figure 1).

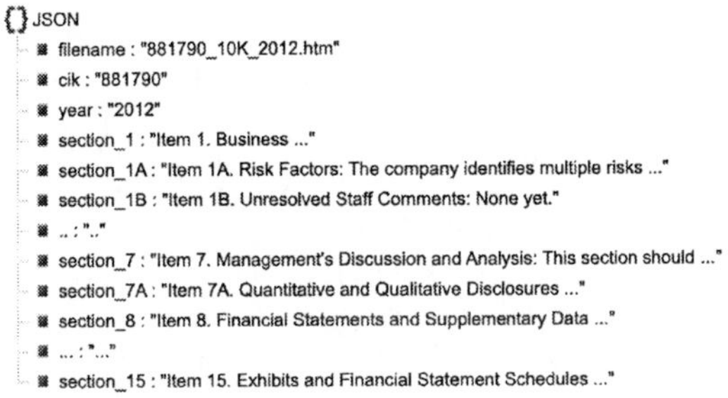

Figure 1: An example of a 10-K report in JSON format as downloaded and extracted by EDGAR-CRAWLER; *filename* is the downloaded 10-K file; *cik* is the Company Index Key; *year* is the corresponding Fiscal Year.

3.2 Word embeddings

To facilitate financial NLP research, we used EDGAR-CORPUS to train WORD2VEC embeddings (EDGAR-W2V), which can be used for downstream tasks, such as financial text classification or summarization. We used WORD2VEC's skip-gram model (Mikolov et al., 2013a,b) with default parameters as implemented by GENSIM (Řehůřek and Sojka, 2010) to generate 200-dimensional WORD2VEC embeddings for a vocabulary of 100K words. The word tokens are generated using SPACY (Honnibal et al., 2020). We also release EDGAR-W2V.[6]

To illustrate the quality of EDGAR-W2V embeddings, in Figure 2 we visualize sampled words from seven different entity types, i.e., *location*, *industry*, *company*, *year*, *month*, *number*, and *financial term*, after applying dimensionality reduction with the UMAP algorithm (McInnes et al., 2018). The

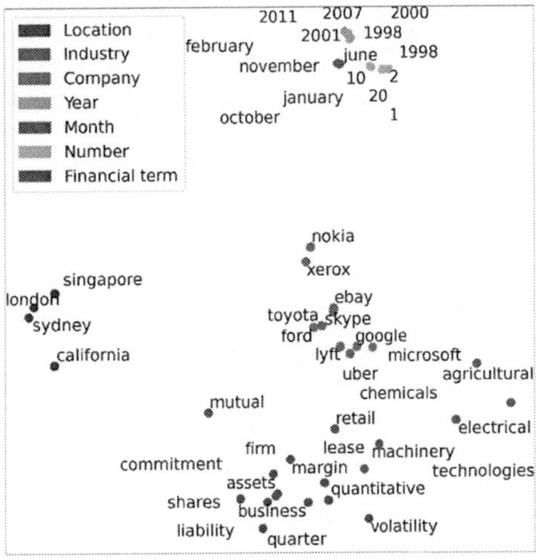

Figure 2: Visualization of the EDGAR-W2V embeddings. Different colors indicate different entity types.

financial terms are randomly sampled from the Investopedia Financial Terms Dictionary.[7] In addition, companies and industries are randomly sampled from well-known industry sectors and publicly traded stocks. Finally, the words belonging to the remaining entity types are randomly sampled from gazetteers. Figure 2 shows that words belonging to the same entity type form clear clusters in the 2-dimensional space indicating that EDGAR-W2V embeddings manage to capture the underlying financial semantics of the vocabulary.

To further highlight the semantics captured by EDGAR-W2V embeddings, we retrieved the 5 nearest neighbors, according to cosine similarity, for commonly used financial terms (Table 3).[8] As shown, all the nearest neighbors are highly related to the corresponding term. For instance, the word *economy* is correctly associated with terms indicating the slowdown of the economy happening during the past few years, e.g., *downturn*, *recession*, or *slowdown*. Also, *market* is correctly related with

economy	*competitor*	*market*	*national*	*investor*
downturn	competitive	marketplace	association	institutional
recession	competing	industry	regional	shareholder
slowdown	dominant	prices	nationwide	relations
sluggish	advantages	illiquidity	american	purchaser
stagnant	competition	prevailing	zions	creditor

Table 3: Sample words from EDGAR-W2V embeddings (top row) and their corresponding nearest neighbors (columns) based on cosine similarity.

[6]The EDGAR-W2V embeddings are available at: `https://zenodo.org/record/5524358`

[7]`https://www.investopedia.com/financial-term-dictionary-4769738`.

[8]We exclude obvious top-scoring neighbors of singular/plural pairs such as *market/markets or investor/investors*.

words such as *marketplace*, *industry*, and *prices*.

4 Experiments on financial NLP tasks

We also compare EDGAR-W2V embeddings against generic GloVe (Pennington et al., 2014) embeddings[9] and the financial embeddings of Tsai et al. (2016) in three financial NLP tasks. For each task, we use the same model and we only alter the embeddings component. In addition, we use the same pre-processing during the creation of the vocabulary of the embeddings in each case.

FinSim-3 (Juyeon Kang and Gan, 2021) provides a set of business and economic terms and the task is to classify them into the most relevant hypernym from a set of 17 possible hypernyms from the Financial Industry Business Ontology (FIBO).[10] Example hypernyms include *Credit Index*, *Bonds*, and *Stocks*. We tackle the problem with a multinomial logistic regression model, which, given the embedding of an economic term, classifies the term to one of the 17 possible hypernyms. Since FinSim-3 is a recently completed challenge, the true labels for the test data were not available. Therefore, we use a stratified 10-fold cross-validation. We report accuracy and the average rank of the correct hypernym as evaluation measures. For the latter, the 17 hypernyms are sorted according to the model's probabilities. A perfect model, i.e., one that would always rank the correct hypernym first, would have an average rank of 1.

Financial tagging (FinT) is an in-house sequence labeling problem for financial documents. The task is to annotate financial reports with word-level tags from an accounting taxonomy. To tackle the problem, we use a BILSTM encoder operating over word embeddings with a shared multinomial logistic regression that predicts the correct tag for each word from the corresponding BILSTM state. We report the F1 score micro-averaged across all tags.

FiQA Open Challenge (Maia et al., 2018) is a sentiment analysis regression challenge over financial texts. It contains financial tweets annotated by domain experts with a sentiment score in the range [-1, 1], with 1 denoting the most positive score. For this problem, we employ a BILSTM encoder which operates over word embeddings, and a linear regressor operating over the last hidden state of the BILSTM. Since we do not have access to the test set in this task, we use a 10-fold cross-validation. We evaluate the results using Mean Squared Error (MSE) and R-squared (R^2).

Across all tasks, EDGAR-W2V outperforms GloVe, showing that in-domain knowledge is critical in financial NLP problems (Table 4). The gains are more substantial in FinSim-3 and FinT, which rely to a larger extent on understanding highly technical economics discourse. Interestingly, the in-domain embeddings of Tsai et al. (2016) are comparable to the generic GloVe embeddings in two of the three tasks. One possible reason is that Tsai et al. (2016) employed stemming during the creation of the embeddings vocabulary, which might have contributed noise to the models due to loss of information.

	FinSim-3		FinT	FiQA	
	Acc. ↑	Rank ↓	F1 ↑	MSE ↓	R^2 ↑
GloVe	85.3	1.26	75.8	0.151	0.119
Tsai et al. (2016)	84.9	1.27	75.3	0.142	0.169
EDGAR-W2V (ours)	**87.9**	**1.21**	**77.3**	**0.141**	**0.176**

Table 4: Results across financial NLP tasks, with different word embeddings. We report averages over 3 runs with different random seeds. The standard deviations were very small and are omitted for brevity.

5 Conclusions and Future Work

We introduced and released EDGAR-CORPUS, a novel NLP corpus for the financial domain. To the best of our knowledge, EDGAR-CORPUS is the largest financial corpus available. It contains textual data from annual reports published in EDGAR, the repository for all US publicly traded companies, covering a period of more than 25 years. All the reports are split into their corresponding items (sections) and are provided in a clean, easy-to-use JSON format. We also released EDGAR-CRAWLER, a toolkit for downloading and extracting the reports. To showcase the impact of EDGAR-CORPUS, we used it to train and release EDGAR-W2V, which are financial WORD2VEC embeddings. After illustrating the quality of EDGAR-W2V embeddings, we also showed their usefulness in three financial NLP tasks, where they outperformed generic GloVe embeddings and other financial embeddings.

In future work, we plan to extend EDGAR-CRAWLER to support additional types of documents (e.g., 10-Q, 8-K) and to leverage EDGAR-CORPUS to explore transfer learning for the financial domain, which is vastly understudied.

[9]We use the 200-dimensional GloVe embeddings from `https://nlp.stanford.edu/data/glove.6B.zip`.

[10]`https://spec.edmcouncil.org/fibo/`.

Disclaimer

This publication contains information in summary form and is therefore intended for general guidance only. It is not intended to be a substitute for detailed research or the exercise of professional judgment. Member firms of the global EY organization cannot accept responsibility for loss to any person relying on this article.

References

Chung-Chi Chen, Hen-Hsen Huang, Hiroya Takamura, and Hsin-Hsi Chen, editors. 2020. *Proceedings of the Second Workshop on Financial Technology and Natural Language Processing*. Kyoto, Japan.

Tobias Daudert and Sina Ahmadi. 2019. CoFiF: A corpus of financial reports in French language. In *Proceedings of the First Workshop on Financial Technology and Natural Language Processing*, pages 21–26, Macao, China.

Mahmoud El-Haj, Vasiliki Athanasakou, Sira Ferradans, Catherine Salzedo, Ans Elhag, Houda Bouamor, Marina Litvak, Paul Rayson, George Giannakopoulos, and Nikiforos Pittaras, editors. 2020. *Proceedings of the 1st Joint Workshop on Financial Narrative Processing and MultiLing Financial Summarisation*. Barcelona, Spain (Online).

Priyank Gandhi, Tim Loughran, and Bill McDonald. 2019. Using Annual Report Sentiment as a Proxy for Financial Distress in U.S. Banks. *Journal of Behavioral Finance*, 20(4):424–436.

Sunita Goel and Jagdish Gangolly. 2012. Beyond the numbers: Mining the annual reports for hidden cues indicative of financial statement fraud. *Intelligent Systems in Accounting, Finance and Management*, 19(2):75–89.

Sunita Goel and Özlem Uzuner. 2016. Do sentiments matter in fraud detection? estimating semantic orientation of annual reports. *Intelligent Systems in Accounting, Finance and Management*, 23:215–239.

Udo Hahn, Véronique Hoste, and Ming-Feng Tsai, editors. 2018. *Proceedings of the First Workshop on Economics and Natural Language Processing*. Melbourne, Australia.

Udo Hahn, Véronique Hoste, and Zhu Zhang, editors. 2019. *Proceedings of the Second Workshop on Economics and Natural Language Processing*. Hong Kong.

Sebastian G.M. Händschke, Sven Buechel, Jan Goldenstein, Philipp Poschmann, Tinghui Duan, Peter Walgenbach, and Udo Hahn. 2018. A corpus of corporate annual and social responsibility reports: 280 million tokens of balanced organizational writing. In *Proceedings of the First Workshop on Economics and Natural Language Processing*, pages 20–31, Melbourne, Australia.

Matthew Honnibal, Ines Montani, Sofie Van Landeghem, and Adriane Boyd. 2020. spaCy: Industrial-strength Natural Language Processing in Python.

Sandra Bellato Juyeon Kang, Ismail El Maarouf and Mei Gan. 2021. Finsim-3: The 3rd shared task on learning semantic similarities for the financial domain. In *Proceedings of the Third Workshop on Financial Technology and Natural Language Processing*, Held Online.

Apostolos G. Katsafados, Ion Androutsopoulos, Ilias Chalkidis, Emmanouel Fergadiotis, George N. Leledakis, and Emmanouil G. Pyrgiotakis. 2021. Using textual analysis to identify merger participants: Evidence from the u.s. banking industry. *Finance Research Letters*, page 101949.

Apostolos G. Katsafados, Ion Androutsopoulos, Ilias Chalkidis, Manos Fergadiotis, George N. Leledakis, and Emmanouil G. Pyrgiotakis. 2020. Textual Information and IPO Underpricing: A Machine Learning Approach. MPRA Paper 103813, University Library of Munich, Germany.

Shimon Kogan, Dimitry Levin, Bryan R. Routledge, Jacob S. Sagi, and Noah A. Smith. 2009. Predicting risk from financial reports with regression. In *Proceedings of Human Language Technologies: The 2009 Annual Conference of the North American Chapter of the Association for Computational Linguistics*, pages 272–280, Boulder, Colorado.

Heeyoung Lee, Mihai Surdeanu, Bill MacCartney, and Dan Jurafsky. 2014. On the importance of text analysis for stock price prediction. In *Proceedings of the Ninth International Conference on Language Resources and Evaluation (LREC'14)*, pages 1170–1175, Reykjavik, Iceland.

Tim Loughran and Bill McDonald. 2016. Textual analysis in accounting and finance: A survey. *Journal of Accounting Research*, 54(4):1187–1230.

Macedo Maia, S. Handschuh, A. Freitas, Brian Davis, R. McDermott, M. Zarrouk, and A. Balahur. 2018. Www'18 open challenge: Financial opinion mining and question answering. *Companion Proceedings of the The Web Conference 2018.*

Leland McInnes, John Healy, Nathaniel Saul, and Lukas Grossberger. 2018. Umap: Uniform manifold approximation and projection. *The Journal of Open Source Software*, 3(29):861.

Tomás Mikolov, Kai Chen, Greg Corrado, and Jeffrey Dean. 2013a. Efficient estimation of word representations in vector space. In *1st International Conference on Learning Representations, ICLR 2013, Scottsdale, Arizona, USA, May 2-4, 2013, Workshop Track Proceedings*.

Tomás Mikolov, Ilya Sutskever, Kai Chen, Gregory S. Corrado, and Jeffrey Dean. 2013b. Distributed representations of words and phrases and their compositionality. In *Advances in Neural Information Processing Systems 26: 27th Annual Conference on Neural Information Processing Systems 2013. Proceedings of a meeting held December 5-8, 2013, Lake Tahoe, Nevada, United States*, pages 3111–3119.

Ryan Moriarty, Howard Ly, Ellie Lan, and Suzanne McIntosh. 2019. Deal or no deal: Predicting mergers and acquisitions at scale. *2019 IEEE International Conference on Big Data (Big Data)*, pages 5552–5558.

Jeffrey Pennington, Richard Socher, and Christopher Manning. 2014. GloVe: Global vectors for word representation. In *Proceedings of the 2014 Conference on Empirical Methods in Natural Language Processing (EMNLP)*, pages 1532–1543, Doha, Qatar.

Lynnette Purda and David Skillicorn. 2015. Accounting variables, deception, and a bag of words: Assessing the tools of fraud detection. *Contemporary Accounting Research*, 32(3):1193–1223.

Radim Řehůřek and Petr Sojka. 2010. Software Framework for Topic Modelling with Large Corpora. In *Proceedings of the LREC 2010 Workshop on New Challenges for NLP Frameworks*, pages 45–50, Valletta, Malta. `http://is.muni.cz/publication/884893/en`.

Ming-Feng Tsai, Chuan-Ju Wang, and Po-Chuan Chien. 2016. Discovering finance keywords via continuous-space language models. *ACM Transactions on Management Information Systems*, 7(3).

The Global Banking Standards QA Dataset (GBS-QA)

Kyunghwan Sohn
KAIST
Daejeon, South Korea
sony0125@kaist.ac.kr

Sunjae Kwon*
University of Massachusetts
Amherst, MA, USA
sunjaekwon@cs.umass.edu

Jaesik Choi
KAIST
Daejeon, South Korea
jaesik.Choi@kaist.ac.kr

Abstract

A domain specific question answering (QA) dataset dramatically improves the machine comprehension performance. This paper presents a new Global Banking Standards QA dataset (GBS-QA) in the banking regulation domain. The GBS-QA has three values. First, it contains actual questions from market players and answers from global rule setter, the Basel Committee on Banking Supervision (BCBS) in the middle of creating and revising banking regulations. Second, financial regulation experts analyze and verify pairs of questions and answers in the annotation process. Lastly, the GBS-QA is a totally different dataset with existing datasets in finance and is applicable to stimulate transfer learning research in the banking regulation domain.

1 Introduction

Global banking standards have been strictly organized and gradually evolved over time to reflect the changes of financial environment and new risks emerged. The Basel Committee on Banking Supervision (BCBS) which is one of international rule setters governs to create and revise the international banking standards in cooperation with member countries and international financial supervisory agencies.

Creating new rules and revising current standards require clear communications with related parties such as financial supervisory authorities and market players over the globe. In the process of this work, Frequently Asked Questions (FAQs) are formally constructed and disclosed in order to help understand better how to implement provisions in practice. The FAQs contains questions from market players and answers from the BCBS. However, original pairs of questions and answers in the FAQs are not standardized so that they need to be re-organized and revised in order to become qualified practices on the corresponding provisions. Considering that financial regulations are directly influential to the market and they require expertise to interpret and understand the context in the FAQs, financial regulation experts should be involved.

We propose a new Global Banking Standards QA dataset (GBS-QA). The GBS-QA has three values. First, given that GBS-QA is composed of actual questions and answers in practice, both market players and regulators find it quite useful at work as additional guidelines. Second, financial regulation experts participate in this study to construct revised QA pairs which can be properly applied into the NLP model. Third, the GBS-QA is a totally different dataset with existing datasets in finance and is applicable to stimulate transfer learning research in the banking regulation domain.

This paper is constructed as follows. Related work is reviewed in Section 2. The process of collecting and annotating the GBS-QA is described in Section 3. The experimental results of the pre-trained language model and its domain-adaptive model on GBS-QA are revealed in Section 4.

2 Related work

There have been many researches on constructing new datasets in various domains and utilizing them on their own purpose. In finance, financial news sentiment dataset (Ding et al., 2015) and financial opinion mining and questions answering dataset (Chen et al., 2020) are widely utilized. However, since these are basically rooted from financial news and general narratives in financial reports, they are not equipped with terminology in financial regulation and of course are not qualified for doing tasks in financial regulation domain.

Aside from construction of new datasets, how to make AI-enabled NLP models be more understandable and explainable is one of top priorities. Recently centered on medical domain, text entailment(Abacha and Demner-Fushman, 2016; Fei

* He engaged in this work when he was in KAIST.

Proceedings of the Third Workshop on Economics and Natural Language Processing, pages 19–25
Punta Cana and online, November 11.

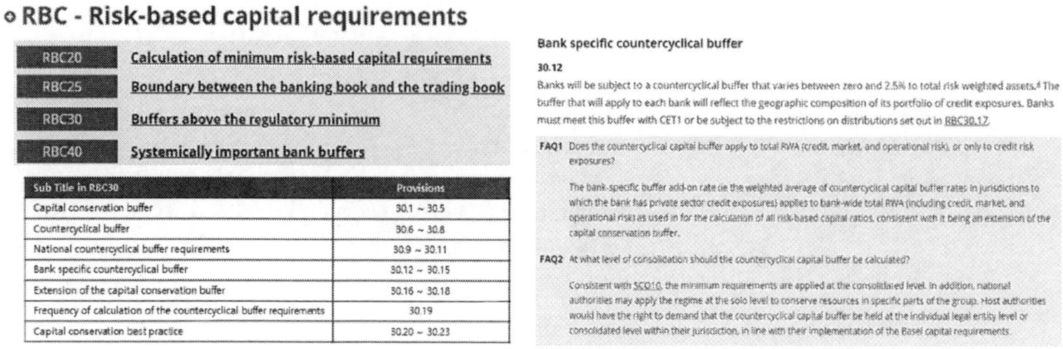
o RBC - Risk-based capital requirements

RBC20	Calculation of minimum risk-based capital requirements
RBC25	Boundary between the banking book and the trading book
RBC30	Buffers above the regulatory minimum
RBC40	Systemically important bank buffers

Sub Title in RBC30	Provisions
Capital conservation buffer	30.1 ~ 30.5
Countercyclical buffer	30.6 ~ 30.8
National countercyclical buffer requirements	30.9 ~ 30.11
Bank specific countercyclical buffer	30.12 ~ 30.15
Extension of the capital conservation buffer	30.16 ~ 30.18
Frequency of calculation of the countercyclical buffer requirements	30.19
Capital conservation best practice	30.20 ~ 30.23

Bank specific countercyclical buffer

30.12

Banks will be subject to a countercyclical buffer that varies between zero and 2.5% to total risk weighted assets.[4] The buffer that will apply to each bank will reflect the geographic composition of its portfolio of credit exposures. Banks must meet this buffer with CET1 or be subject to the restrictions on distributions set out in RBC30.17.

FAQ1 Does the countercyclical capital buffer apply to total RWA (credit, market, and operational risk), or only to credit risk exposures?

The bank-specific buffer add-on rate (ie the weighted average of countercyclical capital buffer rates in jurisdictions to which the bank has private sector credit exposures) applies to bank-wide total RWA (including credit, market, and operational risk) as used in for the calculation of all risk-based capital ratios, consistent with it being an extension of the capital conservation buffer.

FAQ2 At what level of consolidation should the countercyclical capital buffer be calculated?

Consistent with SCO10, the minimum requirements are applied at the consolidated level. In addition, national authorities may apply the regime at the solo level to conserve resources in specific parts of the group. Host authorities would have the right to demand that the countercyclical capital buffer be held at the individual legal entity level or consolidated level within their jurisdiction, in line with their implementation of the Basel capital requirements.

Figure 1: An Example of provisions, questions and answers in GBS-QA

et al., 2021) and deep neural reasoning(Han et al., 2021) are applied to do question answering tasks and combination of these approaches and input medical text contributes to achieve the goal of enhancing interpretability and explainability. From a perspective of few-shot setting, few-shot textual entailment framework combined with graphical structure in data also shows its effectiveness in the downstream tasks(Yin et al., 2020).

In addition, domain-adaptive pretraining is proposed as one of the guaranteed way to lead to performance gains (Ding et al., 2015) in domain-specific tasks. FinBERT (Andrew and Gao, 2007) and BioBERT (Lee et al., 2020), for example, are types of domain-adaptive models.

3 GBS-QA

GBS-QA is collected from the BCBS website[1]. The BCBS framework comprises the 14 standards and each standard has its provisions and the associated FAQs which are matched with the corresponding provisions. As shown in Figure 1, Risk-based capital requirements (RBC) which is one of the standards contains 4 sub-categories and each sub-category has a varying number of provisions with different length. The provision of 30.12, for example, raises two questions from market players so that the BCBS answers these questions with detailed explanations.

Overview of a GBS-QA construction process follows Figure 2. Starting from BCBS framework, all standards and the associated FAQs are automatically filtered out of the BCBS website. These data are organized and preprocessed by human annotation process. Human annotation includes organizing provisions, matching the provisions with the corresponding FAQs and reviewing questions and answers in a reconciled manner. This review is conducted by independent annotators which consists of five financial regulation experts. From the human annotation process, pairs of questions and answers are classified into four types which include 1) Binary answerable type, 2) WH type, 3) How type and 4) Conditional type. Upon question classification, questions are revised into "Binary answerable type" and answers are labelled into "Yes" or "No" to corresponding questions according to the GBS-QA classification guideline in Appendix A. After completing the whole process in Figure 2, GBS-QA is constructed as a set of questions and answers in banking regulation domain.

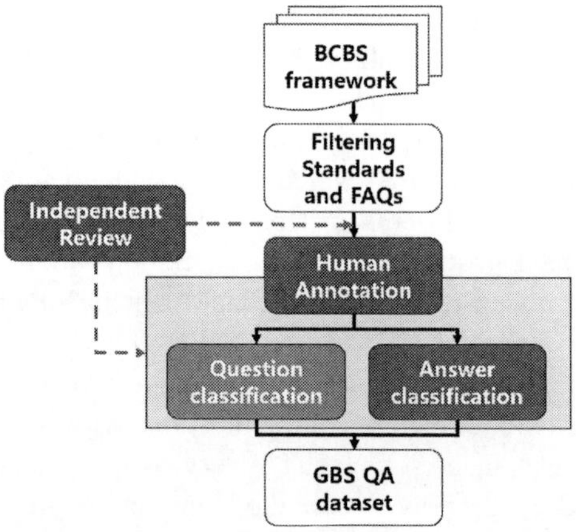

Figure 2: Overview of a GBS-QA construction process.

3.1 Automatic filtering of standards, questions and answers

The BCBS website provides a well-structured platform. From web crawling, data is collected by filtering "basel_navigations_standard_selection", "basel_paragraphs", "faqs_and_footnotes" and "basel_faq".

[1]https://www.bis.org/basel_framework/

3.2 Human Annotation

Human annotation mainly covers question classification and answer classification. This annotation process is conducted by five financial experts independently. Since it requires expertise in interpreting international banking regulations, annotators should be financial regulation experts who are qualified for this task. In the beginning, guideline is set to make it transparent and consistent for them to annotate questions and answers. The guideline is described in Appendix A. In compliance with the guideline, reviewing all pairs of questions and answers is implemented and then classifying questions and answers is followed. After constructing a dataset of questions and answers individually, five outcomes are compared and pairs are chosen throughout majority voting. Kappa statistics (Gururangan et al., 2020) is used as quantitative metric.

3.2.1 Question classification

Questions raised in the process of creating or revising standards are intended to make the corresponding provisions clearer with additional explanations in order to help market players to implement them compliantly. Given that answers are directly influential to market, they are supposed to be transparent and concise based on attached references.

Considering the characteristics of pairs of questions and answers in the BCBS framework, we reach to a conclusion that if all the questions are revised to be answered with "Yes" or "No", the revised questions can be added to the corresponding provisions and ultimately become additional provisions. The question of "What is the difference between (the jurisdiction of) “ultimate risk” and (the jurisdiction of) “immediate counterparty” exposures?", for example, can be transformed into "Is it correct that the difference between "ultimate risk" and "immediate counterparty" exposures means that ... ?" and the meaning phrase or sentence becomes additional information. The point is to determine if certain behavior is compliant with regulation or not and answers in the FAQs can be regarded as qualified provisions interpreted from the BCBS.

To transform the questions to be answerable with "Yes" or "No, question type should be analyzed and classified in the beginning. In this paper, we propose four question types which include 1) Binary answerable type, 2) WH type, 3) How type and 4) Conditional type. The definitions of four types are as follows. Examples are described in Appendix B.

1. **Type1 : Binary answerable type**
   A question which is answerable with "Yes" or "No".

2. **Type2 : WH type**
   A question which starts with "What", "Where", "Why" and "When" or has same nuance to all "WH".

3. **Type3 : How type**
   A question which starts with "How".

4. **Type4 : Conditional type**
   A question which is not answerable with "Yes" or "No" in general. However, if certain condition is met, this question becomes Type1.
   [Example]
   [Q] Can subordinated loans be included in regulatory capital?
   [A] As long as the subordinated loans meet all the criteria required for Additional Tier 1 or Tier capital, it is correct.

According to the annotation guideline in Appendix A, questions in Type2, Type3 and Type4 are transformed into new questions which can be answerable with "Yes" or "No" as same as Type1. Type2 and Type3 have specific phrase or sentence as the corresponding answer. In this case, the questions are simply revised into the sentence structure of "Is it correct that ..." or "Does it mean that ...". Type4 can be answerable as same as Type2 if certain conditions are met. In this regard, the condition captured from the context of the answer is put in front of or at the end of the original question with "if", "in cases where" and "as long as".

3.2.2 Answer classification

In line with question classification, answer classification is implemented by five annotators independently.

3.2.3 Classification result

Total number of pairs of questions and answers in the GBS-QA is 186. Question type distribution is shown in Table 1. Type1 accounts for 39% at the highest ratio and Type4 secondly ranks with 30% in the GBS-QA. The coverage ratio of "Yes" is 70%, whearas that of "No" is 30%.

Total	Type1	Type2	Type3	Type4
186	72(39%)	36(19%)	23(12%)	55(30%)

Table 1: Question type distribution

3.3 Comparison with other datasets in finance

The GBS-QA is quite different from other datasets in finance as shown in Figure 3. Comparing top 4 words among three datasets, GBS-QA contains the words of "capital", "risk", "bank", "Tier" which are closely related to banking regulations whereas FiQA includes "stock", "money", "company" and "credit" and PhraseBank covers "company", "profit", "net" and "sales". FiQA focuses on stock market and PhraseBank deals with corporate financial performance.

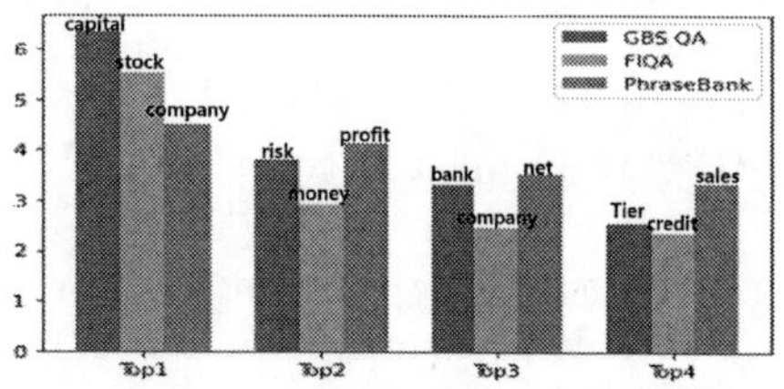

Figure 3: top 4 words distribution of GBS-QA, FiQA and PhraseBank.

In addition, in top 100 words, jaccard similarity of GBS-QA with the other two datasets remarks 0.10 and 0.05 respectively. Especially, the top 10 words in GBS-QA do not have any significant intersection with others. It implies that words distribution of GBS-QA is far away from the existing datasets in finance.

3.4 Important issues on GBS-QA

One of core parts in constructing the GBS-QA is how to revise the original questions to be answerable with "Yes" or "No" without significant loss of information in the original pairs of questions and answers. It is quite difficult to measure how much information is lost in this transforming process. However, if it is guaranteed that revised questions contain correct phrases or sentences in the original answers, it could tell that there is little loss of information in a qualitative manner.
Among four types of questions proposed in the section 3.2.1, Type3 (How type) and Type4 (conditional type) are much harder to transform the original questions because they require complete understanding on the context of answers in order to extract correct phrases or sentences concisely. In this regard, before disclosing the GBS-QA, it needs more effort to thoroughly review all QA pairs. Eventually the GBS-QA should be confirmed by the BCBS.

4 Model Architecture

The experiments aim to show that GBS-QA can be applicable to stimulate transfer learning on the classification task. Considering uniqueness and expertise of GBS-QA, domain-adaptive language models which are trained with all provisions in current standards and all answers are used to do this task.

As shown in Figure 4, it starts from pre-trained models such as RoBERTa (Liu et al., 2019) and ELECTRA(Clark et al., 2020). By training domain knowledge of banking standards, pre-trained models are evolved into post-trained model which is qualified for dealing with GBS-QA. Next, these post-trained models are fine-tuned for classification task with pairs of questions and answers("Yes" or "No) and the associated provisions. The final model is called BankReg QA model.

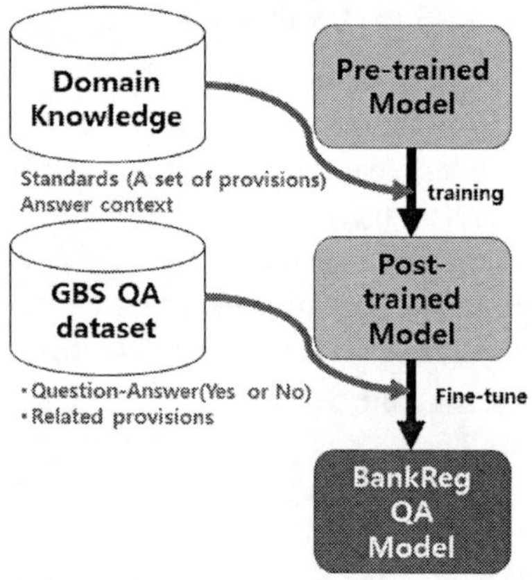

Figure 4: Overview of a BankReg QA model construction process.

5 Experiments

Due to lack of data points in the GBS-QA, there is no significant difference in experimental results between pre-trained and post-trained model in the GBS-QA. Moreover, some questions have longer length than 512 which is maximum length in the model and the other questions require interpretation of equations to calculate risk factors or risk exposure so that the models can not handle them properly. However, the post-trained model shows slightly lower performance in both FiQA and PhraseBank dataset.

6 Conclusion

We propose a new QA dataset which is called GBS-QA in the banking regulation domain. The

GBS-QA contains pairs of questions and answers re-organized and verified by financial regulation experts. Extra information extracted from the GBS-QA can become qualified practices on the associated provisions in the regulation. From the analysis and experiments, the GBS-QA shows that it has a different words distribution compared to other existing datasets in finance and it can be applicable in the NLP models.

7 Future Work

First of all, GBS-QA consists of high quality but relatively small number of QA pairs. Therefore, it is necessary to expand the size of the dataset. However, it requires tremendous cost to label large-scale data by qualified financial experts. Semi-supervised approaches can be one possible way to constuct large-scale data with minimal cost. We can consider to use a bootstrapping that iteratively expands data based on good quality seed data. In addition, we can utilize a relationship among provisions. This relationship can be drawn as a graph and the graphical structure can be used in training and fine-tuning. Lastly, studies on text entailment and non monotonic reasoning are applicable to analyzing and understanding financial regulation in the NLP tasks.

Acknowledgements

This work was supported by Institute of Information communications Technology Planning Evaluation (IITP) grant funded by the Korea government (MSIT) (No.2019-0-00075, Artificial Intelligence Graduate School Program (KAIST))

References

Asma Ben Abacha and Dina Demner-Fushman. 2016. Recognizing question entailment for medical question answering. In *AMIA Annual Symposium Proceedings*, volume 2016, page 310. American Medical Informatics Association.

Galen Andrew and Jianfeng Gao. 2007. Scalable training of L1-regularized log-linear models. In *Proceedings of the 24th International Conference on Machine Learning*, pages 33–40.

Chung-Chi Chen, Hen-Hsen Huang, and Hsin-Hsi Chen. 2020. Fine-grained financial opinion mining: A survey and research agenda. *arXiv preprint arXiv:2005.01897*.

Kevin Clark, Minh-Thang Luong, Quoc V Le, and Christopher D Manning. 2020. Electra: Pre-training text encoders as discriminators rather than generators. *arXiv preprint arXiv:2003.10555*.

Xiao Ding, Yue Zhang, Ting Liu, and Junwen Duan. 2015. Deep learning for event-driven stock prediction. In *Twenty-fourth international joint conference on artificial intelligence*.

Hao Fei, Yuanpei Guo, Bobo Li, Donghong Ji, and Yafeng Ren. 2021. Adversarial shared-private model for cross-domain clinical text entailment recognition. *Knowledge-Based Systems*, 221:106962.

Suchin Gururangan, Ana Marasović, Swabha Swayamdipta, Kyle Lo, Iz Beltagy, Doug Downey, and Noah A Smith. 2020. Don't stop pretraining: Adapt language models to domains and tasks. *arXiv preprint arXiv:2004.10964*.

Zhongyi Han, Benzheng Wei, Xiaoming Xi, Bo Chen, Yilong Yin, and Shuo Li. 2021. Unifying neural learning and symbolic reasoning for spinal medical report generation. *Medical Image Analysis*, 67:101872.

Jinhyuk Lee, Wonjin Yoon, Sungdong Kim, Donghyeon Kim, Sunkyu Kim, Chan Ho So, and Jaewoo Kang. 2020. Biobert: a pre-trained biomedical language representation model for biomedical text mining. *Bioinformatics*, 36(4):1234–1240.

Yinhan Liu, Myle Ott, Naman Goyal, Jingfei Du, Mandar Joshi, Danqi Chen, Omer Levy, Mike Lewis, Luke Zettlemoyer, and Veselin Stoyanov. 2019. Roberta: A robustly optimized bert pretraining approach. *arXiv preprint arXiv:1907.11692*.

Wenpeng Yin, Nazneen Fatema Rajani, Dragomir Radev, Richard Socher, and Caiming Xiong. 2020. Universal natural language processing with limited annotations: Try few-shot textual entailment as a start. *arXiv preprint arXiv:2010.02584*.

A Annotation guideline

This annotation guideline contains a set of process to do question classification and answer classification. Question classification means that every question is categorized into one of pre-determined types considering context of questions and answers in a reconciled manner. The four types are as follow.

1. **Type1 : Binary answerable type**
   A question which is answerable with "Yes" or "No" without critical difficulty.

2. **Type2 : WH type**
   A question which starts with "What", "Where", "Why" and "When" or has similar nuance to all "WH". Specific phrase or

sentence is an answer to the corresponding question.

3. **Type3 : How type**
   A question which starts with "How". Interpretation or explanation is an answer to the corresponding question.

4. **Type4 : Conditional type**
   A question which is not answerable with "Yes" or "No" in general. However, if certain condition is met, this question becomes Type1.

Question classification is solely dependent on experts' viewpoint and interpretation from scratch. In order to verify the classification results from five independent annotators, it follows majority voting and reliability test with Kappa statistics.

One of the biggest challenges is how to revise questions into Type1. To save time and effort, one leading annotator does transform the questions in Type2, Type3 and Type4. Type2 and Type3 follows that firstly the phrase or sentence or a set of sentences in the context of the corresponding answer is identified and new question is constructed with the sentence structure of "Is it correct that ..." or "Does it mean that ...". These structures are considered quite simple. However, we all agree that it is one of the most effective and intuitively understandable approach. Type4 is revised by adding the condition captured in the context of the corresponding answer in front of or at the end of the questions with "If + condition". Upon question classification, answers are labelled into "Yes" or "No" at the end.

B Examples of question types

B.1 Type1: Binary answerable type

1. **original question**
   Regarding CAP10.11(16), consider a bank that issues capital out of a foreign subsidiary, and wishes to use such capital to meet both the solo requirements of the foreign subsidiary and include the capital in the consolidated capital of the group. Is it correct that the relevant authority in jurisdiction of the consolidated supervisor must have the power to trigger write-down / conversion of the instrument in addition to the relevant authority in the jurisdiction of the foreign subsidiary?

2. **original answer**
   Yes, this is correct.

B.2 Type2: WH type

original question
What is the difference between (the jurisdiction of) "ultimate risk" and (the jurisdiction of) "immediate counterparty" exposures?

original answer
The concepts of "ultimate risk" and "immediate risk" are those used by the BIS' International Banking Statistics . The jurisdiction of "immediate counterparty" refers to the jurisdiction of residence of immediate counterparties, while the jurisdiction of "ultimate risk" is where the final risk lies. For the purpose of the countercyclical capital buffer, banks should use, where possible, exposures on an "ultimate risk" basis.

revised question
Is it correct that the jurisdiction of "immediate counterparty" refers to the jurisdiction of residence of immediate counterparties, while the jurisdiction of "ultimate risk" is where the final risk lies?

revised answer
Yes

B.3 Type3: How type

original question
How is the final bank-specific buffer add-on calculated?

original answer
The final bank-specific buffer add-on amount is calculated as the weighted average of the countercyclical capital buffer add-on rates applicable in the jurisdiction(s) in which a bank has private sector credit exposures (including the bank's home jurisdiction) multiplied by total risk-weighted assets. The weight for the buffer add-on rate applicable in a given jurisdiction is the credit risk charge that relates to private sector credit exposures allocated to that jurisdiction, divided by the bank's total credit risk charge that relates to private sector credit exposures across all jurisdictions. Where the private sector credit exposures (as defined in RBC30.13(FAQ1)) to a jurisdiction, including the home jurisdiction, are zero, the weight to be allocated to the particular jurisdiction would be zero.

revised question
Is it correct that the final bank-specific buffer add-on amount is calculated as the weighted average of the countercyclical capital buffer add-on rates applicable in the jurisdiction(s) in which a bank has private sector credit exposures (including the

bank's home jurisdiction) multiplied by total risk-weighted assets?

revised answer

Yes

B.4 Type4: Conditional type

original question

Can subordinated loans be included in regulatory capital?

original answer

Yes. As long as the subordinated loans meet all the criteria required for Additional Tier 1 or Tier 2 capital, banks can include these items in their regulatory capital.

revised question

As long as the subordinated loans meet all the criteria required for Additional Tier 1 or Tier 2 capital, can subordinated loans be included in regulatory capital?

revised answer

Yes

Corporate Bankruptcy Prediction with Domain-Adapted BERT

Alex Gunwoo Kim*
Seoul National University
Graduate School of Business
kimgunwoo95@snu.ac.kr

Sangwon Yoon*
Artificial Society Inc.
swyoon@artificial.sc

Abstract

This study performs BERT-based analysis, which is a representative contextualized language model, on corporate disclosure data to predict impending bankruptcies. Prior literature on bankruptcy prediction mainly focuses on developing more sophisticated prediction methodologies with financial variables. However, in our study, we focus on improving the quality of input dataset. Specifically, we employ BERT model to perform sentiment analysis on MD&A disclosures. We show that BERT outperforms dictionary-based predictions and Word2Vec-based predictions under time-discrete logistic hazard model, k-nearest neighbor (kNN-5), and linear kernel support vector machine (SVM). Further, instead of pretraining the BERT model from scratch, we apply self-learning with confidence-based filtering to corporate disclosure data. We achieve the accuracy rate of 91.56% and demonstrate that the domain adaptation procedure brings a significant improvement in prediction accuracy.

1 Introduction

Predicting imminent corporate bankruptcies has been of great importance both in academia and in industry. Early studies on bankruptcy prediction focuses on identifying financial variables that precede impending insolvencies. Altman (1968) finds out that z-score, a composite measure of several financial variables, predicts imminent insolvencies. Since then, numerous papers document additional financial variables that seem to predict bankruptcies (Ding et al., 2012; Bharath and Shumway, 2008; Dwyer et al., 2004). Among 39 distinct financial variables, Tian et al. (2015) choose seven key variables that effectively predict bankruptcies within 12 months by LASSO.

However, in contrast to the fact that the majority of corporate disclosures contain non-financial information, textual disclosures have received relatively less attention. Following Li (2008)'s call for research on textual corporate disclosures, there have been numerous attempts (Tetlock et al., 2008; Li, 2010; Mayew et al., 2015) to analyze the textual sentiments of corporate disclosures. They commonly find that textual non-financial information has orthogonal informational value to the existing financial information. However, the majority of the analyses are based on the dictionary-based approach suggested by Loughran and McDonald (2011).

In our study, we perform a BERT-based analysis on corporate disclosure data. BERT (Devlin et al., 2018) is the pre-trained language model based on the self-attention mechanism of Transformers (Vaswani et al., 2017). BERT and its improved versions such as GLUE (Wang et al., 2018), SQUAD (Rajpurkar et al., 2016), and RACE (Lai et al., 2017), have achieved state-of-the-art results in several NLP downstream tasks. In this research, we analyze the management, discussion, and analysis (MD&A) section of corporate disclosures and extract its context-specific sentiment. We then predict bankruptcies that occur within 12 months from the issuance of annual reports using the sentiment variables produced by BERT-based model. The reasons why we choose MD&A sections to be our target of BERT-based analysis are as follows.

First, managers are obliged to express their opinions regarding the future performance of firms in MD&A sections. Therefore, MD&A is a rich source of information to analyze managerial assessment regarding a firm's ability to operate as a going concern. Second, negative future predictions are likely to be accompanied by other positive explanations (see Appendix A, Jung and Kwon, 1988). Therefore, even though humans can interpret implicit negative nuance in the written disclosures, the traditional dictionary-based approach likely leads

*Equal contribution.

Proceedings of the Third Workshop on Economics and Natural Language Processing, pages 26–36
Punta Cana and online, November 11.

to an erroneous conclusion. Lastly, MD&A sections are required when preparing 10-K filings for all firms. Therefore, we mitigate the sample selection bias by confining our analysis to observations archived in SEC filings.

Our paper makes several contributions to the existing line of literature. To our best knowledge, this is by far the first study to predict corporate outcomes other than stock market returns with BERT-based sentiment analysis. Unsophisticated investors have difficulty in understanding corporate disclosures since the disclosures are complex in nature (Bartov et al., 2000). Therefore, the dictionary-based approach displays a trivial limitation in analyzing disclosure texts. We expect that context-specific linguistic analysis will accurately examine the contextual sentiment of corporate disclosures. Specifically, by comparing the ability to predict impending bankruptcies, we show that BERT-based analysis outperforms analyses based on dictionary (key word lists) and word level embedding.

Second, there is no BERT model trained on corporate disclosures and the open-source BERT model which is trained on the closest domain is Fin-BERT (Araci, 2019). Fin-BERT is trained using financial news data. However, since the corporate disclosures and the financial news texts are in a similar but different domain, Fin-BERT is not perfectly suitable for interpreting corporate disclosures. We need to ensure that the data distributions of the training domain and the test domain are the same to improve the performance of machine learning models. Violation of this requirement, which is known as domain shift (Shimodaira, 2000), leads to underperformance of models (Glorot et al., 2011). Language models that are trained in two stages of pre-training and fine-tuning such as BERT, satisfy this assumption only when they are pre-trained and fine-tuned with a subset of their domain. Domain shift harms BERT model performance substantially (Lee et al., 2020; Beltagy et al., 2019). The most trivial way to overcome this problem is to pre-train BERT language model from scratch. However, language model pre-training is highly time and resource-consuming and it is inefficient to pre-train language models for only specific tasks.

Another way to deal with domain shift in BERT application is to fine-tune the model with labeled data from the target domain. However, in reality, labeled data for fine-tuning is often not available. In such cases, unsupervised domain adaption is a good alternative (Kim et al., 2020; Kundu et al., 2020). In this paper, we apply self-learning, one of the key methodologies of unsupervised domain adaption. We show that if the distance between the source and target domains is close enough, supervising a BERT-based classification model with self-generated pseudo-labels filtered with confidence level leads to a significant improvement in performance.

2 Related Studies

2.1 Bankruptcy predictions

In his seminal study, Altman (1968) finds that financial variables disclosed in annual reports predict bankruptcies. Shumway (2001) shows that in addition to financial statement-related variables, stock market-related variables such as market capitalization and stock price are also associated with future bankruptcies. However, considering that financial variables convey imperfect corporate information (Tennyson et al., 1990), prior literature extracts information from narrative disclosures. Cecchini et al. (2010) employ a complex vector space model to predict bankruptcies with MD&A disclosures. However, they remain silent on whether textual information has additional predictive ability to financial variables. Mayew et al. (2015) find that narrative disclosures indeed contain information which is orthogonal to the information provided by financial variables. They utilize words lists provided by Loughran and McDonald (2011) to analyze general tone of MD&A disclosures.

Related to prediction methodology, Wilson and Sharda (1994) use neural network with financial variables to predict bankruptcies. Premachandra et al. (2011) introduce data envelopment analysis (DEA) and show that bankrupt firms exhibit relatively lower operating efficiency. Shin et al. (2005) find that SVM is effective in predicting notable corporate events including bankruptcies and Chen et al. (2013) develop an adaptive fuzzy k-nearest neighbor method for insolvency prediction. Overall, prior literature has been successful in developing machine learning models that predict bankruptcies with considerable accuracy. However, few research focuses on improving the quality of input variables. Specifically, less effort has been made to produce precise semantic tone analysis with narrative disclosures.

2.2 Text classification

The most traditional method of text classification is the dictionary-based approach. The Harvard Psychological Dictionary is the most commonly used source in open domain text classification. Loughran and McDonald (2011) propose a dictionary specialized in the finance domain. However, dictionary-based approach has a limitation that it is difficult to create a dictionary that covers all the keywords needed for text classification and that the frequency of certain keywords does not necessarily contain sufficient information to classify sentences. Therefore, methods based on word embedding are suggested as alternatives.
Word embedding assigns a vector which encodes the meaning of the word to each text. Text classification methods based on word embedding include frequency-based methods as Tf-Idf (Salton and Buckley, 1988) and prediction-based embedding methods as Word2Vec (Mikolov et al., 2013). Word2vec, in particular, places each word in a vector space which approximates its semantic space. This algebraic transformation allows the vector operations among words. Therefore, we may set a word vector as the initial value of neural network and further classify sentences by exploring their contextual information. Kim et al. (2014) prove that CNN structure, combined with Word2Vec embedding, can be used to classify sentences.
Language models based on Recurrent Neural Network(RNN) (Liu et al., 2016) and its variations (Zhou et al., 2015; Wang et al., 2018) are also used on text classification. However, recently, Transformer-based language models as BERT (Devlin et al., 2018) and GPT-2(Radford et al., 2019) outperform RNN-based methods and have drawn attention with their performance in generic benchmarks. These models apply self-attention to generate contextualized embedding. Especially BERT, the origin of many SOTA (State–Of–The–Art) models, pre-trains contextual embedding model with masked LM tasks and sentence prediction tasks, and is then fine-tuned to be applied to downstream tasks.

2.3 Domain adaptation

In its early stage, domain adaptation takes a form of semi-supervised learnings. Semi-supervised domain adaptation is used when labeled data exists in the target domain but when its amount is not sufficient. For instance, Saenko et al. (2010) and Kulis et al. (2011) use metric learnings to solve domain shifts. In specific, they adopt methods to learn task-specific distance metrics with labeled data and assign labels to unlabeled data based on the learned distance.
However, in reality, we may not be able to find domains with labeled data. In such a case, unsupervised domain adaptation (UDA) can be an attractive alternative. The subspace-based methods consider both source and target domain a subspace of single domain space. On the other hand, a more popular approach in UDA is to consider source and target domain separate spaces and try to align the distributions of these. Some works first compare the mean of samples from each domain in Hilbert space and assign a weight to each sample of source domain (Gretton et al., 2012) or select samples in the source domain to minimize the maximum mean discrepancy of the two domains (Gong et al., 2013). But when source and target domains are significantly different, we may not expect these methods to perform well. To deal with this problem, other studies (Pan et al., 2010; Baktashmotlagh et al., 2013; Sun et al., 2016) map data from both domains to a latent space to deal with this problem.
Recently, with the advent of deep learning, feature extraction from raw data becomes an important process in every task. And the models that learn domain invariant features have become the mainstream in UDA (Ganin et al., 2016; Saito et al., 2018; Long et al., 2017). However, these methods require the data from the source domain to extract domain invariant features. Therefore, self-learning can be an alternative since the source domain data is not required in the setting. The most important consideration in self-learning is how to generate or filter accurate pseudo-labels. Kim et al. (2020) propose confidence-based filtering and similarity-based pseudo-labeling method in the image classification task. However, their methodology cannot be directly applied to NLP tasks since word embedding is more implicit and multidimensional than image features. Recently, Yoon et al. (2021) prove that fine-tuning the original model with pseudo-labels that are filtered based on confidence level increases accuracy in the target domain in the token classification task. To our best knowledge, our research is the first to show that self-learning without using samples from the source domain significantly improves model performance in sentence classification tasks.

3 Methodoloy

3.1 Sentiment analysis[1]

3.1.1 Dictionary-based approach

Loughran and McDonald (2011) develop word lists specifically suited for 10-K filings. They provide word lists that contain negative words and positive words, respectively. Following their methodology to calculate the tone of textual disclosures, we count the numbers of positive and negative words in each MD&A section and scale them by the number of total words in each section (*DICTPOS* and *DICTNEG*). Although the analysis provides value-relevant information, the measures are comparatively less accurate in that they do not consider context-specific tone of the texts. We calculate the tone variables with Python.

3.1.2 Word2Vec

Word2Vec is a prediction-based word embedding method which trains by predicting center words with context words (CBoW) or vice versa (Skip-Gram). After training, each word in a corpus corresponds one-on-one to a vector that contains its semantic information. Kim et al. (2014) achieve a remarkable performance on text classification by employing a structure with 1-layer convolutional neural network (CNN) and a fully connected output layer to classify sentences. This model takes pre-trained Word2Vec embedding as its input and the width of the filter in CNN equals the dimension of the word embedding. In our research, we replicate the CNN–static model of Kim et al. (2014) in which the Word2Vec model freezes during the training. We use Word2Vec weight trained on the 10-K corpus of 1996-2013 (Tsai et al., 2016), and train the network with the financial sentiment analysis dataset provided by Malo et al. (2014) which consists of 4,846 sentences. The model takes each sentence as input and assigns probability to each of three classes: positive, negative, and neutral. We sum the probabilities of all sentences in a document and normalize them to calculate the sentiment score of each document (*W2VPOS* and *W2VNEG*). We use nltk sentence tokenizer[2] to split each document to sentences, gensim package[3] to load Word2Vec embedding, and Pytorch to implement CNN-based classifier. We use Cross-Entropy loss function and Adam optimizer. We train model for 60 epochs, with batch size 50. We set sentence length to 50 words in both training phase and inference phase.

3.1.3 BERT

BERT is a pre-trained language model with bidirectional transformers, which can be applied to downstream tasks after supervised fine-tuning with relatively low resources. We utilize the model structure based on the original BERT model (Devlin et al., 2018) and the fine-tuned weight of Fin-BERT (Araci, 2019) trained for financial sentiment analysis. Fin-BERT is pre-trained on the subset of Reuters TRC2 dataset which includes financial press articles and fine-tuned on the financial sentiment analysis dataset provided by Malo et al. (2014), which is identical to the dataset that we use to train the network of Word2Vec model. Similarly, the model takes each sentence as its input and assigns probability to each of three classes: positive, negative, and neutral. We sum the probabilities of all sentences in a document and normalize them to calculate the sentiment score of each document (*BERTPOS* and *BERTNEG*). Similarly, we use nltk sentence tokenizer and Huggingface Transformers package[4] with Pytorch to implement BERT. We set max sentence length to 512, which is the max length limit of BERT.

3.1.4 Unsupervised domain adaptation

We apply self-learning, one of the unsupervised domain-adaptation methods, to our BERT-based model. The self-learning procedure follows the three-step approach. First, we generate pseudo-labels with sentences from MD&A sections. Then we filter out "reliable" samples based on the self-confidence of the sentences. Since it is well known that erroneous labels may deteriorate the performance of the models, we filter the samples with high self-confidence. Specifically, we proxy for self-confidence with self-entropy (Zou et al., 2018; Saporta et al., 2020), Lastly, we perform supervised learning using the newly-obtained pseudo labels. Refer to Figure 1 for visual representation of the algorithm. We use the following equation to calculate self-entropy:

$$H(s_i) = -\frac{1}{\log M} \sum_{n=0}^{2} l_n(s_i) \log l_n(s_i)$$

[1]For dictionary-based approach, we primarily utilize the following: https://github.com/rflugum/10K-MDA-Section. For the remainder, refer to our anonymized github: https://anonymous.4open.science/r/BankruptcyBert-CC19/

[2]https://www.nltk.org

[3]https://radimrehurek.com/gensim/

[4]https://huggingface.co

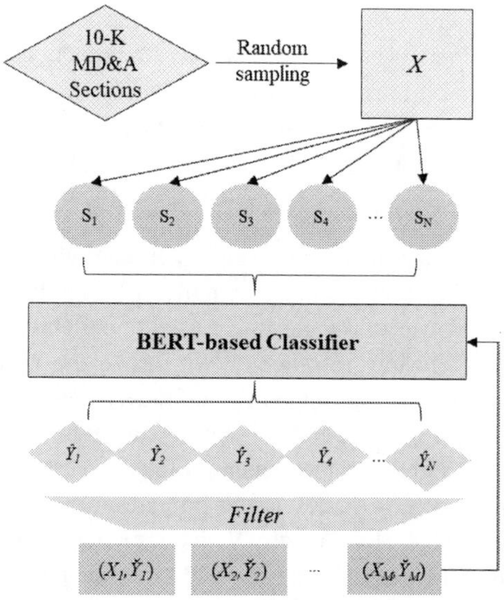

Figure 1: This figure portrays the pipeline of our domain adaptation method. First, we randomly sample 1,200 documents from the corporate fillings from 1995 to 2020. We label this set of narrative disclosures X. Then we generate pseudo-labels $\widehat{Y}$ by applying a BERT-based classifier to every sentence in X (denoted as s_i). To prevent noisy pseudo-labels from harming the model performance, we filter out only the 'reliable' samples $(X, \check{Y})$ by their normalized self-entropy. Then we supervise the BERT-based classifier with reliable samples.

,where s_i denotes each sentence and $l_n(s_i)$ denotes the probability that s_i belongs to class n ($n = 0, 1, 2$). Here, we calculate $l_n(s_i)$ with the BERT-based classification model that we use in section 3.1.3. Then we normalize the self-entropy by scaling the value with $\log M$, which is the natural logarithm of the number of labels (here, $M = 3$). We define three classes 0, 1, and 2. Each class represents positive, negative, or neutral, respectively.

We obtain 59,389 cleansed MD&A filings merged with financial variables. Then we generate pseudo-labels by randomly picking 1,200 documents and doing inference on all sentences in the documents. In specific, we collect and analyze 589,858 distinct sentences. Next, we filter the results with the threshold of self-entropy 0.2 and discard the observations with self-entropy over 0.2. We obtain 38,703 reliable sentences through this process (6.56% of the sentence domain). We train the model for 2 epochs with batch size 32 and set the learning rate to be $5e^{-5}$. We use Cross-Entropy loss and Adam optimizer. After training the model, the inference follows the same procedures as the previous two models and we generate sentiment variables *DAPTPOS* and *DAPTNEG*.

3.2 Classification model

We implement three basic machine-learning based classifiers (hazard time-discrete logistic model, SVM, and kNN) to evaluate the additional informativeness of textual data. Since models as DNN or RNN achieve state-of-the-art prediction accuracy only with financial variables, it is difficult to show the effect of adding textual variables. Therefore, we compare the relative performance of the baseline classifiers to highlight the incremental prediction accuracy from adding BERT-based sentiment variables.

3.2.1 Hazard model

We use proportional hazards model (Fine and Gray, 1999) to calculate prediction accuracy. Shumway (2001) finds that maximum log-likelihood estimation of discrete-time logistic regression yields consistent estimates. In specific, we estimate the following discrete-time logistic regression with maximum-likelihood estimation:

$$\log h_i(t) = \beta X_i(t)$$

$h_i(t)$ refers to the risk of bankruptcy for firm i at time t. $X_i(t)$ refers to a vector of firm i at time t that consists of variables that are known to precede bankruptcies. In our study X includes financial variables and MD&A sentiments. Specifically, we first run the regression with only financial variables (*FIN*). Then we add dictionary-based variables (*FIN*, *DICTPOS*, and *DICTNEG*), Word2Vec-based variables (*FIN*, *W2VPOS*, and *W2VNEG*), BERT-based variables (*FIN*, *BERTPOS*, and *BERTNEG*), and domain-adapted BERT-based variables (*FIN*, *DAPTPOS*, and *DAPTNEG*), respectively. Using the obtained coefficients, we calculate the fitted values of $\log h_i(t)$ ($\log \widehat{h_i(t)}$) and classify the observation to be bankrupt if $\log \widehat{h_i(t)} > 0.5$ and non-bankrupt otherwise. Continuous variables are winsorized at 1% level to minimize the effect of outliers on regression results.

3.2.2 k-Nearest Neighbors and Support Vector Machine

To further enhance the classification performance, we employ k-nearest neighbors (kNN) and Support Vector Machine (SVM) algorithms, following prior literature.

kNN is a simple non-parametric classification

method. First, we calculate the Euclidean distance between any two pair of observations. That is for observation vectors X_1 and X_2, we compute

$$d(X_1, X_2) = \sqrt{X_1 \cdot X_2}$$

, where $\cdot$ denotes the inner product of the two vectors. Specifically, in our research, vector X_i includes variables that precede insolvencies. We start from five financial variables and sequentially include sentiment variables calculated using different sentiment analysis models. Then, the algorithm computes the distances between observation X_i which belongs to the test set and all other observations that belong to the train set. Next, it chooses k smallest distances from the observation X_i and label the distances. In our research, we set $k = 5$. The algorithm classifies X_i to be bankrupt if the number of bankrupt labels is greater than the number of non-bankrupt labels.

Next, SVM aims at finding a hyperplane that divides the dataset into distinct categories with the largest margin. Let X_i be a training data and two classes are labeled with y_i as either +1 or -1. We solve the following minimization problem with respect to hyperplane w:

$$\min \frac{1}{2} \|w\|^2 + C \sum_{i=1}^{M} \xi_i$$

,where $y_i(wX_i + b) \geq 1 - \xi_i$. Here, ξ denotes a slack variable and C is a regularization parameter. In our setting, we set $C = 1e^{-5}$. Further, we choose linear kernel for SVM classification. Linear kernel reduces the cost of computation but yields comparatively less accurate results. In our sample, univariate analysis results in section 4.1 indicate that linear kernel is acceptable to classify the dataset. We choose the most basic models of kNN and SVM since the primary purpose of our research is to compare the relative performance of text sentiment classification models.

3.3 Accuracy calculation

We report two distinct accuracy measures to compare the performance of our models. A1 is the ratio of the number of observations that are classified as non-bankrupt (CNB) under each model to the number of total non-bankrupt (NB) observations (A1 = CNB/NB). On the other hand, A2 is the ratio of the number of observations that are classified as bankrupt (CB) under each model to the number of total bankrupt observations (B) (A2 = CB/B).

For hazard model, we also report adjusted R-square (Nagelkerke et al., 1991; Cox and Snell, 2018).

$$R^2 = 1 - \exp\left[\frac{2\left(\log l(Fit) - \log l(Null)\right)}{n}\right]$$

$\log l(Fit)$ and $\log l(Null)$ refer to the maximum log likelihoods of the fitted model and null model containing only the intercept term, respectively. Then, the equation can be rewritten as

$$-\log\left(1 - R^2\right) = 2\left[\frac{\log l(Fit) - \log l(Null)}{n}\right]$$

	BRUPT=1	*BRUPT=0*	Difference (t-stat)
	(1)	(2)	(1) - (2)
WC	-0.5558	0.2091	-0.7649***
			(-3.91)
RE	-0.3977	0.0450	-0.4427***
			(-3.47)
SALE	1.0161	0.9607	0.0554**
			(2.15)
MVE	1.8010	10.3129	-8.5119***
			(-8.83)
EBIT	-0.7172	0.4907	-1.2079***
			(-3.17)
DICTPOS	0.0069	0.0072	-0.0003***
			(-3.36)
DICTNEG	0.0182	0.0136	0.0046***
			(17.79)
W2VPOS	0.3786	0.4042	-0.0256***
			(-5.53)
W2VNEG	0.0969	0.0558	0.0411***
			(3.21)
BERTPOS	0.1833	0.2257	-0.0424***
			(-12.04)
BERTNEG	0.2433	0.2140	0.0293***
			(9.41)
DAPTPOS	0.1421	0.2362	-0.0941***
			(-13.21)
DAPTNEG	0.3512	0.1528	0.1984***
			(10.55)
n	520	58,867	

Table 1: This table reports univariate analysis results. Column (1) reports the mean of the variables when *BRUPT*=1. Column (2) reports the mean of the variables when *BRUPT*=0. The last column reports the differences in mean values (Column (1) – Column (2)). We also report t-statistics that examine the statistical significance of the differences in the parenthesis. *, **, and *** indicate that the difference is statistically significant under 1%, 5%, and 10% confidence level, respectively.

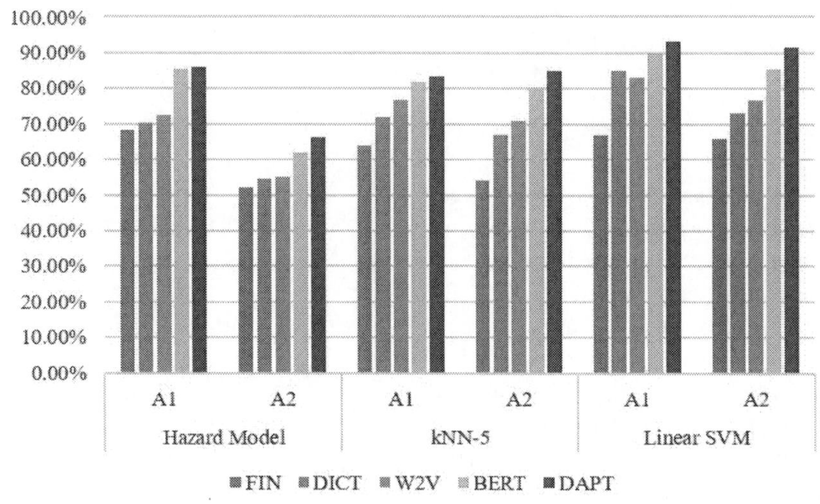

Figure 2: This figure displays the relative accuracy prediction of the models. Refer to Section 3 for detailed definitions of *FIN, DICT, W2V, BERT* and *DAPT*. A1 measures the accuracy of predicting non-bankrupt firm-years and A2 measures the accuracy of predicting bankrupt firm-years. We display the prediction performance measured with hazard discrete logistic regression model, kNN-5, and linear SVM.

4 Empirical Experiments

4.1 Data

We first identify bankrupt firm-years from Compustat. The dataset provides us with the dates when firms file for bankruptcy and the dates when the bankruptcy procedure is complete. In our analysis, we use the dates when firms first file for bankruptcy as bankruptcy years. Then, following Altman (1968) and Mayew et al. (2015), we compute five key financial variables that are known to precede bankruptcies (*WC, RE, EBITDA, MVE,* and *SALE*). *WC* refers to the ratio of working capital to total asset. *RE* refers to retained earnings to total liability. *EBITDA* refers to earnings before interest, tax, depreciation, and amortization scaled by total asset. *MVE* is the market value of equity scaled by total liability. *SALE* is the ratio of sales revenue to total asset.

Next, we construct our main variables by extracting MD&A sections from annual reports. Specifically, we inspect 10-K, 10-KSB, 10-K405, and 10KSB40 filings and search for MD&A sections (Item 6 or Item 7). During the collection process, we exclude html notations, tables, and page numbers. This process ensures that we analyze only the textual components from MD&A sections. Our sample period spans from 1995 to 2020 since SEC started to require firms to disclose electronic (machine-readable) filings from 1995. *BRUPT* is an indicator variable that equals one for observations that face bankruptcy within 365 days from their issuance of annual report, and zero otherwise. We require all financial variables and MD&A section texts for each observation and obtain 59,389 distinct observations. Among the sample, we identify 520 bankrupt firm-year observations (*BRUPT*=1). We acquire financial data from Compustat database and filing texts from SEC archive.

To evaluate the performance of SVM and kNN models, we split the sample into three subsets: 60% assigned to train set, 20% to validation set, and 20% to test set. However, since the data that we use is panel, randomly assigning 20% of the sample to the test set may bias our results. That is, the model may learn from future information and use it to predict the same future. To mitigate this concern, we implement time-based split. That is, we choose 104 latest bankruptcy observations from 2018 to 2020 and randomly choose 104 non-bankruptcy observations from the same time period. To further ensure that our results are not driven by random sample selection, we repeat the selection procedure 100 times and report the average accuracy with its standard deviation.

In SVM, we test 10 different hyperparameters ranging from 0 to 1 and compare their relative performances. Next, for kNN model, we experiment five different hyperparameters (k). Since the model follows the majority rule, we examine odd parameters

Vars	Hazard Model			kNN-5		Linear SVM	
	R2	A1	A2	A1	A2	A1	A2
FIN	16.23%	68.20%	52.23%	63.88%	53.99%	66.83%	65.82%
				(0.06)	(0.05)	(0.03)	(0.03)
FIN+DICT	21.33%	70.25%	54.55%	72.01%	66.98%	85.11%	73.28%
				(0.03)	(0.03)	(0.05)	(0.06)
FIN+W2V	23.51%	72.39%	55.23%	76.75%	70.93%	83.20%	76.73%
				(0.05)	(0.04)	(0.02)	(0.04)
FIN+BERT	24.83%	85.44%	62.00%	81.73%	80.32%	89.98%	85.20%
				(0.05)	(0.05)	(0.03)	(0.06)
FIN+DAPT	**26.38%**	**86.12%**	**66.12%**	**83.22%**	**85.08%**	**93.26%**	**91.56%**
				(0.06)	(0.04)	(0.04)	(0.02)

Table 2: This table reports the relative prediction accuracy of the models. We input the set of variables (*FIN, DICT, W2V, BERT*, and *DAPT*) in each of the three classification models. A1 equals (1 – Type I error rate) and A2 equals (1 – Type II error rate). We repeat the sampling experiment 100 times for each model and report the standard deviation of the accuracy rate in parenthesis.

3, 5, 7, 9, and 11. We then set the regularization parameter C in SVM to be $1e^{-5}$ and the number of nearest neighbors k to be 5.

4.2 Results

To ensure that the selected variables move in accordance with *BRUPT*, we report the univariate analysis results depending on the variable *BRUPT* (See Table 1).

As evidenced by Altman (1968) and other prior studies, we find higher *WC, RE, MVE*, and *EBIT*, and lower *SALE* for non-bankrupt firms. Further, we demonstrate that *DICTNEG, W2VNEG, BERTNEG*, and *DAPTNEG* are higher for bankrupt firms and *DICTPOS, W2VPOS, BERTPOS*, and *DAPTPOS* are higher for non-bankrupt firms. This confirms that managers are likely to disclose negative-tone MD&A sections before imminent bankruptcies. More importantly, untabulated tests including quadratic terms do not find any evidence that there exists non-linear relationship between *BRUPT* and other independent variables. Taken together, univariate analysis results imply that we may choose linear kernel for SVM classification.

Table 2 and Figure 2 report the relative performance of the models. Consistent with the prior literature (Zhou et al., 2012; Wu et al., 2007), SVM generally performs the best among the three classifiers. Also, A1 is generally higher than A2 in all model specifications, implying that the models generally predict non-bankrupt firms more accurately than bankrupt firms.

Our main finding is that BERT-based analysis outperforms dictionary-based analysis and Word2Vec-based analysis. This indicates that context-specific sentiment analysis produces more accurate tone of the texts than non-context specific methods. Specifically, SVM with BERT-based sentiment variables display the bankruptcy prediction accuracy (A2) of 85.20%. Further, we observe that R-square increases as we proceed from analyzing only financial variables (16.23%) to including domain-adapted BERT-based sentiment variables (26.38%). Comparing this result with prior literature that utilizes SVM to predict corporate bankruptcies, we obtain relatively high accuracy. For instance, Zhou et al. (2012) obtain the accuracy rate of approximately 75% by analyzing financial variables with DSSVM and GASVM models. Taken together, our results imply that textual information has predictive ability which is orthogonal to the existing set of financial variables and that adding high-quality textual information in the classifiers significantly improves the prediction accuracy.

Next, we also find that domain-adaptation further improves prediction accuracy. Domain-adapted BERT-based analysis yields the best accuracy rate (A2) of 91.56% with linear SVM classifier among the models. These results strongly indicate that context-specific sentiment analysis of corporate disclosure texts provides more value-relevant information.

5 Conclusion

In our study, we examine whether context-specific textual sentiment analysis (BERT) improves the accuracy of corporate bankruptcy prediction. We utilize five financial variables calculated from the stock market and annual reports that are known to precede impending insolvencies. Further, we collect and examine a large sample of MD&A narrative disclosures from 1995 to 2020 to test whether textual sentiment is helpful in predicting financial distress. We find that textual sentiment has additional predictive ability to well-known financial variables. Most importantly, we show that BERT-based analysis outperforms dictionary-based analysis suggested by Loughran and McDonald (2011) and Word2Vec-based analysis combined with convolutional neural network. Further, we acknowledge the domain shifting problem of current BERT model. To assuage such a limitation, we perform domain-adaptation to the existing financial BERT model. This approach reduces computational costs compared to pre-training the BERT model with a new corpus and, at the same time, significantly improves the prediction accuracy.

6 Acknowledgement

The authors deeply appreciate helpful comments from Bok Baik and Yang Hoon Kim. Further, the authors appreciate the GPU support from Artificial Intelligence.

References

Edward I Altman. 1968. Financial ratios, discriminant analysis and the prediction of corporate bankruptcy. *The journal of finance*, 23(4):589–609.

Dogu Araci. 2019. Finbert: Financial sentiment analysis with pre-trained language models. *arXiv preprint arXiv:1908.10063*.

Mahsa Baktashmotlagh, Mehrtash T Harandi, Brian C Lovell, and Mathieu Salzmann. 2013. Unsupervised domain adaptation by domain invariant projection. In *Proceedings of the IEEE International Conference on Computer Vision*, pages 769–776.

Eli Bartov, Suresh Radhakrishnan, and Itzhak Krinsky. 2000. Investor sophistication and patterns in stock returns after earnings announcements. *The Accounting Review*, 75(1):43–63.

Iz Beltagy, Kyle Lo, and Arman Cohan. 2019. Scibert: A pretrained language model for scientific text. *arXiv preprint arXiv:1903.10676*.

Sreedhar T Bharath and Tyler Shumway. 2008. Forecasting default with the merton distance to default model. *The Review of Financial Studies*, 21(3):1339–1369.

Mark Cecchini, Haldun Aytug, Gary J Koehler, and Praveen Pathak. 2010. Detecting management fraud in public companies. *Management Science*, 56(7):1146–1160.

Hui-Ling Chen, Chang-Cheng Huang, Xin-Gang Yu, Xin Xu, Xin Sun, Gang Wang, and Su-Jing Wang. 2013. An efficient diagnosis system for detection of parkinson's disease using fuzzy k-nearest neighbor approach. *Expert systems with applications*, 40(1):263–271.

David Roxbee Cox and E Joyce Snell. 2018. *Analysis of binary data*. Routledge.

Jacob Devlin, Ming-Wei Chang, Kenton Lee, and Kristina Toutanova. 2018. Bert: Pre-training of deep bidirectional transformers for language understanding. *arXiv preprint arXiv:1810.04805*.

A Adam Ding, Shaonan Tian, Yan Yu, and Hui Guo. 2012. A class of discrete transformation survival models with application to default probability prediction. *Journal of the American Statistical Association*, 107(499):990–1003.

Douglas W Dwyer, Ahmet E Kocagil, and Roger M Stein. 2004. Moody's kmv riskcalc v3. 1 model. *White paper, Moody's, https://www. moodys. com/sites/products/ProductAttachments/RiskCalc*, 203.

Jason P Fine and Robert J Gray. 1999. A proportional hazards model for the subdistribution of a competing risk. *Journal of the American statistical association*, 94(446):496–509.

Yaroslav Ganin, Evgeniya Ustinova, Hana Ajakan, Pascal Germain, Hugo Larochelle, François Laviolette, Mario Marchand, and Victor Lempitsky. 2016. Domain-adversarial training of neural networks. *The journal of machine learning research*, 17(1):2096–2030.

Xavier Glorot, Antoine Bordes, and Yoshua Bengio. 2011. Domain adaptation for large-scale sentiment classification: A deep learning approach. In *ICML*.

Boqing Gong, Kristen Grauman, and Fei Sha. 2013. Connecting the dots with landmarks: Discriminatively learning domain-invariant features for unsupervised domain adaptation. In *International Conference on Machine Learning*, pages 222–230. PMLR.

Arthur Gretton, Karsten M Borgwardt, Malte J Rasch, Bernhard Schölkopf, and Alexander Smola. 2012. A kernel two-sample test. *The Journal of Machine Learning Research*, 13(1):723–773.

Woon-Oh Jung and Young K Kwon. 1988. Disclosure when the market is unsure of information endowment of managers. *Journal of Accounting research*, pages 146–153.

Kwanho Kim, Beom-suk Chung, Yerim Choi, Seungjun Lee, Jae-Yoon Jung, and Jonghun Park. 2014. Language independent semantic kernels for short-text classification. *Expert Systems with Applications*, 41(2):735–743.

Youngeun Kim, Sungeun Hong, Seunghan Yang, Sungil Kang, Yunho Jeon, and Jiwon Kim. 2020. Associative partial domain adaptation. *arXiv preprint arXiv:2008.03111*.

Brian Kulis, Kate Saenko, and Trevor Darrell. 2011. What you saw is not what you get: Domain adaptation using asymmetric kernel transforms. In *CVPR 2011*, pages 1785–1792. IEEE.

Jogendra Nath Kundu, Naveen Venkat, R Venkatesh Babu, et al. 2020. Universal source-free domain adaptation. In *Proceedings of the IEEE/CVF Conference on Computer Vision and Pattern Recognition*, pages 4544–4553.

Guokun Lai, Qizhe Xie, Hanxiao Liu, Yiming Yang, and Eduard Hovy. 2017. Race: Large-scale reading comprehension dataset from examinations. *arXiv preprint arXiv:1704.04683*.

Jinhyuk Lee, Wonjin Yoon, Sungdong Kim, Donghyeon Kim, Sunkyu Kim, Chan Ho So, and Jaewoo Kang. 2020. Biobert: a pre-trained biomedical language representation model for biomedical text mining. *Bioinformatics*, 36(4):1234–1240.

Feng Li. 2008. Annual report readability, current earnings, and earnings persistence. *Journal of Accounting and economics*, 45(2-3):221–247.

Feng Li. 2010. Textual analysis of corporate disclosures: A survey of the literature. *Journal of accounting literature*, 29(1):143–165.

Pengfei Liu, Xipeng Qiu, and Xuanjing Huang. 2016. Recurrent neural network for text classification with multi-task learning. In *Proceedings of the Twenty-Fifth International Joint Conference on Artificial Intelligence (IJCAI-16)*, pages 2873–2879.

Mingsheng Long, Zhangjie Cao, Jianmin Wang, and Michael I Jordan. 2017. Conditional adversarial domain adaptation. *arXiv preprint arXiv:1705.10667*.

Tim Loughran and Bill McDonald. 2011. When is a liability not a liability? textual analysis, dictionaries, and 10-ks. *The Journal of finance*, 66(1):35–65.

Pekka Malo, Ankur Sinha, Pekka Korhonen, Jyrki Wallenius, and Pyry Takala. 2014. Good debt or bad debt: Detecting semantic orientations in economic texts. *Journal of the Association for Information Science and Technology*, 65(4):782–796.

William J Mayew, Mani Sethuraman, and Mohan Venkatachalam. 2015. Md&a disclosure and the firm's ability to continue as a going concern. *The Accounting Review*, 90(4):1621–1651.

Tomas Mikolov, Kai Chen, Greg Corrado, and Jeffrey Dean. 2013. Efficient estimation of word representations in vector space. *arXiv preprint arXiv:1301.3781*.

Nico JD Nagelkerke et al. 1991. A note on a general definition of the coefficient of determination. *Biometrika*, 78(3):691–692.

Sinno Jialin Pan, Ivor W Tsang, James T Kwok, and Qiang Yang. 2010. Domain adaptation via transfer component analysis. *IEEE transactions on neural networks*, 22(2):199–210.

Inguruwatt M Premachandra, Yao Chen, and John Watson. 2011. Dea as a tool for predicting corporate failure and success: A case of bankruptcy assessment. *Omega*, 39(6):620–626.

A Radford, J Wu, R Child, D Luan, D Amodei, and I Sutskever. 2019. Language models are unsupervised multitask learners.

Pranav Rajpurkar, Jian Zhang, Konstantin Lopyrev, and Percy Liang. 2016. Squad: 100,000+ questions for machine comprehension of text. *arXiv preprint arXiv:1606.05250*.

Kate Saenko, Brian Kulis, Mario Fritz, and Trevor Darrell. 2010. Adapting visual category models to new domains. In *European conference on computer vision*, pages 213–226. Springer.

Kuniaki Saito, Kohei Watanabe, Yoshitaka Ushiku, and Tatsuya Harada. 2018. Maximum classifier discrepancy for unsupervised domain adaptation. In *Proceedings of the IEEE conference on computer vision and pattern recognition*, pages 3723–3732.

Gerard Salton and Christopher Buckley. 1988. Term-weighting approaches in automatic text retrieval. *Information processing & management*, 24(5):513–523.

Antoine Saporta, Tuan-Hung Vu, Matthieu Cord, and Patrick Pérez. 2020. Esl: Entropy-guided self-supervised learning for domain adaptation in semantic segmentation. *arXiv preprint arXiv:2006.08658*.

Hidetoshi Shimodaira. 2000. Improving predictive inference under covariate shift by weighting the log-likelihood function. *Journal of statistical planning and inference*, 90(2):227–244.

Kyung-Shik Shin, Taik Soo Lee, and Hyun-jung Kim. 2005. An application of support vector machines in bankruptcy prediction model. *Expert systems with applications*, 28(1):127–135.

Tyler Shumway. 2001. Forecasting bankruptcy more accurately: A simple hazard model. *The journal of business*, 74(1):101–124.

Baochen Sun, Jiashi Feng, and Kate Saenko. 2016. Return of frustratingly easy domain adaptation. In *Proceedings of the AAAI Conference on Artificial Intelligence*, volume 30.

B Mack Tennyson, Robert W Ingram, and Michael T Dugan. 1990. Assessing the information content of narrative disclosures in explaining bankruptcy. *Journal of Business Finance & Accounting*, 17(3):391–410.

Paul C Tetlock, Maytal Saar-Tsechansky, and Sofus Macskassy. 2008. More than words: Quantifying language to measure firms' fundamentals. *The journal of finance*, 63(3):1437–1467.

Shaonan Tian, Yan Yu, and Hui Guo. 2015. Variable selection and corporate bankruptcy forecasts. *Journal of Banking & Finance*, 52:89–100.

Ming-Feng Tsai, Chuan-Ju Wang, and Po-Chuan Chien. 2016. Discovering finance keywords via continuous-space language models. *ACM Transactions on Management Information Systems (TMIS)*, 7(3):1–17.

Ashish Vaswani, Noam Shazeer, Niki Parmar, Jakob Uszkoreit, Llion Jones, Aidan N Gomez, Łukasz Kaiser, and Illia Polosukhin. 2017. Attention is all you need. In *Advances in neural information processing systems*, pages 5998–6008.

Alex Wang, Amanpreet Singh, Julian Michael, Felix Hill, Omer Levy, and Samuel R Bowman. 2018. Glue: A multi-task benchmark and analysis platform for natural language understanding. *arXiv preprint arXiv:1804.07461*.

Rick L Wilson and Ramesh Sharda. 1994. Bankruptcy prediction using neural networks. *Decision support systems*, 11(5):545–557.

Chih-Hung Wu, Gwo-Hshiung Tzeng, Yeong-Jia Goo, and Wen-Chang Fang. 2007. A real-valued genetic algorithm to optimize the parameters of support vector machine for predicting bankruptcy. *Expert systems with applications*, 32(2):397–408.

Sangwon Yoon, Yanghoon Kim, and Kyomin Jung. 2021. Self-adapter at semeval-2021 task 10: Entropy-based pseudo-labeler for source-free domain adaptation. *Proceedings of the 15th International Workshop on Semantic Evaluation*.

Chunting Zhou, Chonglin Sun, Zhiyuan Liu, and C.M. Francis Lau. 2015. A c-lstm neural network for text classification. *CoRR*.

Jian Zhou, Xibing Li, and Xiuzhi Shi. 2012. Long-term prediction model of rockburst in underground openings using heuristic algorithms and support vector machines. *Safety science*, 50(4):629–644.

Yang Zou, Zhiding Yu, BVK Kumar, and Jinsong Wang. 2018. Unsupervised domain adaptation for semantic segmentation via class-balanced self-training. In *Proceedings of the European conference on computer vision (ECCV)*, pages 289–305.

A Sample MD&A

The following is an excerpt from an MD&A section of 10-K report of Learning Tree International, disclosed on September 30, 1996. Learning Tree International filed a bankruptcy in 1997.

In response to the continued **strength** in enrollments, the Company has further accelerated its development of new course titles, **expanded** its future direct mailing plans to capture additional market share and has taken steps to expand the number of classrooms in its education centers. However, there can be **no assurance** that the Company will be able to **achieve** an increase in market share after making such expenditures or will maintain its growth in revenues, **profitability** or market share in the future.

Positive words are colored in **RED** and negative words are colored in **BLUE**. Humans can interpret that this document conveys negative implication. However, there are 1 negative word and 4 positive words according to Loughran and McDonald (2011) word lists. In contrast, BERT-based sentiment vector of the paragraph equals (1.0365, 2.2161, 1.1704). Normalization yields *BERTPOS* = 0.2343 and *BERTNEG* = 0.5000. Therefore, BERT-based analysis outperforms the traditional dictionary-based approach.

Is Domain Adaptation Worth Your Investment? Comparing BERT and FinBERT on Financial Tasks

Bo Peng, Emmanuele Chersoni, Yu-Yin Hsu, Chu-Ren Huang
Department of Chinese and Bilingual Studies, The Hong Kong Polytechnic University,
Yuk Choi Road 11, Hung Hom, Kowloon, Hong Kong
{peng-bo.peng,emmanuele.chersoni,yu-yin.hsu,churen.huang}.polyu.edu.hk

Abstract

With the recent rise in popularity of Transformer models in Natural Language Processing, research efforts have been dedicated to the development of domain-adapted versions of BERT-like architectures.

In this study, we focus on FinBERT, a Transformer model trained on text from the financial domain. By comparing its performances with the original BERT on a wide variety of financial text processing tasks, we found continual pretraining from the original model to be the more beneficial option. Domain-specific pretraining from scratch, conversely, seems to be less effective.

1 Introduction

The Transformer architectures have taken the field of Natural Language Processing (NLP) by storm, leading to remarkable performance leaps in several tasks (Vaswani et al., 2017; Devlin et al., 2019).

The first-generation Transformers were mainly trained on general corpora, such as Wikipedia or Common Crawl. However, considering domain adaptations, many researchers have later injected domain-specific knowledge in such architectures, leading to the publication of Transformers trained on different types of in-domain text, e.g., scientific articles (Beltagy et al., 2019), biomedical text (Lee et al., 2020; Gu et al., 2020), clinical notes (Alsentzer et al., 2019), and patent corpora (Lee and Hsiang, 2020).

Since language technologies have seen increasingly frequent use in accounting and finance (Loughran and McDonald, 2016), it is not surprising that several attempts have been made to adapt Transformers to the financial domain (Araci, 2019; Yang et al., 2020; Liu et al., 2020).

In this study, we test the FinBERT model by Yang et al. (2020) on a variety of tasks in the field of financial NLP, including sentiment analysis, causality detection, numeral understanding, and numeral attachment, and we study the impact of different types of pretraining on the system performance. We obtained the best results with a FinBERT model with pretraining continuing from the original BERT and with the same general-domain vocabulary, while a model trained anew on financial corpora and with a domain-adapted vocabulary performed similarly to BERT Base.

2 Related Work

Although financial NLP is a relatively recent field, it already has an active research community, which has regularly introduced new shared tasks and benchmarks in recent years, e.g., sentence boundary detection in financial documents (Azzi et al., 2019; Wan et al., 2019; Au et al., 2021), hypernymy detection (El Maarouf et al., 2021; Mansar et al., 2021), document causality detection (Mariko et al., 2020), document structure extraction (Juge et al., 2019; Bentabet et al., 2020), and document summarization (Zheng et al., 2020). Given the success of Transformer models in general-domain NLP, it is not surprising that they are also a popular choice for many systems competing in financial tasks (Chen et al., 2020).

To adapt the original BERT to sentiment analysis in the financial domain, Araci (2019) was the first to propose a FinBERT model by further pretraining BERT Base on the financial subset of the Reuters TRC2 corpus. The evaluation, carried out on the Financial Phrase Bank (Malo et al., 2014) and the FiQA sentiment scoring dataset (Maia et al., 2018), demonstrated that FinBERT largely outperformed all the LSTM-based baselines and was slightly better than the original model.

The second FinBERT model, introduced by Yang et al. (2020), followed two different training strategies. The first version (FinBERT BaseVocab) was further pretrained from a BERT Base checkpoint on three financial corpora (i.e., the Corporate Reports 10-K & 10-Q from the Securities

Proceedings of the Third Workshop on Economics and Natural Language Processing, pages 37–44
Punta Cana and online, November 11. ©2021 Association for Computational Linguistics

Exchange Commission, [1] the Earnings Call Transcripts from the Seeking Alpha website, [2] and the Analyst Reports from the Investext database), and the second (FinBERT FinVocab) was trained afresh on the same three corpora but with new vocabulary specific to the financial domain, not inheriting it from the original BERT. They evaluated the models on the same sentiment analysis datasets, in conjunction with the opinion mining data from Huang et al. (2014), and reported improved performance over BERT Base, especially when using the FinBERT model with the domain-adapted vocabulary.

In this study, we chose to test the FinBERT system used in Yang et al. (2020), which has two publicly available versions, in order to directly compare the impact of the two different domain adaptation strategies and to evaluate them on more semantic tasks. The previous studies (Araci, 2019; Yang et al., 2020) focused their evaluation exclusively on sentiment analysis. However, sentiment analysis is a general task that is not necessarily ideal for observing the advantages of domain adaptation because the expressions of sentiment might not reflect the in-domain language. For example, in the biomedical domain, several tasks have recently been shown to benefit from training from scratch on an in-domain text and from a domain-specific vocabulary (Gu et al., 2020; Portelli et al., 2021). Therefore, besides sentiment analysis, we decided to evaluate our models on three semantic tasks that are more specific to the financial domain: document causality detection (Mariko et al., 2020), numeral understanding (Chen et al., 2019b), and numeral attachment (Chen et al., 2020).

3 Experimental Setting

3.1 Tasks and Datasets

The following section describes all the tasks related to the study, and the datasets to be evaluated. Descriptive statistics for the latter are provided in Table 1. More details about the class distributions are in Appendix A.

3.1.1 Sentiment Analysis

Sentiment Analysis stands out as one of the most popular tasks in NLP. To compare our models in the financial domain, we selected three different datasets. The Financial PhraseBank (Malo et al., 2014) is a standard dataset for sentiment classification composed of 4,840 sentences selected from financial news and annotated for Positive, Negative, and Neutral sentiment by 16 different annotators with experience in the financial domain. The dataset comes with the original annotations: for our study, we evaluated on a subset of 2,264 instances with at least 75% of annotator agreement.

We also used the FinTextSen dataset from SemEval 2017 Task 5 that dedicates itself to sentiment analysis on financial microblogs (Cortis et al., 2017). The dataset consists of 2,488 microblog messages retrieved from Twitter and StockTwits in March 2016. Each instance contains the following information: the message, a cashtag, and a sentiment score. The latter was originally a continuous score, but we used the dataset version by Daudert et al. (2018), who clustered the scores to obtain a 3-class annotation (Positive, Negative, and Neutral), to maintain consistency with the other sets.

Finally, the StockSen dataset (Xing et al., 2020) is composed of 20,675 financial tweets extracted from the StockTwits platform between June and August 2019, all of which were annotated with either Positive or Negative sentiments.

3.1.2 Financial Document Causality Detection

For Document Causality Detection, we used the dataset of the FinCausal shared task 2020 (Mariko et al., 2020). The dataset is made of texts extracted from a 2019 corpus of financial news provided by Qwan, with each instance annotated with binary labels to indicate whether it described a causal relation. For example, in (1), the italicized part was annotated as the cause for the fall of the GDP.

(1) *Things got worse when the Wall came down.* GDP fell 20% between 1988 and 1993.

We refer to the dataset for subtask 1, which is a simple binary classification task (class 1 if the text includes a causal relation and 0 otherwise).

3.1.3 Numeral Understanding

Understanding numerals is of key importance for the automatic processing of financial documents. In coincidence with the FinNum shared task, Chen et al. (2019b) released a microblogs dataset extracted from StockTwits, in which numerals are annotated with 7 high-level categories (i.e., **Monetary, Percentage, Option, Indicator, Temporal, Quantity, and Product/Version**) and 17 more

[1] https://www.sec.gov/edgar.shtml.
[2] https://seekingalpha.com/.

Datasets	Train	Dev	Test	Classes	Max Length
Financial Phrase Bank (Malo et al., 2014)	2,264	\	\	3	81
FinTextSen (Daudert et al., 2018)	2,488	\	\	3	476
StockSen (Xing et al., 2020)	14,457	6,218	\	2	370
Causality Detection (Mariko et al., 2020)	13,478	\	8,580	2	1,460
FinNum-1 subtask 1/2 (Chen et al., 2019b)	4,072	457	786	7/17	48
FinNum-2 (Chen et al., 2019a)	7,187	2,109	1,044	2	120

Table 1: Descriptive statistics for all the experimental datasets: train and test splits, classes, max text length.

fine-grained classes, which are sub-classes of the same categories. The labels have been identified based on the taxonomy by Chen et al. (2018), and the annotation was carried out by two domain experts. The dataset only includes examples on which the annotators reached an agreement. Examples (2a) and (2b) illustrate, respectively, the Monetary and the Product/Version category (the numeral expression to be classified is in bold).

(2) a. $FB (**110.20**) is starting to show some relative strength and signs of potential B/O on the daily.

b. iPhone **6** may not be as secure as Apple thought.. $AAPL

We address both the subtasks of FinNum (e.g., the 7-class and the 17-class classification tasks); that is, the tweets containing n financial numbers and the corresponding category labels will be copied n times. The details of the reconstructed data are also illustrated in Table 1.

3.1.4 Numeral Attachment

The numeral attachment task was introduced during the FinNum-2 competition (Chen et al., 2019a). The authors built a dataset of financial microblogs extracted from StockTwits, in which, given a target cashtag and a target numeral, a system predicts whether the numeral is attached to the cashtag. For example, in (3), the second numeral in the sentence is attached to the $NE cashtag, while the first one is not.

(3) **$NE**, last time oil was over *$65* you were close to *$8*.

Therefore, for each instance, the system must perform a binary classification task (i.e., 1 if the numeral is attached to the cashtag, and 0 otherwise).

3.2 Models

In this study, two baseline models were used. One is the **BERT Base** (Devlin et al., 2019), which consists of a series of stacked Transformer encoders. It was trained using both a masked language modeling objective and a next sentence prediction objective on a concatenation of the Books Corpus (Zhu et al., 2015) and the English version of Wikipedia. The other one is a traditional Support Vector Machine (SVM) baseline (Noble, 2006), where the input representation is the element-wise addition of the word vectors of each word in the sentence. We used the publicly available FastText vectors by Grave et al. (2018).

As for the FinBERT models, we used **FinBERT BaseVocab** (FV w/ BV) and **FinBERT FinVocab** (FB w/ FV) (Yang et al., 2020). The former was initialized from the original BERT Base (i.e., it also uses the same general-domain vocabulary) and then further pretrained on financial corpora, and the latter was trained afresh on financial corpora for 1M iterations and uses a domain-specific financial vocabulary.

Following the methodology by Devlin et al. (2019), all models used a linear layer with $softmax$ as a classification layer and the cross-entropy loss as a loss function. The texts were directly fed to the models after some simple preprocessing steps. For all models, we replaced the URLs with the special token [URL]. For the Numeral Understanding task, the texts and the target numbers were concatenated with the special token [SEP] after the tokenization. Finally, in the Numeral Attachment task, we followed Moreno et al. (2020) by adding the special tokens **£** and **§** to the beginning and the end of the *$cashtag*, and the target number, respectively.

3.3 Evaluation Metrics

All the models have been evaluated in terms of Macro F1-score and Micro F1-score. In this study,

Datasets	SVM		FB w/ BV		FB w/ FV		BERT Base	
	Micro-F1(%)	Macro-F1 (%)	Micro-F1(%)	Macro-F1 (%)	Micro-F1 (%)	Macro-F1 (%)	Micro-F1 (%)	Macro-F1 (%)
Financial Phrase Bank	61.62	33.55	**96.86±1.43**	**95.51±2.32**	96.69±1.1	95.39±1.54	96.60±1.06	95.15±1.52
FinTextSen	69.53	36.81	**84.48±2.34**	56.81±3.59	83.08±3.25	57.34±7.65	83.04±2.58	**60.83±10.94**
StockSen	73.21	42.90	**79.48±0.7**	**69.69±0.41**	76.37±0.57	69.38±0.75	78.72±0.92	68.78±0.48
Causality Detection	94.07	59.84	94.28±0.68	**79.79±0.81**	**94.51±0.31**	79.68±0.71	94.24±0.6	79.65±0.74
FinNum-1 subtask 1	63.27	34.69	**94.38±0.29**	**89.41±0.79**	93.51±0.72	87.11±1.07	94.07±0.48	88.04±1.39
FinNum-1 subtask 2	48.76	24.40	**88.84±0.51**	**80.71±0.82**	87.45±0.67	80.66±1.62	88.12±0.63	79.4±1.5
FinNum-2	82.69	51.64	85.67±0.55	67.56±2.12	**85.78±0.52**	**67.84±2.8**	85.07±0.44	66.51±1.91

Table 2: Comparative results in terms of Micro-F1 and Macro-F1 (top scores per dataset/metric are in **bold**), with standard deviations for the BERT models.

Datasets	FB w/ BV vs. BERT Base		FB w/ FV vs. BERT Base		FB w/ BV vs. FB w/ FV	
	Micro-F1(%)	Macro-F1(%)	Micro-F1(%)	Macro-F1(%)	Micro-F1(%)	Macro-F1(%)
Financial Phrase Bank	0.26	0.36	0.09	0.24	0.17	0.12
FinTextSen	1.44	-4.02	0.04	-3.49	1.4	-0.53
StockSen	0.76	0.91	-2.35	0.6	3.11	0.31
Causality Detection	0.04	0.14	0.27	0.03	-0.23	0.11
FinNum-1 subtask 1	0.31	1.37	-0.56	-0.93	0.87	2.3
FinNum-1 subtask 2	0.72	1.31	-0.67	1.26	1.39	0.05
FinNum-2	0.6	1.05	0.71	1.33	-0.11	-0.28
Sentiment Analysis	0.82	-0.92	-0.74	-0.88	1.56	-0.03
Numeral Understanding	0.52	1.34	-0.62	0.17	1.13	1.18

Table 3: Performance gaps for each dataset and metric. In the last two lines, we also report the aggregate performance for the group of sentiment analysis datasets (Financial Phrase Bank, FinTextSen and StockSen) and for the numeral understanding ones (FinNum-1 subtask 1 and 2).

the latter is equivalent to the traditional Accuracy metric, due to treating each task as a multi-class classification task. For the datasets without an official train-test split (e.g., FinTextSen and Financial Phrase Bank), we ran a 10-fold cross-validation and reported the average score. However, due to the instability of BERT fine-tuning on small datasets (Zhang et al., 2020), even the results of multiple runs on the same split may heavily fluctuate. Therefore, we reported the average scores after 10 runs, even for the datasets with an official train-test split.

4 Results and Discussion

The full results are shown in Table 2. Firstly, we observe that all the pretrained BERT models outperformed the SVM baseline in all the financial datasets. Secondly, many models reported large standard deviations on some of the datasets, especially the sentiment analysis ones. It can be observed that FinBERT BaseVocab reports the best performance in almost all the datasets, generally outperforming BERT Base. Excluding the FinTextSen dataset, in which BERT Base is the top-scoring model, FinBERT BaseVocab achieves an average increase of 0.85 of Macro F1-score on the other benchmarks. On the other hand, FinBERT FinVocab performed similarly to BERT Base, sometimes showing small improvements and sometimes lagging behind the original model. It achieved the top score only in the numeral attachment task and in causality detection, the latter only for the Micro-F1. [3] Moreover, the performance increase for FinBERT BaseVocab was more noticeable on the datasets on numerals, while the performances of FinBERT FinVocab were more irregular, performing slightly better than BERT Base and the BaseVocab model on FinNum2 (numeral attachment), but lagging behind both on FinNum subtask 1 (numeral understanding).

Table 3 summarizes the performance comparison between the Transformer models, where it can be seen that FinBert BaseVocab typically improves over the other models for both metrics (the FinTextSen dataset being the only exception). However, it should also be noticed that the differences between models are sometimes small compared to the standard deviations in Table 2, which invites to be cautious in drawing firm conclusions.

4.1 Error Analysis

We ran a qualitative error analysis of the instances that were misclassified by our models for the tasks of sentiment analysis, numeral attachment, and

[3] It should be pointed out that in the Causality data the class distribution is very unbalanced, with almost 93% of negative instances (see Appendix A), and thus Macro-F1 is a more reliable score.

Text instance	Task	Golden Label	Misclassified by
$AAPL Force in VWAP is strong with this one.....no break since it fell below.....awesome	StockSen	0	All
$GOOG $AMZN $FB Trump is not going to do anything to these companies. He wouldn t risk crashing the market before the election. That anti-trust talk is just smoke and mirrors.	StockSen	1	FB w/ BV
£$HMNY£ it's over. No one is going back. Once people get a deal. *§30§* years ago I sold Toyotas for full sticker only. The world changes!	FinNum-2	0	All
£$SPY£ Tax reform scam is code word for bailout. After *§8§* years, the CBs are still pumping. They want to transfer wealth. Don't let them.	FinNum-2	0	All
When they signed up in 2008, the government invested R52-million to fund the workers shares.	Causality Detection	0	All
The existing $500 - $600 billion of public support for agriculture must be redirected to more inclusive, resilient and low carbon production and innovative technologies and finance to enhance the resilience of small-scale producers.	Causality Detection	0	BertBase

Table 4: Error cases for different tasks, together with the right label and the models that misclassified the instance.

causality detection. Table 4 displays some of the examples that we extracted.

For Sentiment Analysis, we extracted some misclassified examples from StockSen and noticed that the polarity of some tweets is mistaken by the classifiers because of irony, such as the final exclamation *awesome* on the first row in Table 4. In some other cases, like the one on the second row, the words associated with a negative polarity (e.g., *risk, crashing*) might be misleading the systems, while the tweet is actually positive.

In the numeral attachment task, where the target cashtag is in bold, and the target numeral in italics, the models seem to experience problems in assigning the correct interpretations to numerals, especially when they appear in temporal adjuncts (e.g., the examples on the third and the fourth rows).

The error sources seem to be more varied and more difficult to identify in the causality detection task. However, we encountered a few cases like the examples on the fifth and the sixth rows, where a *to*-infinitive construction is used for expressing goals. Given the semantic similarity between cause and goal, it seems plausible that the construction has confused the classifiers, leading them to erroneously assign the instances to the positive class.

5 Conclusions

In this paper, we compared the original BERT model with the financially adapted models by Yang et al. (2020). Domain adaptation was generally confirmed to be beneficial and, unlike what has been recently observed in the biomedical domain (Gu et al., 2020; Portelli et al., 2021), the model benefiting from continuous pretraining from BERT Base showed more consistent improvements across tasks and datasets. This suggests that the models take advantage from exposure to financial text, but the tasks do not necessarily require a specialized vocabulary. On the negative side, fluctations in the results confirmed that there is some degree of instability in the fine-tuning of BERT-like models on relatively small datasets (Zhang et al., 2020).

In our future work, we plan to investigate also the contextualized embeddings produced by the domain-adapted Transformers. Word embeddings have been used in tasks with important applications in the financial domain, such as the identification of semantic relations (Chersoni et al., 2016; Xiang et al., 2020), which is useful for building domain ontologies (El Maarouf et al., 2021; Mansar et al., 2021; Chersoni and Huang, 2021), and the unsupervised detection of semantic changes in diachronic data, e.g., annual reports of traded companies (Giulianelli et al., 2020; Montariol et al., 2021; Masson and Montariol, 2021). In this perspective, a promising research direction would be to analyze how different domain adaptation strategies affect the quality of the embedding representations.

Acknowledgments

We would like to thank Tobias Daudert, Frank Xing, and Chung-Chi Chen for sharing their datasets with us, and the four anonymous reviewers for their insightful feedback. This research was made possible by the University Postdoc Matching Fund (W16H) and Project of Strategic Importance (ZE2J) at the Hong Kong Polytechnic University.

References

Emily Alsentzer, John R Murphy, Willie Boag, Wei-Hung Weng, Di Jin, Tristan Naumann, and Matthew McDermott. 2019. Publicly Available Clinical BERT Embeddings. In *Proceedings of the NAACL Workshop on Clinical Natural Language Processing*.

Dogu Araci. 2019. FinBERT: Financial Sentiment Analysis with Pre-trained Language Models. *arXiv preprint arXiv:1908.10063*.

Willy Au, Abderrahim Ait-Azzi, and Juyeon Kang. 2021. FinSBD-2021: The 3rd Shared Task on Structure Boundary Detection in Unstructured Text in the Financial Domain. In *Companion Proceedings of the Web Conference*.

Abderrahim Ait Azzi, Houda Bouamor, and Sira Ferradans. 2019. The FinSBD-2019 Shared Task: Sentence Boundary Detection in Pdf Noisy Text in the Financial Domain. In *Proceedings of the IJCAI Workshop on Financial Technology and Natural Language Processing*.

Iz Beltagy, Kyle Lo, and Arman Cohan. 2019. SciBERT: A Pretrained Language Model for Scientific Text. *arXiv preprint arXiv:1903.10676*.

Najah-Imane Bentabet, Rémi Juge, Ismail El Maarouf, Virginie Mouilleron, Dialekti Valsamou-Stanislawski, and Mahmoud El-Haj. 2020. The Financial Document Structure Extraction Shared Task (FinToc 2020). In *Proceedings of the Joint Workshop on Financial Narrative Processing and MultiLing Financial Summarisation*.

Chung-Chi Chen, Hen-Hsen Huang, and Hsin-Hsi Chen. 2019a. Numeral Attachment with Auxiliary Tasks. In *Proceedings of the 42nd International ACM SIGIR Conference on Research and Development in Information Retrieval*, pages 1161–1164.

Chung-Chi Chen, Hen-Hsen Huang, Yow-Ting Shiue, and Hsin-Hsi Chen. 2018. Numeral Understanding in Financial Tweets for Fine-grained Crowd-based Forecasting. In *IEEE/WIC/ACM International Conference on Web Intelligence (WI)*, pages 136–143. IEEE.

Chung-Chi Chen, Hen-Hsen Huang, Hiroya Takamura, and Hsin-Hsi Chen. 2019b. Overview of the NTCIR-14 FinNum Task: Fine-grained Numeral Understanding in Financial Social Media Data. In *Proceedings of the 14th NTCIR Conference on Evaluation of Information Access Technologies*, pages 19–27.

Chung-Chi Chen, Hen-Hsen Huang, Hiroya Takamura, and Hsin-Hsi Chen. 2020. Overview of the NTCIR-15 FinNum-2 Task: Numeral Attachment in Financial Tweets. *Development*, 850(194):1–044.

Emmanuele Chersoni and Chu-Ren Huang. 2021. PolyU-CBS at the FinSim-2 Task: Combining Distributional, String-Based and Transformers-Based Features for Hypernymy Detection in the Financial Domain. In *Companion Proceedings of the Web Conference*, pages 316–319.

Emmanuele Chersoni, Giulia Rambelli, and Enrico Santus. 2016. CogALex-V Shared Task: ROOT18. In *Proceedings of the COLING Workshop on Cognitive Aspects of the Lexicon*.

Keith Cortis, André Freitas, Tobias Daudert, Manuela Huerlimann, Manel Zarrouk, Siegfried Handschuh, and Brian Davis. 2017. Semeval-2017 Task 5: Fine-grained Sentiment Analysis on Financial Microblogs and News. In *Proceedings of SemEval*.

Tobias Daudert, Paul Buitelaar, and Sapna Negi. 2018. Leveraging News Sentiment to Improve Microblog Sentiment Classification in the Financial Domain. In *Proceedings of the EMNLP Workshop on Economics and Natural Language Processing*.

Jacob Devlin, Ming-Wei Chang, Kenton Lee, and Kristina Toutanova. 2019. BERT: Pre-training of Deep Bidirectional Transformers for Language Understanding. In *Proceedings of NAACL*.

Ismail El Maarouf, Youness Mansar, Virginie Mouilleron, and Dialekti Valsamou-Stanislawski. 2021. The FinSim 2020 Shared Task: Learning Semantic Representations for the Financial Domain. In *Proceedings of the IJCAI Workshop on Financial Technology and Natural Language Processing*.

Mario Giulianelli, Marco Del Tredici, and Raquel Fernández. 2020. Analysing Lexical Semantic Change with Contextualised Word Representations. In *Proceedings of ACL*.

Edouard Grave, Piotr Bojanowski, Prakhar Gupta, Armand Joulin, and Tomas Mikolov. 2018. Learning Word Vectors for 157 Languages. In *Proceedings of LREC*.

Yu Gu, Robert Tinn, Hao Cheng, Michael Lucas, Naoto Usuyama, Xiaodong Liu, Tristan Naumann, Jianfeng Gao, and Hoifung Poon. 2020. Domain-specific Language Model Pretraining for Biomedical Natural Language Processing. *arXiv preprint arXiv:2007.15779*.

Allen H Huang, Amy Y Zang, and Rong Zheng. 2014. Evidence on the Information Content of Text in Analyst Reports. *The Accounting Review*, 89(6):2151–2180.

Rémi Juge, Imane Bentabet, and Sira Ferradans. 2019. The FinToc-2019 Shared Task: Financial Document Structure Extraction. In *Proceedings of the Financial Narrative Processing Workshop*.

Jieh-Sheng Lee and Jieh Hsiang. 2020. Patent Classification by Fine-tuning BERT Language Model. *World Patent Information*, 61:101965.

Jinhyuk Lee, Wonjin Yoon, Sungdong Kim, Donghyeon Kim, Sunkyu Kim, Chan Ho So, and Jaewoo Kang. 2020. BioBERT: A Pre-trained Biomedical Language Representation Model for Biomedical Text Mining. *Bioinformatics*, 36(4):1234–1240.

Zhuang Liu, Degen Huang, Kaiyu Huang, Zhuang Li, and Jun Zhao. 2020. FinBERT: A Pre-trained Financial Language Representation Model for Financial Text Mining. In *Proceedings of IJCAI*.

Tim Loughran and Bill McDonald. 2016. Textual Analysis in Accounting and Finance: A Survey. *Journal of Accounting Research*, 54(4):1187–1230.

Macedo Maia, Siegfried Handschuh, André Freitas, Brian Davis, Ross McDermott, Manel Zarrouk, and Alexandra Balahur. 2018. WWW'18 Open Challenge: Financial Opinion Mining and Question Answering. In *Companion Proceedings of The Web Conference*, pages 1941–1942.

Pekka Malo, Ankur Sinha, Pekka Korhonen, Jyrki Wallenius, and Pyry Takala. 2014. Good Debt or Bad Debt: Detecting Semantic Orientations in Economic Texts. *Journal of the Association for Information Science and Technology*, 65(4):782–796.

Youness Mansar, Juyeon Kang, and Ismail El Maarouf. 2021. The FinSim-2 2021 Shared Task: Learning Semantic Similarities for the Financial Domain. In *Companion Proceedings of the Web Conference*, pages 288–292.

Dominique Mariko, Estelle Labidurie, Yagmur Ozturk, Hanna Abi Akl, and Hugues de Mazancourt. 2020. Data Processing and Annotation Schemes for FinCausal Shared Task. *arXiv preprint arXiv:2012.02498*.

Corentin Masson and Syrielle Montariol. 2021. Detecting Omissions of Risk Factors in Company Annual Reports. In *Proceedings of the IJCAI Workshop on Financial Technology and Natural Language Processing*.

Syrielle Montariol, Alexandre Allauzen, and Asanobu Kitamoto. 2021. Variations in Word Usage for the Financial Domain. In *Proceedings of the IJCAI Workshop on Financial Technology and Natural Language Processing*.

Jose G Moreno, Emanuela Boros, and Antoine Doucet. 2020. TLR at the NTCIR-15 FinNum-2 Task: Improving Text Classifiers for Numeral Attachment in Financial Social Data. In *Proceedings of the 15th NTCIR Conference on Evaluation of Information Access Technologies, Tokyo*, pages 8–11.

William S Noble. 2006. What is a Support Vector Machine? *Nature Biotechnology*, 24(12):1565–1567.

Beatrice Portelli, Edoardo Lenzi, Emmanuele Chersoni, Giuseppe Serra, and Enrico Santus. 2021. BERT Prescriptions to Avoid Unwanted Headaches: A Comparison of Transformer Architectures for Adverse Drug Event Detection. In *Proceedings of EACL*.

Ashish Vaswani, Noam Shazeer, Niki Parmar, Jakob Uszkoreit, Llion Jones, Aidan N Gomez, Łukasz Kaiser, and Illia Polosukhin. 2017. Attention Is All You Need. In *Advances in Neural Information Processing Systems*, pages 5998–6008.

Mingyu Wan, Rong Xiang, Emmanuele Chersoni, Natalia Klyueva, Kathleen Ahrens, Bin Miao, David Clive Broadstock, Jian Kang, Hing Wah Yung, and Chu-Ren Huang. 2019. Sentence Boundary Detection of Financial Data with Domain Knowledge Enhancement and Cross-lingual Training. In *Proceedings of The First Workshop on Financial Technology and Natural Language Processing: The FinSBD Shared Task*.

Rong Xiang, Emmanuele Chersoni, Luca Iacoponi, and Enrico Santus. 2020. The CogALex Shared Task on Monolingual and Multilingual Identification of Semantic Relations. In *Proceedings of the COLING Workshop on Cognitive Aspects of the Lexicon*.

Frank Xing, Lorenzo Malandri, Yue Zhang, and Erik Cambria. 2020. Financial Sentiment Analysis: An Investigation into Common Mistakes and Silver Bullets. In *Proceedings of COLING*.

Yi Yang, Mark Christopher Siy Uy, and Allen Huang. 2020. FinBERT: A Pretrained Language Model for Financial Communications. *arXiv preprint arXiv:2006.08097*.

Tianyi Zhang, Felix Wu, Arzoo Katiyar, Kilian Q Weinberger, and Yoav Artzi. 2020. Revisiting Few-sample BERT Fine-tuning. In *Proceedings of ICLR*.

Siyan Zheng, Anneliese Lu, and Claire Cardie. 2020. SUMSUM@ FNS-2020 Shared Task. In *Proceedings of the Joint Workshop on Financial Narrative Processing and MultiLing Financial Summarisation*.

Yukun Zhu, Ryan Kiros, Rich Zemel, Ruslan Salakhutdinov, Raquel Urtasun, Antonio Torralba, and Sanja Fidler. 2015. Aligning Books and Movies: Towards Story-like Visual Explanations by Watching Movies and Reading Books. In *Proceedings of the IEEE International Conference on Computer Vision*, pages 19–27.

A Appendix

Figure 1 shows the pie charts illustrating the distribution of classes for all the benchmark datasets.

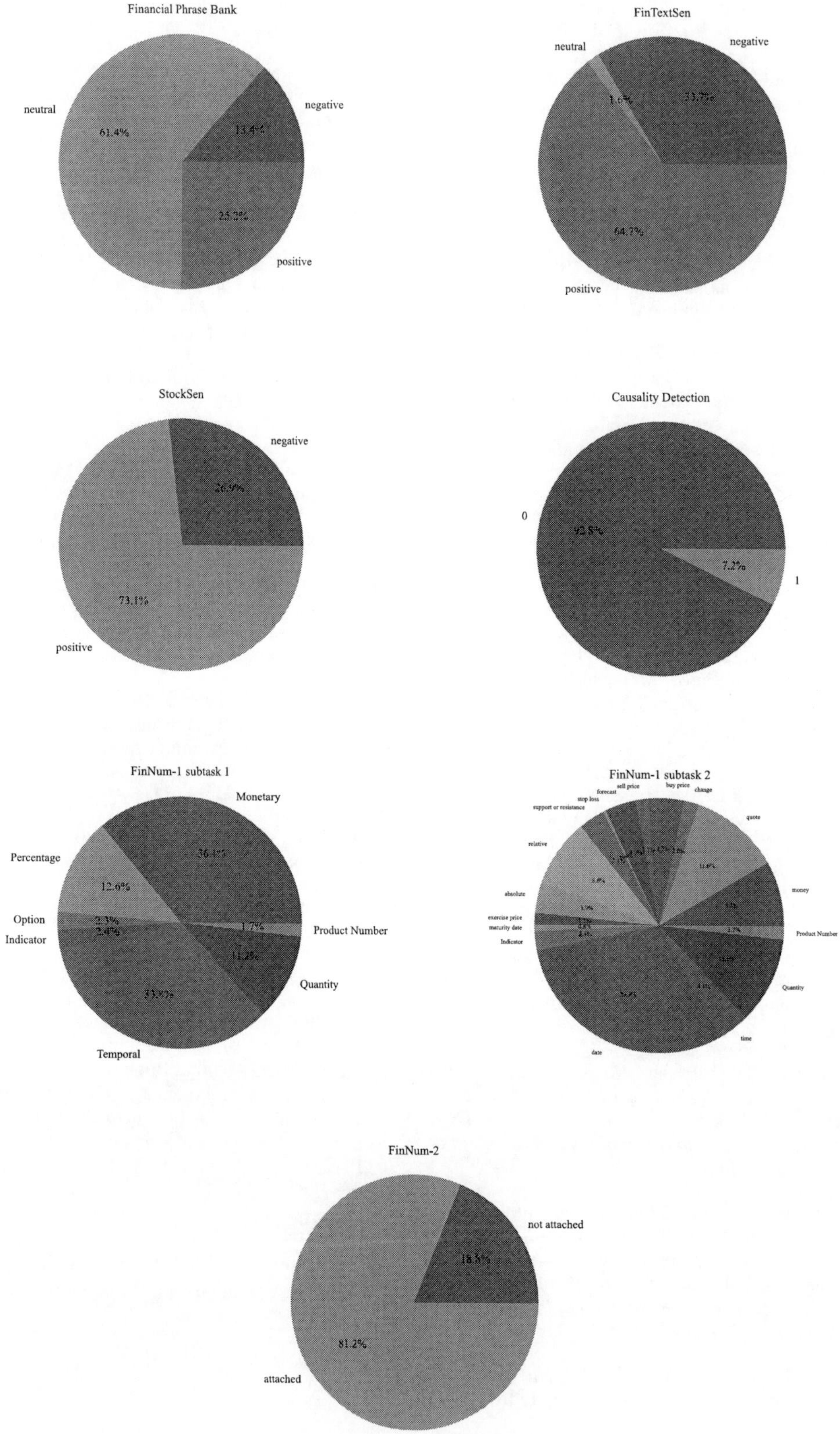

Figure 1: Class distribution for each of the evaluation datasets.

From Stock Prediction to Financial Relevance: Repurposing Attention Weights to Assess News Relevance Without Manual Annotations

Luciano Del Corro* **Johannes Hoffart***
Max Planck Institute for Informatics, Saarbrücken, Germany
{corrogg, jhoffart}@mpi-inf.mpg.de

Abstract

We present a method to automatically identify financially relevant news using stock price movements and news headlines as input. The method repurposes the attention weights of a neural network initially trained to predict stock prices to assign a relevance score to each headline, eliminating the need for manually labeled training data. Our experiments on the four most relevant US stock indices and 1.5M news headlines show that the method ranks relevant news highly, positively correlated with the accuracy of the initial stock price prediction task.

1 Introduction

Events such as lawsuits, the unveiling of a newly discovered technology, the introduction of new legislation, or previous market movements can have a significant impact on stock prices. A quick and informed reaction to such an event is crucial for financial analysts.

Information overload is pervasive in the financial industry, hindering the analysts' ability to incorporate the most relevant events into their decision process. One of the main natural language understanding challenges across many industries is to prioritize incoming information, reducing the risk of missing important events.

In this paper, we propose a novel method to identify relevant financial news. The key insight is that this can be achieved without relying on manually created relevance judgments, instead leveraging the correlation of news events and stock prices. The core idea is to train an attention-based neural network on the stock prediction task, using the price movement as label. The input of the network is a set of events in the form of news headlines (embedded using BERT (Devlin et al., 2019)), and the output is the price movement of a specific stock index with respect to the previous day (i.e., DOWN, STAY, UP), mediated by an attention layer (Bahdanau et al., 2015). The layer acts as an input selector, computing the weight for each headline on a given day. These weights are repurposed to score and thus rank news headlines according to financial relevance. As each weight solely depends on the headline itself, we can use it to compare headlines across the entire dataset.

We evaluated our method on the most prominent US stock indices (S&P500, Dow Jones, Russell 1000, and Nasdaq) and 1.5 million headlines (1994-2010) from Gigaword (Graff et al., 2003). A first automatic evaluation confirmed a positive correlation between stock prediction accuracy and relevance scores (via the attention weight). In a second, manual evaluation, we labeled 1000 headlines and found that the method ranks relevant events highly: A network trained on the Dow Jones stock index prices, for example, resulted in 89% relevant events in the top 200 ranks, compared to only 19% relevant events in a uniform sample of headlines.

2 Related Work

Stock price prediction from news. The feasibility of predicting stock prices from news has been debated (Merello et al., 2018) as the news can affect the price before it is published. In our case this is not an issue as it only matters that the price change is reflected in the news, not the timing; news about price movements are indeed relevant. Multiple approaches explored alternatives to extract price signals from news such as sentiment analysis, semantic parsing, etc (Gidófalvi, 2001; Schumaker and Chen, 2009; Xie et al., 2013; Li et al., 2014; Peng and Jiang, 2016). Here we use contextualized embeddings plus attention to extract those signals.

Extraction of financial events. Previous work focused on the explicit representation of events, either in a canonical or semi-canonical way (Ding et al., 2014, 2015, 2016; Peng and Jiang, 2016; Jacobs et al., 2018), or non-canonicalized (Ein-Dor et al.,

* equal contribution

Proceedings of the Third Workshop on Economics and Natural Language Processing, pages 45–49
Punta Cana and online, November 11.

2019; Shi et al., 2019). Events are represented as structured facts (Ding et al., 2014), via embeddings (Ding et al., 2015) or keywords (Shi et al., 2019), and are usually pre-selected based on explicit company mentions (Shi et al., 2019). Most approaches differ from ours in that events are input for stock prediction as ultimate goal, while we use stock prediction to identify relevant events. Our end-to-end approach allows us to automatically select the relevant events avoiding involved preprocessing, compromise on the representation of the event, or the use of an underlying extraction system.

Attention as explanation. A debate has erupted around the idea of using the attention mechanism (Bahdanau et al., 2015) to explain output. Serrano and Smith (2019) and Jain and Wallace (2019) concluded that attention weights should not be used to explain a decision, and Wiegreffe and Pinter (2019) developed a set of tests to determine weight consistency. In our specific case, we found that the results on the stock price prediction are related to the attention weights performance as relevance scores, and have merit when used for ranking. However, we acknowledge the need to go into deeper analysis to understand score stability in future work.

3 Training the attention layer for event scoring

The idea is to make use of universal key attention mechanism as in Yang et al. (2016) to learn a headline relevance weight by predicting the stock price movement. Once the network is trained we can use the unnormalized weights of the attention layer as a global relevance score for the news headlines.

As input we use all daily headlines and their categories. The output is DOWN, STAY, UP with respect to the next trading session open price. The full network is displayed in Figure 1.

Each headline $hl_1, \ldots, hl_k$ consisting of a (padded) sequence of N tokens $\{w_i\}_{i=1,\ldots,N}$, is encoded into vectors $\{\mathbf{hhl}_i\}_{i=1,\ldots,N}$ of length 768 via the BERT-base-uncased model pooled output:

$$\mathbf{hhl}_i = \text{BERT}(hl_i)$$

Each headline comes with a category label $hc_1, hc_2, \ldots$ (details in Section 4) embedded into a randomly initialized vector of length 30

$$\mathbf{hhc}_i = \text{embed}(hc_i),$$

Both vectors are concatenated

$$\mathbf{h}_i = \mathbf{hhl}_i \oplus \mathbf{hhc}_i$$

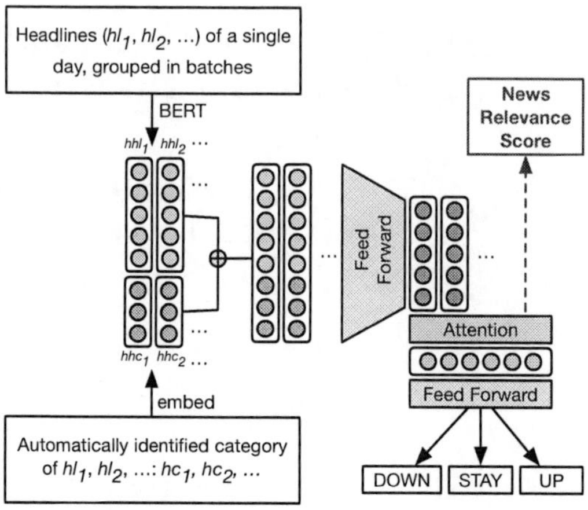

Figure 1: Neural Network Layout

and projected to a vector $\mathbf{h}_{p_i}$ of length 100 by a fully connected feed forward with ELU activation

$$\mathbf{h}_{p_i} = \text{FF}_{\text{ELU}}(\mathbf{h}_i)$$

Following Yang et al. (2016), an attention layer computes normalized weights for each headline in the input day via a universal key, $\mathbf{H}_{p_d} := \{\mathbf{h}_{p_i}\}_{i=1,\ldots,k}$, and aggregates them according to those weights.

$$\mathbf{h}_{a_d} = \text{Attention}(\mathbf{H}_{p_d})$$

The final label l_i (DOWN, STAY, UP) is computed using a feed forward layer with softmax activation

$$l_i = \text{FF}_{\text{softmax}}(\mathbf{h}_{a_d})$$

Every input layer is normalized, and weights are initialized using *He*. The dropout rate is 0.25. All weights are fine-tuned on the task. We ran on 3 Tesla V100 with a total batch size of 15. The model has a total of $\sim$110M parameters.

4 Evaluation

Dataset. AP headlines of English Gigaword (Graff et al., 2003) and the most prominent US stock indices: S&P500, Dow Jones, Nasdaq, and Russell[1], totaling 3777 trading sessions (1994–2010) and 1,532,260 headlines, with a daily average of 405.68, a standard deviation of 134.49, a minimum of 1 and a maximum of 1213.

News Classification. We trained a classifier on TagMyNews (Vitale et al., 2012) to classify the

[1] `https://finance.yahoo.com/quote/%5EGSPC/history?p=%5EGSPC`

headlines into 6 categories: 'business', 'entertainment', 'health', 'sci-tech', 'sport', 'us' and 'world'. The input of the BERT based model is a single headline and the output a class score (dropout=0.25, batch size=120, maximum headline length=15 tokens). The best model F1 was 0.85 (20% test size), in line with state-of-the-art (Zeng et al., 2018). We assigned a single class to each headline (0.5 threshold). Table 1 shows the distribution per category.

Category	Number of articles	%
world	596,899	38,96
sport	275,585	17.99
business	231,083	15.08
us	211,570	13.81
unclassified	66,891	4.37
entertainment	54,607	3.56
sci-tech	54,057	3.53
health	41,568	2.70

Table 1: Distribution of news per category

Preprocessing. Given resource constraints, we are limited to 115 headlines per day, with a maximum length of 15 tokens. To account for more than 115 headlines, we created stratified subsets on headline categories to generate several data points per day. We discarded days with less than 25 headlines for the four most prominent categories, dropping 511 data points (13.53%), and removed headlines with less than 20 characters. To assign price movement labels, we set thresholds that minimize the distance between the majority and minority class to balance the distributions. We searched for a symmetric threshold between [0.1%, 1%] at 0.1 intervals, see Table 2 for the final values.

Stock Index	Threshold	DOWN	STAY	UP
S&P500	+/- 0.3%	30.91%	33.61%	35.48%
Dow Jones	+/- 0.3%	30.53%	33.23%	36.23%
Russell 1000	+/- 0.3%	29.47%	34.38%	36.15%
Nasdaq	+/- 0.3%	30.48%	29.83%	39.69%

Table 2: Thresholds and class distributions

4.1 Event relevance

The goal is to understand if the attention layer's unnormalized weights can be used to generate meaningful global news relevance scores; we understand meaningful as a score that favors news reflecting stronger price movement signals, either ex-ante or ex-post the price change, as in both cases the news would be relevant; we do not control for endogeneity. We ran two experiments: one to understand which news categories provide better signals, and the second to check if they effectively receive higher scores. We also performed a manual evaluation over the top 200 headlines for each index plus a uniform random sample, totaling 1000 headlines.

Categories with stronger signals. We ran the network on each news category separately to predict the price movement. We selected the model with the maximum accuracy over 20 epochs. Table 3 shows the results for all categories. 'business' headlines are more informative, achieving the highest accuracy on most of the stock indices. Interestingly, 'sci-tech' news is the best category for Nasdaq, which specializes in technology. However, the top accuracy for this index lags well behind the others. This fact will be reflected in the relevance scores in the following experiment.

News Category	S&P500	Dow Jon.	Russ. 1000	Nasd.
business	**57.88**	**61.97**	**55.92**	43.64
us	40.13	42.02	39.59	38.45
world	41.83	39.66	38.73	44.89
sports	38.94	36.36	38.94	44.09
sci-tech	36.74	37.05	36.90	**44.96**
entertainment	34.57	37.98	38.14	42.33
health	34.57	34.26	35.81	40.78
all	52.92	54.99	54.49	45.22

Table 3: Max stock prediction accuracy per category

Scoring news headlines. Now we need to understand if the attention weights are consistent with results in Table 3; we expect 'business' headlines to have a relatively higher score. We trained the network on the entire set of news and used the attention layer to score 271,520 headlines across all categories in the test set. We selected the model with the minimum loss, patience of two epochs. Table 4 shows the results for the top 10, 100, 1,000, and 2,500 headlines. It shows the fraction of business headlines up to that rank, and the increase compared to the fraction of business news in the whole set. For the indices with higher accuracy in the previous experiment (S&P500, Dow Jones, and Russell 1000), the scores significantly skew the distribution at the top ranks towards business news by between 534.65%–471.09% at Rank 10 and between 419.31%–84.14% at Rank 2500. For Nasdaq, with a previously lower performance, the scores do not seem to provide a clear pattern, indicating that the stock prediction performance might reflect the quality of scores.

Stock Index	@Rank 10	@Rank 100	@Rank 1000	@Rank 2500
S&P500	90.00% / +471.09%	91.82% / +482.62%	87.50% / +455.22%	81.30% / +415.88%
Dow Jones	85.00% / +439.36%	63.00% / +299.76%	40.95% / +159.84%	29.02% / +84.14%
Russell 100	100.00% / +534.54%	92.33% / +485.90%	87.40% / +454.59%	81.84% / +419.31%
Nasdaq	0.06% / -61.93%	14.20% / -9.90%	16.46% / +4.45%	16.512% / +4.78%

Table 4: Percentage of 'business' news at rank / Percentage increase compared to base distribution of 15.76%

Rank	Headline	Rank	Headline
1	Dow Drops 176; Nasdaq Tumbles 179	14	Stocks, Dollar Lower on Strong Economic Report ...
2	U.S. stocks drop as bond market signals slowdown; Dow ...	15	Dow Down 60.50; Nasdaq Off 8.78
3	U.S. stocks drop on profit-taking, poor Time Warner ...	16	Stocks dip as traders await Fed meeting details
4	Dollar Lower, Stocks Fall in Early Trading	17	Dow Drops 17; Nasdaq Down Fraction
5	Stocks fall despite manufacturing pickup ...	18	Dollar Weaker, Stocks Fall ...
6	Nasdaq Falls 95; Dow Up 8	19	Dollar, Stocks Traded Lower Eds ...
7	Stocks Fall, Dollar Traded Higher ...	20	Stocks Fall Back, Dollar Lower ...
8	Stocks fall in early trading	21	Stocks fall on concerns over Wall Street and local ec...
9	U.S. stocks turn lower as investors take profits from ...	22	Dollar, Stocks Lower in Early Tokyo Trading ...
10	Dow closes below 10,000; Nasdaq at lowest level ...	23	Nasdaq Ends Down 147; Dow Up 25
11	Stocks lower on Wall Street amid mixed global picture ...	24	U.S. stocks end mostly lower after GDP report ...
12	Financial shares fall on delay, restatement of results	25	Dow Up 70.20; Nasdaq Falls 71.28
13	Stocks Plunge on Profit-Taking, Dollar Inches Higher ...	26	London Shares Lower ...

Table 5: Top results for S&P500

Rank	Headline
1	Latam stocks lower on slowdown concerns
2	Stocks end lower amid worries after House OKs plan
3	Latam stocks plunge on slowdown concerns
4	World markets drop on worries of US-led slowdown
5	French economy enters recession
6	US economy sheds most jobs since 2003
7	Manhattan apartment sales drop further
8	India ' s key stock index drops 4 percent
9	Japan stocks slide on worries about US economy
10	Hon Kong stocks drop on US worries
11	Credit markets still tight after bailout approval
12	US cuts off family planning group in Africa
13	Employers cut 159,000 jobs, most in over 5 years
14	Russian shares fall sharply
15	US Congress OKs bailout bill and Bush signs its

Table 6: Top 15/219 – S&P500 – October 3, 2008

4.2 Anecdotal data

Table 5 shows the top 26 headlines over the whole timespan, ranked using the unnormalized attention layer weights of the model trained for S&P500 with all news categories. The examples show that the model scores market-relevant headlines highly. We see mostly headlines reflecting general market trends. Results for an iconic date, October 3, 2008, in which the US House passed the 2008 bailout show the same trend (Table 6). As for a single day, specific news about stock movements are not many, top-ranking has space for other relevant economic or political events.

4.3 Manual evaluation

We labeled the top 200 test set headlines for each index plus 200 uniformly sampled. Two annotators classified them as relevant or non-relevant. In total, there were only 19 (1.9%) discrepancies that were resolved via mutual agreement. Table 7 shows the relevance results and the high inter-annotator agreement. As before, financially relevant news score higher for the best performing indices compared to Nasdaq and the uniform sample.

Stock Index	Relevant	Not Relevant	Cohen's kappa
S&P500	**100%**	0%	1
Dow Jones	**89%**	11%	0.88
Russell 1000	**87%**	13%	0.94
Nasdaq	25.5%	**73.5%**	0.95
Uniform	19%	**81%**	0.90

Table 7: Manual evaluation on top 200 headlines

5 Conclusion and future work

We presented an exploratory analysis to rank financially relevant events without manually labeled data. We showed that when a simple neural network is able to extract informative signals from news, the attention layer was able to score higher the most relevant news. Future work needs to focus on a more fine-grained analysis of the data and understanding the stability of the scores.

Acknowledgments

We gratefully acknowledge the support of NVIDIA Corporation with the donation of the Titan V GPU used for this research.

References

Dzmitry Bahdanau, Kyunghyun Cho, and Yoshua Bengio. 2015. Neural machine translation by jointly learning to align and translate. In *ICLR*.

Jacob Devlin, Ming-Wei Chang, Kenton Lee, and Kristina Toutanova. 2019. BERT: Pre-training of deep bidirectional transformers for language understanding. In *NAACL-HLT*, pages 4171–4186.

Xiao Ding, Yue Zhang, Ting Liu, and Junwen Duan. 2014. Using structured events to predict stock price movement: An empirical investigation. In *EMNLP*, pages 1415–1425.

Xiao Ding, Yue Zhang, Ting Liu, and Junwen Duan. 2015. Deep learning for event-driven stock prediction. In *IJCAI*, IJCAI'15, page 2327–2333.

Xiao Ding, Yue Zhang, Ting Liu, and Junwen Duan. 2016. Knowledge-driven event embedding for stock prediction. In *COLING*, pages 2133–2142.

Liat Ein-Dor, Ariel Gera, Orith Toledo-Ronen, Alon Halfon, Benjamin Sznajder, Lena Dankin, Yonatan Bilu, Yoav Katz, and Noam Slonim. 2019. Financial event extraction using Wikipedia-based weak supervision. In *Second Workshop on Economics and Natural Language Processing*, pages 10–15.

Győző Gidófalvi. 2001. Using news articles to predict stock price movements.

David Graff, Junbo Kong, Ke Chen, and Kazuaki Maeda. 2003. English gigaword. *Linguistic Data Consortium, Philadelphia*, 4(1):34.

Gilles Jacobs, Els Lefever, and Véronique Hoste. 2018. Economic event detection in company-specific news text. In *First Workshop on Economics and Natural Language Processing*, pages 1–10.

Sarthak Jain and Byron C. Wallace. 2019. Attention is not explanation. In *NAACL-HLT*, pages 3543–3556.

Xiaodong Li, Haoran Xie, Li Chen, Jianping Wang, and Xiaotie Deng. 2014. News impact on stock price return via sentiment analysis. *Know.-Based Syst.*, 69(1):14–23.

S. Merello, A. Picasso Ratto, Y. Ma, O. Luca, and E. Cambria. 2018. Investigating timing and impact of news on the stock market. In *2018 IEEE International Conference on Data Mining Workshops (ICDMW)*, pages 1348–1354.

Yangtuo Peng and Hui Jiang. 2016. Leverage financial news to predict stock price movements using word embeddings and deep neural networks. In *NAACL-HLT*, pages 374–379.

Robert P. Schumaker and Hsinchun Chen. 2009. Textual analysis of stock market prediction using breaking financial news: The azfin text system. *ACM Trans. Inf. Syst.*, 27(2).

Sofia Serrano and Noah A. Smith. 2019. Is attention interpretable? In *ACL*, pages 2931–2951.

Lei Shi, Zhiyang Teng, Le Wang, Yue Zhang, and Alexander Binder. 2019. Deepclue: Visual interpretation of text-based deep stock prediction. *IEEE TKDE*, 31:1094–1108.

Daniele Vitale, Paolo Ferragina, and Ugo Scaiella. 2012. Classification of short texts by deploying topical annotations. In *ECIR*, page 376–387.

Sarah Wiegreffe and Yuval Pinter. 2019. Attention is not not explanation. In *EMNLP-IJCNLP*, pages 11–20.

Boyi Xie, Rebecca J. Passonneau, Leon Wu, and Germán G. Creamer. 2013. Semantic frames to predict stock price movement. In *ACL*, pages 873–883.

Zichao Yang, Diyi Yang, Chris Dyer, Xiaodong He, Alex Smola, and Eduard Hovy. 2016. Hierarchical attention networks for document classification. In *NAACL-HLT*, pages 1480–1489.

Jichuan Zeng, Jing Li, Yan Song, Cuiyun Gao, Michael R. Lyu, and Irwin King. 2018. Topic memory networks for short text classification. In *EMNLP*, pages 3120–3131.

Privacy enabled Financial Text Classification using Differential Privacy and Federated Learning

Priyam Basu and **Tiasa Singha Roy**
Manipal Institute of Technology
{priyam.basu1, tiasa.singharoy}@learner.manipal.edu

Rakshit Naidu
Carnegie Mellon University
rnemakal@andrew.cmu.edu

Zumrut Muftuoglu
Yildiz Technical University
zumrutmuftuoglu@gmail.com

Abstract

Privacy is important considering the financial Domain as such data is highly confidential and sensitive. Natural Language Processing (NLP) techniques can be applied for text classification and entity detection purposes in financial domains such as customer feedback sentiment analysis, invoice entity detection, categorisation of financial documents by type etc. Due to the sensitive nature of such data, privacy measures need to be taken for handling and training large models with such data. In this work, we propose a contextualized transformer (BERT and RoBERTa) based text classification model integrated with privacy features such as Differential Privacy (DP) and Federated Learning (FL). We present how to privately train NLP models and desirable privacy-utility tradeoffs and evaluate them on the Financial Phrase Bank dataset.

1 Introduction

Divulging personally identifiable information during a business transaction has become a commonplace occurrence for most individuals. This activity can span from sharing of bank account numbers, loan account numbers, and credit/debit card numbers, to providing non-financial personally identifiable information such as name, social security number, driver's license number, address, and e-mail address. Maintaining the privacy of confidential customer information has become essential for any firm which collects or stores personally identifiable data. The financial services industry operates and deals with a significant amount of confidential client and customer data for daily business transactions. Though many organizations are taking strides to improve their privacy practices, and consumers are becoming more privacy-aware, it remains a tremendous burden for users to manage their privacy (Anton et al., 2004).

NLP has major applications in the finance industry for many tasks such as detection of entities for gross tax calculation from invoice and payroll data, categorising different kinds of financial documents based on type, grouping of financial documents based on semantic similarity, sentiment analysis of financial text (Vicari and Gaspari, 2020), conversational bots for banking systems, investment recommendation engines etc.

Text Classification can be extended to many NLP applications including sentiment analysis, question answering, and topic labeling . For example, financial or government institutions that wish to train a chatbot for their clients cannot be allowed to upload all text data from the client-side to their central server due to strict privacy protection statements (Liu et al., 2021). At this point, applying the federated learning paradigm presents an approach to solve the dilemma due to its advances in privacy preservation and collaborative training where the central server can train a powerful model with different local labeled data at client devices without uploading the raw data considering increasing privacy concerns in public.

The goal of this paper is to propose a privacy enabled text classification system, combining state-of-the-art transformers (BERT and RoBERTa) with differential privacy, on both centralized and FL based setups, exploring different privacy budgets to investigate the privacy-utility trade-off and see how they perform when trying to classify financial document-based text sequences. For the federated setups, we try to explore both IID (Independent and Identically Distributed) and non-IID distributions of data.

2 Related Work

Deep learning techniques have often been used to learn text representations via neural models by language application. The input text can give us individual demographic information about the author. Sentiment analysis can be used for the classification or categorization of financial documents. Xing

Proceedings of the Third Workshop on Economics and Natural Language Processing, pages 50–55
Punta Cana and online, November 11.

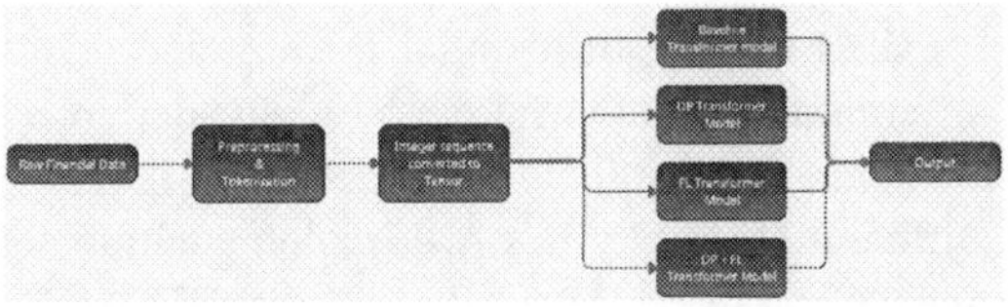

Figure 1: Pipeline

et al. investigate the error patterns of some widely acknowledged sentiment analysis methods in the finance domain. Mishev et al. perform more than one hundred experiments using publicly available datasets, labeled by financial experts. In their work, Liu et al. propose a domain-specific language model pre-trained on large-scale financial corpora and evaluate it on the Financial Phrase Bank dataset. Araci presents a BERT-based model which is pre-trained on a large amount of finance-based data in his study.

Studies have been conducted on training differentially private deep models with the formal differential privacy approach in the literature (Abadi et al., 2016; McMahan et al., 2018; Yu et al., 2019). Fernandes et al. discuss the security through differential privacy in textual data. (Panchal, 2020) in his work portrays the use of DP in the generation of contextually similar messages for Honey encryption which encrypts messages using low min-entropy keys such as passwords. Federated learning is another privacy-enhancing approach (McMahan et al., 2017; Yang et al., 2019; Kairouz et al., 2021; Jana and Biemann, 2021; Priyanshu and Naidu, 2021), which relies on distributed training of models on devices and sharing of model gradients. Liu et al. show how FL can be used for decentralized training of heavy pre-trained NLP models. Basu et al. in their work have shown a detailed benchmark comparison of multiple BERT based models with DP and FL for depression detection. Jana and Biemann in their work show a differentially private sequence tagging system in a federated learning setup.

3 Dataset

The key arguments for the low utilization of statistical techniques in financial sentiment analysis have been the difficulty of implementation for practical applications and the lack of high- quality training data for building such models. Especially in the case of finance and economic texts, annotated collections are a scarce resource and many are reserved for proprietary use only. For this reason, we use the Financial Phrase Bank dataset (Malo et al., 2014) which was also used for benchmarking the pre-trained FinBERT model for sentiment analysis (Araci, 2019). The dataset includes approximately 5000 phrases/sentences from financial news texts and company press releases. The objective of the phrase level annotation task is to classify each example sentence into a positive, negative or neutral category by considering only the information explicitly available in the given sentence. Since the study is focused only on financial and economic domains, the annotators were asked to consider the sentences from the viewpoint of an investor only; i.e. whether the news may have a positive, negative or neutral influence on the stock price. As a result, sentences that have a sentiment that is not relevant from an economic or financial perspective are considered neutral.

Given a large number of overlapping annotations (5 to 8 annotations per sentence), there are several ways to define a majority vote-based gold standard. To provide an objective comparison, the authors have formed 4 alternative reference datasets based on the strength of majority agreement. For the purpose of this task, we use those sentences with 75% or more agreement. The final dataset has 3453 sentences in total out of which 60% belong to the neutral class, 28% belong to the positive class and 12% belong to the positive class.

4 Preliminaries

Today, the text is the most widely used communication instrument.For years, researchers are studies focusing on implementing different approaches that make possible machines to imitate human reading (Ly et al., 2020). Natural Language Processing(NLP) lays a bridge between computers and natural languages by helping machines to analyze human language (Manning and Schütze, 1999) .Devlin et al. developed a model which is based on bidirectional encoder representation (Alyafeai et al., 2020). RoBERTa is a modified form of BERT (Liu et al., 2019).

4.1 BERT

Transformer-based models have been used since they use a self-attention mechanism and process the entire input data at once instead of as a sequence to capture long-term dependencies for obtaining contextual meaning. Bidirectional Encoder Representations from Transformers (BERT)(Devlin et al., 2018) tokenizes words into sub-words (using WordPiece) which are then given as input to the model. It also uses positional embeddings to replace recurrence.

4.2 RoBERTa

Robustly Optimized BERT-Pretraining Approach (RoBERTa) (Liu et al., 2019) is a state-of-the-art transformer model which improves BERT (Devlin et al., 2018) that uses a multi-headed attention mechanism which enables it to capture long term dependencies. It essentially fine-tunes the original BERT model along with data manipulation and uses Byte-Pair Encoding for utilizing the character and word level representations and removed Next Sentence Prediction (NSP) to match or even slightly improve downstream task performance.

4.3 Differential Privacy

Differential Privacy (DP) is a privacy standard which allows data use in any analysis by presenting mathematical guarantee (Dwork and Roth, 2014). It provides strong confidentiality in statistical databases and machine learning approaches through mathematical definition. This definition is an acceptable measure of privacy concern (Dwork, 2008).

Definition 1.1 : *M and E denote a random mechanism and each event (output) respectively. D and D' are defined neighboring datasets having difference with one record. (ε, δ) protects confidentiality (Dwork, 2011). M gives (ε, δ)-differential privacy for and D and D' if M satsifies:*

$$\Pr\left[M\left(D\right) \in E\right] \leq e^{\epsilon} \cdot \Pr\left[M\left(D'\right) \in E\right] + \delta \quad (1)$$

where ε denotes the privacy budget and δ represents the probability of error.

4.3.1 The Privacy Budget

The privacy guarantee level of M is controlled through privacy budget of ϵ (Haeberlen et al., 2011).There are two widely used privacy budget compositions as the sequential composition and the parallel composition.

The ratio between the two mechanisms ($M(D)$ and $M(D')$) limits by e^{ε}. For $\delta = 0$, M gives ε-differential privacy by its strictest definition. In other case, for some low probability cases, (ε,δ)-differential privacy provides latitude to invade strict ε-differential privacy. ε-differential privacy is called as pure differential privacy and (ε, δ)-differential privacy, where $\delta > 0$, is called as *approximate differential privacy* (Beimel et al., 2014). Differential privacy has two implementation settings: Centralized DP (CDP) via DP-SGD and Local DP (LDP) (Qu et al., 2021).

In CDP, a trusted data curator answers queries or releases differentially private models by using randomisation algorithms (Dwork and Roth, 2014). In this article, we use DP-SGD (Differentially Private Stochastic Gradient Descent) (Abadi et al., 2016) to train our models.

4.4 Federated Learning

As conventional centralized learning systems require that all training data produced on different devices be uploaded to a server or cloud for training, it may give rise to serious privacy concerns (Privacy, 2017). FL allows training an algorithm in a decentralized way (McMahan et al., 2017, 2016). It ensures multiple parties collectively train a machine learning model without exchanging the local data (Li et al., 2021). To define mathematically, it is assumed that there are N parties, and each party is showed with T_i, where $i \in [1, N]$. For the non-federated setting, each party uses its local data and depicted by D_i to train a local model M_i and send the local model parameters to the server. The predictive data is sent only the local model parameters to the FL server. Most centralized setups have just the IID assumption for train test data but in a federated learning based decentralized setup, non-IID poses the problem of high skewness of different devices due to different data distribution (Liu et al., 2021).

In federated language modeling, existing works (Yang et al., 2018) use FedAvg as the federated optimization algorithm. In FedAvg, gradients that are computed locally over a large population of clients are aggregated by the server to build a novel global model. Every client is trained by locally stored data and computes the average gradient with the current global model via one or more steps of SGD.

Applying FL to text classification can cause problems such as designing proper aggregating algorithms for handling the gradients or weights uploaded by different client models. Zhu et al. proposed a text classification using the standard FedAvg algorithm to update the model parameter with local trained models. Model compression has also been introduced to federated classification tasks due to the dilemma of computation restraints on the client-side, where an attempt to reduce the model size on the client-side to enable the real application of federated learning was made. For overcoming the communication dilemma of FL, central server can successfully train the central model with only one or a few rounds of communication under poor communication scenarios in a one-shot or few-shot setting.

5 Experimental Results

In the scope of the study, the FinBERT (pre-trained) model is used as the base model. Two NLP models were trained by implementing DP and FL. In this section, the results presented in the tables are discussed. The results placed in the tables are the average and the standard deviation of the results obtained after running the models thrice.

The dataset was split into train set and test set with 80:20 train test ratio. BERT and RoBERTa based models were used for the language modelling part. It should be noted that the table contain the average and the standard deviation of the results obtained after running the models 3 times. Table 1 shows a comparison according to epsilon values between both the language models using Centralized DP and in a Federated Learning set up. The Opacus library was used along with PyTorch for the experiments. We implement DP, FL and DP-FL on BERT and RoBERTa for $\epsilon = 0.5, 5, 15, 20, 25$. Our baseline model (with no noise) achieves an accuracy of **67.71%** and **68.37%** on BERT and RoBERTa respectively.

In baseline mode, we can see that RoBERTa has a slight improvement over BERT because of its robustness owing to a heavier pre-training procedure. We also notice that with the increase in epsilon values, the amount of standard deviation decreases as the model approaches towards its vanilla variant (without DP noise).

Table 2 also shows us the results obtained when DP was applied in a federated learning mode, both in IID (Identical and Independently distributed) and Non-IID data silos. For Non-IID scenarios, we assume 10 shards of size 240 assigned to each client. We run it over 10 clients in total, selecting only a fraction of 0.5 in each round for training. We add DP locally, that is, to each client model at every iteration and aggregate them to perform Federated Averaging. We observe the best accuracies with

Table 1: Averaged Test Accuracies of FL and DPFL models

Setup	Epsilon(ϵ)	BERT	RoBERTa
Centralized DP	0.5	31.5±23.94	31.36 ± 26.35
	5	37.48±20.42	38.34 ±20.08
	15	51.71 ±14.71	51.34 ± 15.45
	20	55.37 ± 5.49	55.54 ± 5.54
	25	60.03 ± 1.37	62.6 ± 4.24
DP-FL IID	0.5	14.57 ± 2.86	20.11 ± 7.68
	5	30 ±25.6	30.04 ± 28.22
	15	40.34 ± 20.55	50.26 ± 20.84
	20	51.05 ± 7.95	54.78 ± 2.99
	25	53.47 ± 6.48	61.38 ± 0.93
DP-FL Non IID	0.5	19.82 ± 5.97	33.13 ± 25.41
	5	35.74 ± 21.48	36.51 ± 26.87
	15	45.87 ± 15.56	49.83 ± 20.6
	20	52.43 ± 4.08	53.36 ± 3.27
	25	58.96 ± 2.56	60.83 ± 0.53

RoBERTa for the centralised DP implementation, particularly with $\epsilon = 25$ with an accuracy of 62.6%. BERT in a centralised DP setting does come close at $\epsilon = 25$ with an accuracy of 60.03%. The results also show that the accuracy decreases by adding FL to the DP implementations.

We also empirically observe that with increase in ϵ , accuracy of the models also increases. This happens because as the value of ϵ increases, privacy decreases with the addition of noise from a smaller range which results in smaller variance. Consequently, the accuracy of the model increases. Inherently, applying DP to deep learning yields loss of utility due to the addition of noise and clipping. We can also observe that the performance of federated language models still lies behind that of centralized ones.

6 Conclusion

Financial data is highly sensitive , hence the risks of collecting and sharing data can limit studies. Financial organizations work with a lot of confidential user data and therefore highly value protecting the data to retain the integrity of the user and we need to delve into research of private training of machine learning models to ensure this. During this study, we benchmark the utility of privacy models while attempting to preserve the performance of SOTA transformer models such as BERT and RoBERTa. Our empirical results show that the models show better performance with increasing ε as expected with the decrease in noise. The models come close to the performance of the baseline models near the higher ε values.The DP + FL shows a similar trend which showcases a greater protection feature without compromising the performance. As future work, we hope to improve our models further by hyper-parameter tuning, freezing partial layers of the NLP model and implementing focal loss on the unbalanced dataset to better the results. The complete code to this paper can be found here: https://www.github.com/tiasa2/Privacy-enabled-Financial-Text-Classification-using-Differential-Privacy-and-Federated-Learning.

References

Martin Abadi, Andy Chu, Ian Goodfellow, H. Brendan McMahan, Ilya Mironov, Kunal Talwar, and Li Zhang. 2016. Deep learning with differential privacy. *Proceedings of the 2016 ACM SIGSAC Conference on Computer and Communications Security.*

Zaid Alyafeai, Maged Saeed AlShaibani, and Irfan Ahmad. 2020. A survey on transfer learning in natural language processing.

A.I. Anton, J.B. Earp, Qingfeng He, W. Stufflebeam, D. Bolchini, and C. Jensen. 2004. Financial privacy policies and the need for standardization. *IEEE Security Privacy*, 2(2):36–45.

Dogu Araci. 2019. Finbert: Financial sentiment analysis with pre-trained language models. *arXiv preprint arXiv:1908.10063.*

Priyam Basu, Tiasa Singha Roy, Rakshit Naidu, Zumrut Muftuoglu, Sahib Singh, and Fatemehsadat Mireshghallah. 2021. Benchmarking differential privacy and federated learning for bert models. *arXiv preprint arXiv:2106.13973.*

Amos Beimel, Kobbi Nissim, and Uri Stemmer. 2014. Private learning and sanitization: Pure vs. approximate differential privacy.

Jacob Devlin, Ming-Wei Chang, Kenton Lee, and Kristina Toutanova. 2018. Bert: Pre-training of deep bidirectional transformers for language understanding. *arXiv preprint arXiv:1810.04805.*

Jacob Devlin, Ming-Wei Chang, Kenton Lee, and Kristina Toutanova. 2019. BERT: Pre-training of deep bidirectional transformers for language understanding. In *Proceedings of the 2019 Conference of the North American Chapter of the Association for Computational Linguistics: Human Language Technologies, Volume 1 (Long and Short Papers)*, pages 4171–4186, Minneapolis, Minnesota. Association for Computational Linguistics.

Cynthia Dwork. 2008. Differential privacy: A survey of results. In *Theory and Applications of Models of Computation*, pages 1–19, Berlin, Heidelberg. Springer Berlin Heidelberg.

Cynthia Dwork. 2011. A firm foundation for private data analysis. *Commun. ACM*, 54(1):86–95.

Cynthia Dwork and Aaron Roth. 2014. The algorithmic foundations of differential privacy. *Found. Trends Theor. Comput. Sci.*, 9(3–4):211–407.

Natasha Fernandes, Mark Dras, and Annabelle McIver. 2019. Generalised differential privacy for text document processing. In *Principles of Security and Trust*, Lecture Notes in Computer Science (including subseries Lecture Notes in Artificial Intelligence and Lecture Notes in Bioinformatics), pages 123–148, Germany. Springer-VDI-Verlag GmbH Co. KG.

Andreas Haeberlen, Benjamin C. Pierce, and Arjun Narayan. 2011. Differential privacy under fire. SEC'11, page 33, USA. USENIX Association.

Abhik Jana and Chris Biemann. 2021. An investigation towards differentially private sequence tagging in a federated framework. In *Proceedings of the Third Workshop on Privacy in Natural Language Processing*, pages 30–35.

Peter Kairouz, H. Brendan McMahan, Brendan Avent, Aurélien Bellet, Mehdi Bennis, Arjun Nitin Bhagoji, Kallista Bonawitz, Zachary Charles, Graham Cormode, Rachel Cummings, Rafael G. L. D'Oliveira, Hubert Eichner, Salim El Rouayheb, David Evans, Josh Gardner, Zachary Garrett, Adrià Gascón, Badih Ghazi, Phillip B. Gibbons, Marco Gruteser, Zaid Harchaoui, Chaoyang He, Lie He, Zhouyuan Huo, Ben Hutchinson, Justin Hsu, Martin Jaggi, Tara Javidi, Gauri Joshi, Mikhail Khodak, Jakub Konečný, Aleksandra Korolova, Farinaz Koushanfar, Sanmi Koyejo, Tancrède Lepoint, Yang Liu, Prateek Mittal, Mehryar Mohri, Richard Nock, Ayfer Özgür, Rasmus Pagh, Mariana Raykova, Hang Qi, Daniel Ramage, Ramesh Raskar, Dawn Song, Weikang Song, Sebastian U. Stich, Ziteng Sun, Ananda Theertha Suresh, Florian Tramèr, Praneeth Vepakomma, Jianyu Wang, Li Xiong, Zheng Xu, Qiang Yang, Felix X. Yu, Han Yu, and Sen Zhao. 2021. Advances and open problems in federated learning.

Qinbin Li, Zeyi Wen, Zhaomin Wu, Sixu Hu, Naibo Wang, Yuan Li, Xu Liu, and Bingsheng He. 2021. A survey on federated learning systems: Vision, hype and reality for data privacy and protection.

Ming Liu, Stella Ho, Mengqi Wang, Longxiang Gao, Yuan Jin, and He Zhang. 2021. Federated learning meets natural language processing: A survey. *arXiv preprint arXiv:2107.12603.*

Yinhan Liu, Myle Ott, Naman Goyal, Jingfei Du, Mandar Joshi, Danqi Chen, Omer Levy, Mike Lewis, Luke Zettlemoyer, and Veselin Stoyanov. 2019. Roberta: A robustly optimized bert pretraining approach.

Zhuang Liu, Degen Huang, Kaiyu Huang, Zhuang Li, and Jun Zhao. 2020. Finbert: A pre-trained financial language representation model for financial text mining. In *IJCAI*, pages 4513–4519.

Antoine Ly, Benno Uthayasooriyar, and Tingting Wang. 2020. A survey on natural language processing (nlp) and applications in insurance.

Pekka Malo, Ankur Sinha, Pekka Korhonen, Jyrki Wallenius, and Pyry Takala. 2014. Good debt or bad debt: Detecting semantic orientations in economic texts. *Journal of the Association for Information Science and Technology*, 65(4):782–796.

Christopher D. Manning and Hinrich Schütze. 1999. *Foundations of Statistical Natural Language Processing*. MIT Press, Cambridge, MA, USA.

H. B. McMahan, Eider Moore, D. Ramage, and B. A. Y. Arcas. 2016. Federated learning of deep networks using model averaging. *ArXiv*, abs/1602.05629.

H. Brendan McMahan, Eider Moore, Daniel Ramage, Seth Hampson, and Blaise Agüera y Arcas. 2017. Communication-efficient learning of deep networks from decentralized data.

H. Brendan McMahan, Daniel Ramage, Kunal Talwar, and Li Zhang. 2018. Learning differentially private recurrent language models.

Kostadin Mishev, Ana Gjorgjevikj, Irena Vodenska, Lubomir T. Chitkushev, and Dimitar Trajanov. 2020. Evaluation of sentiment analysis in finance: From lexicons to transformers. *IEEE Access*, 8:131662–131682.

Kunjal Panchal. 2020. Differential privacy and natural language processing to generate contextually similar decoy messages in honey encryption scheme. *arXiv preprint arXiv:2010.15985*.

Apple Differential Privacy. 2017. Learning with privacy at scale.

Aman Priyanshu and Rakshit Naidu. 2021. Fedpandemic: A cross-device federated learning approach towards elementary prognosis of diseases during a pandemic.

Chen Qu, Weize Kong, Liu Yang, Mingyang Zhang, Michael Bendersky, and Marc Najork. 2021. Privacy-adaptive bert for natural language understanding.

Mattia Vicari and Mauro Gaspari. 2020. Analysis of news sentiments using natural language processing and deep learning. *Ai & Society*, pages 1–7.

Frank Xing, Lorenzo Malandri, Yue Zhang, and Erik Cambria. 2020. Financial sentiment analysis: an investigation into common mistakes and silver bullets. In *Proceedings of the 28th International Conference on Computational Linguistics*, pages 978–987.

Qiang Yang, Yang Liu, Tianjian Chen, and Yongxin Tong. 2019. Federated machine learning: Concept and applications.

Timothy Yang, Galen Andrew, Hubert Eichner, Haicheng Sun, Wei Li, Nicholas Kong, Daniel Ramage, and Françoise Beaufays. 2018. Applied federated learning: Improving google keyboard query suggestions. *arXiv preprint arXiv:1812.02903*.

Lei Yu, Ling Liu, Calton Pu, Mehmet Emre Gursoy, and Stacey Truex. 2019. Differentially private model publishing for deep learning. *2019 IEEE Symposium on Security and Privacy (SP)*.

Xinghua Zhu, Jianzong Wang, Zhenhou Hong, and Jing Xiao. 2020. Empirical studies of institutional federated learning for natural language processing. In *Findings of the Association for Computational Linguistics: EMNLP 2020*, pages 625–634, Online. Association for Computational Linguistics.

Using Word Embedding to Reveal Monetary Policy Explanation Changes

Akira Matsui, Xiang Ren, Emilio Ferrara
University of Southern California
{amatsui, xiangren, emiliofe}@usc.edu

Abstract

Documents have been an essential tool of communication for governments to announce their policy operations. Most policy announcements have taken the form of text to inform their new policies or changes to the public. To understand such policymakers' communication, many researchers exploit published policy documents. However, the methods well-used in other research domains such as sentiment analysis or topic modeling are not suitable for studying policy communications. Their training corpora and methods are not for policy documents where technical terminologies are used, and sentiment expressions are refrained. We leverage word embedding techniques to extract semantic changes in the monetary policy documents. Our empirical study shows that the policymaker uses different semantics according to the type of documents when they change their policy.

1 Introduction

Disentangling how policymakers explain their policy is crucial to understand how policymakers supported by democracy uphold their responsibility. However, extracting such abstract information from policy documents is challenging. First of all, policy documents are often crabbedly written with technical terminologies, meaning that machine learning models trained on general corpora may not work well. In addition, popular text mining techniques for social science such as sentiment analysis or topic modeling may not be applicable. It would be a strong assumption, for example, that changes in policy explanation reflect its sentiments. Even if we observed topic changes in documents during policy changes, it only tells "what" was explained but does not disclose "how" policy explanations changed.

This paper proposes a word embedding-based framework for understanding how policymakers change their explanation when they change their policies. Our framework trains the word embedding model only on policy documents, which allows us to resolve the aforementioned challenges by defining the semantic of the policy words solely on the policy documents. We use our approach to study the monetary policy operation by the Federal Reserve Bank (FRB) in the united states. Our framework reveals how the policymaker explains their policy change in the policy documents and finds that different policy documents have a different role in policy change explanation even though the same policymaker publishes these documents. We also find that our word embedding-based framework can be used to predict policy changes. We summarize our framework and study design at Figure 1.

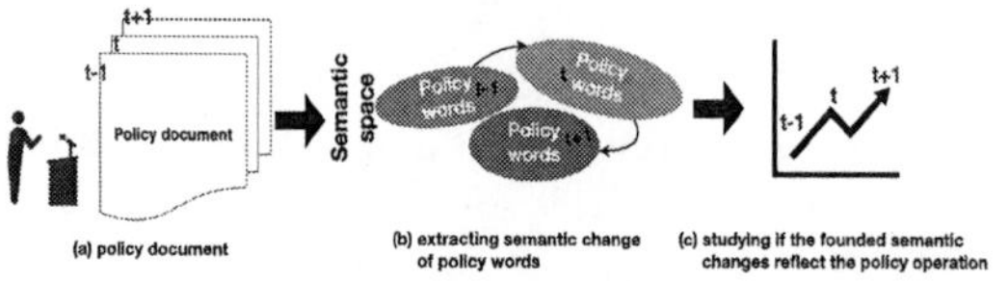

Figure 1: Schematic of our framework and study design

2 Methods and Data

2.1 Word embedding

To extract the policy explanation from the policy documents, we use a dynamic embedding model, focusing on the transition of the semantic of the important words in the policy. The dynamic embedding calculates the semantic differences of the words in the documents over time. Hence, it allows us to study the differences in the semantics of specific policy-related words between two consecutive periods. Word embeddings highlight the semantic movements hidden in corpora, such as gender biases (Garg et al., 2018) or law-of semantics (Hamilton et al., 2016). Comparing the embedding vectors from the corpora over time can yield fallacious analysis because low-dimension embed-

Proceedings of the Third Workshop on Economics and Natural Language Processing, pages 56–61
Punta Cana and online, November 11. ©2021 Association for Computational Linguistics

ding vectors can yield arbitrary orthogonal transformations (Hamilton et al., 2016). To avoid this pitfall, we use the state-of-the-art dynamic word-embedding method that efficiently yields temporal word embeddings (Di Carlo et al., 2019). We construct word-embedding vectors for each time, w_t (30 dimensions).

2.1.1 Introducing the reference words

To obtain interpretable measurement of policy explanation change, we quantify the semantic distance between the policy-related and the reference words. While we can calculate the cosine similarity between the word embedding vectors of the words of interest as (Hamilton et al., 2016), these similarities only describe the degree of semantic changes but not "how" the semantics of policy words change. Instead, we capture the semantic changes of the policy words by calculating how the semantic of policy words are close to the reference words as (Garg et al., 2018).

For the reference words, we use the set of neutral words and the set of positive and negative words from the Subjectivity Lexicon (Wilson, 2005; Wilson et al., 2005). The Subjectivity Lexicon is the annotated polarity dictionary of subjective words: words with explicit polarity (positive and negative), and neutral words [1].

We use these annotated words to calculate the relative distance difference between the semantic of policy words and explicit semantic (positive and negative) words or neutral semantic (neutral) words. We also try another setting of the reference words calculating the relative distance difference between the semantic of policy words and positive semantic words or negative semantic words.

The role of these reference words in this paper is not to measure polarity but rather to measure the degree of the policy-related explanations become explicit during policy changes. To do so, we measure the semantic distance between explicit reference words and policy-related words (the detail to be discussed in Eq 1 in the next subsection). Also, since the embedding vectors of the reference words will be also learned from the policy document, the semantic of such reference words also reflect the text specificity of the policy. With this advantage, our framework overcomes the problem of language model trained on general corpora discussed in the introduction.

2.1.2 Calculating relative distances of the reference words to the policy words

With the trained word embedding model on policy documents, we will measure how the policymaker changes their policy explanation over policy operations. In this study, we calculate the degree of explicit of the policy words that measure the semantic distance between the important policy words and the reference words that have particular stable semantics.

To represent the degree of explicit of policy explanation, we calculate the relative distance between the reference words and the policy words. To easy to follow our analysis, we summarize the selection of reference words in Table 1. Following (Garg et al., 2018), we calculate the semantic differences at each time period t as

$$RT(Ref_1, Ref_2) = \frac{1}{\|\boldsymbol{E}\|} \sum_{\boldsymbol{w}_t^e \in \boldsymbol{E}} \left\| \boldsymbol{w}_t^e - \bar{\boldsymbol{w}}_t^{Ref1} \right\|_2 - \left\| \boldsymbol{w}_t^e - \bar{\boldsymbol{w}}_t^{Ref2} \right\|_2, \quad (1)$$

where $\boldsymbol{w}_t^e$ is the semantic vectors of the policy words p, at time t; $\bar{\boldsymbol{w}}_t^{Refi}$ is the average word embedding vectors of the group i, where Ref_i are the set of subjective words; $\|\boldsymbol{E}\|$ is the number of policy words studied.

Eq 1 calculates the relative similarity of the policy words to the set of words Ref_1 against Ref_2. When Ref_1 is a neutral word and Ref_2 is the concatenation of positive and negative words, a small value of $RT(Ref_1, Ref_2)$ indicates that the policy words are close to the explicit semantic lather than the neutral semantic. We call this variable the degree of explicit. For comparison, we also try to set Ref_2 positive be and Ref_1 be negative, and it takes a small value when the policy words are close to the positive subjective semantic. We call this variable the degree of positive. We will discuss the selection of the policy words in Sec 2.3.

2.2 Vector autoregression model (VAR)

We study whether the calculated degree of explicit policy explanation reflects the actual policy changes over the course of policy operation. The variables of interest, however, have simultaneous interactions with each other. While a semantic shift in policy explanation can follow a change in policy operation, this relation can be the other way around.

[1]For example, the Subjectivity Lexicon annotates "clear","vague" and "completely" as positive, negative, neutral subjective words respectively. The Subjectivity Lexicon is publicly available at (Wilson, 2005).

Table 1: The subjective word choice for Relative distance metrics for policy explanation

	Name	Ref_1	Ref_2
1	**the degree of explicit**	Explicit semantic words (positive and negative words)	Neutral semantic words (neutral words)
2	**the degree of positive**	Negative semantic words	Positive semantic words

Note: The selection of the reference word used in Equation 1. We calculate the relative distance of the word embedding vectors of the policy words and the explicit semantic words, the neutral semantic words (**the degree of explicit**). For an alternative, we also calculate the degree of positive using the relative distance between the policy word and Negative semantic and Positive semantic (**the degree of positive**).

Taking into account this typical challenge in time series analysis, we employ the vector autoregression model (VAR). VAR is a time series model well used in the application of time series analysis in the financial econometric model (Stock and Watson, 2001; Stock et al., 2003).

VAR is a generalized autoregression model widely used for economic time series analysis with multiple variables. An advantage of the VAR model is that the VAR studies the interactions among variables across time periods. We estimate the VAR model that has the following autoregressive structure,

$$y_t = c + \Phi_1 y_{t-1} + \cdots + \Phi_p y_{t-p} + \epsilon_t$$

where c is $n \times 1$ interception vector; Φ is $n \times n$ coefficient matrix; ϵ_t is a error term, $\epsilon_t \sim W.N.(\Sigma)$ and Σ is variance-covariance matrix. Note that y_t is the vector that has the variables of log difference at time t. y_t such as the degree of explicit, the representation of policy operation discussed in the following section.

We use the estimated VAR model to study if a change in the semantic of the policy explanation can follow the policy change. To do so, we conduct impulse response simulation, which is one of the standard methods in financial econometric analysis (Stock and Watson, 2001; Stock et al., 2003). Impulse response simulation investigates how a change in a variable at time t transmits the other variables in the terms after time t, modeling the interactions among variables. In our analysis, we study if a change in the variable of the policy semantic at time t transmit the variables represents the policy change at time $t + 1$ and after[2]. By doing this, we can remove the relation that the policy change at time t leads to some changes in the semantic of the policy explanation t, which is known as simultaneous interactions.

[2](Stock and Watson, 2001) provides a good summary of how to interprets the impulse response analysis with an example in p106.

2.3 Policy words selection and FRB data

This paper will use the data from FRB. The FRB policy documents explain their policy operation as the Federal law requires. Also, it is widely recognized that maintaining transparency is a key to conduct a successful monetary policy operation theoretically and practically (Woodford, 2005; Geraats, 2002; Blinder et al., 2008). In addition, the FRB publishes the statement about their policy operation, which enables us to select what policy words should be studied in our analysis. Lastly, we measure the FRB policy operation by its policy interest rate. These practical and technical advantages allow us to investigate our research question with our framework.

To construct the variable of the policy words' semantics, using Equation 1, we select the specific groups of words that represent the FRB's monetary policy. For selecting such words, we leverage the situation that the FRB discloses their policy goal as *the Fed's mandate* (the Federal Reserve Bank of Chicago, 2020). The Fed's mandate states the three main goals of the monetary policy declared by the FRB: "full employment", "stable prices", and "moderate long-term interest rates" (Bank, 2020c; the Federal Reserve Bank of Chicago, 2020). We select the words related to the Fed's mandate: Employment (unemployment rate, wage); Stable prices (unemployment rate, wage, unemployment, labor, full employment); Interest rates (interest, interest rate). As a sub-analysis, we expand the words to study by adding the other terminologies in economics using a economic dictionary by (Welker, 2020).

We construct our corpus of the FRB documents (Bank, 2020a,b): Beige Book, Tealbook, and Federal Open Market Committee (FOMC) minute. These documents inherently contain information on FRB's policy-making, yet they describe the FRB monetary policy from different perspectives. The FOMC minutes is one of the most relevant documents that communicates the FRB monetary policy operation. FOMC minute is the summary of the FOMC meetings where the FRB committees decide the direction of the FRB monetary policy. The FOMC committee refers to the Tealbook that reports the economic conditions and backgrounds for monetary policy operation. The Beige Book summarizes the US economic conditions reported by each district of the FRB. The text sizes of each document per quarter are as follow; Beige book (mean:13,952 total: 1,018,531); Minute (mean: 11,075 total: 808,501); Tealbook (mean:68,50 total: 5,000,916).

To study whether our framework captures the FRB policy, we need to have a variable that represents the FRB policy. We use the FFR, the interest rate for depository institutions trading federal funds with each other overnight. In this study, we focus on the relationship between the constructed feature and FFR.

Table 2: Comparing the prediction performances

		Economic Dictionary	Fed's mandate
VAR	Deg of explicit	0.033979	**0.033000**
	Deg of positive	0.035895	0.035793
	Cosine dist	0.034892	0.035440
	LSA	0.035426	
	Word count	0.036309	0.037934
LSTM	Deg of explicit	0.043946	0.043875
	Deg of positive	0.043871	0.043743
	Cosine dist	0.043799	0.043633
	LSA	0.043631	
	Word count	0.043682	0.043692
ARIMA	Only using (FFR)	0.037722	

Predicting the policy behavior represented by the Federal Funds Rate (FFR). RMSE of the prediction results (40-time series splits data; smaller is better). **Deg of explicit** and **positive** are the degree of explicit and positive respectively (summarized at Table 1). Cosine distance calculates the distance average embedding of the policy words between periods. **LSA** is used to calculate cosine distance of the document vector by Latent Semantic Analysis (LSA) using Bag of Words. Word count is the number of policy words for each reference words.

3 Results

This section reports the results of the impulse response analysis, and the prediction analysis.

3.1 VAR analysis

We estimate the VAR model with the degree of explicit in policy documents, FFR and U.S. GDP. We present our impulse simulation with the estimated VAR model at Figure 2. Each sub-figure demonstrates how one-standard deviation positive changes in the degree of explicit transmits the policy operation represented by the federal funds rate (FFR). The blue line represents the percent changes in the policy rate derived from a change in the estimated model.

The first left sub-figure at Figure 2(**b**) shows that when the policymaker increases the degree of explicit in the document (Tealbook), they increase their policy rate in the next few quarters (the dotted line represent 95% confidence intervals). On the other hand, the right sub-figure at Figure 2(**b**) demonstrates that when the policymaker increases the degree of explicit, they will decrease the policy rate in the following few quarters. These results imply that even when simultaneously considered, we found the policymaker changes the semantic of the document when they change their policy.

Our results also reveal that the policy documents have different role in explaining policy changes. Minute and Tealbook show opposite direction changes. The results also demonstrate that the model with focused reference words (Fed's Mandate) show relatively clearer result than one with the expanded reference words (Economic Dictionary). The left sub-figure of Figure 2(**a**) does not shows significant policy changes compared to the left sub-figure of Figure 2(**b**). This result imply that the focused policy related words well captures the policy operation than the general terminologies.

3.1.1 Implication of the VAR analysis

The results in Figure 2(**b**) suggest that the policymaker use the different documents according to the phase of policy. The policymaker increases the degree of explicit in Tealbook when they increases the policy rate (tamping down stimulating economy), and they increases the degree of explicit in the minute when they decrease the policy rate (stimulating economy). Those results clearly describe how the policymaker uses the different documents according to the phase of the policy. When they can write the condition of the economy (in the Tealbook) explicitly, the policymaker tamps down their policy. On the other hand, when the committee's discussion of the policy operation (in the minute) is explicit, they stimulate the economy. To summarize those results, the policy implication of the results is that the policymaker uses the economic condition to rational for tamping down their policy, whereas they stimulate the economy when the committee has a explicit discussion in the policy operation meeting (FOMC meeting).

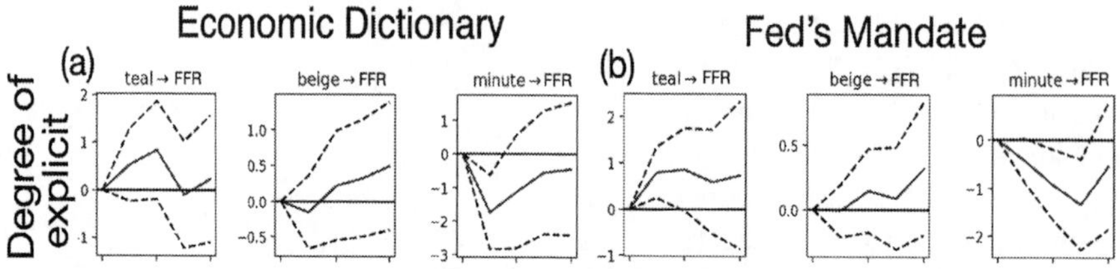

Figure 2: Impulse response analysis

Impulse response to a shock in the neutrality of the policy words in the three documents (**FFR**: Federal Funds Rate;**teal**: Tealbook; **beige**: Beige book; **minute**: FOMC minute). The x-axis represents the time after a change in the degree of explicit occur (quarterly). The y-axis represents the percent change. The dashed lines represent 95% confidence interval. They demonstrate how a change in document transmits to the FFR across the following four quarters. Each column represents policy word selection (the economic dictionary, the Fed's mandate)

3.2 Prediction analysis

We reports the prediction results in Table 2. For semantic calculation, we use two document-level features: the embedding results of Latent Semantic Analysis and the count of the reference words. We study the cosine distance of the embedding vector of each set of reference words. For prediction models, in addition to VAR, we use LSTM and ARIMA models as a baseline. The performances are measured by the root mean square error (RMSE) between forecasts by the models and the actual outcome. To prevent data leakage, we split the data based on time series split.

Table 2 shows that the degree of explicit returns the better performance than the economic dictionary in most cases, which is consistent with the impulse response simulation. We also find that the predictions by the LSTM model do not return clear results and yield relatively inferior results. We believe this is because of the small data size, as discussed in (Makridakis et al., 2018). This is consistent with the fact that the ARIMA model outperforms the LSTM model even when the ARIMA model uses only the FFR. The result also shows that the performance with Fed's mandate is better than we expand the expanded reference words with more general words about economics from the economic dictionary (Welker, 2020).

4 Discussion and Conclusion

This paper has presented the framework to study the policy explanation using the published policy documents. We utilized the word embedding technique to extract the semantic changes of policy-related words. Our framework provided the interpretable analysis, calculating the semantics between the policy words and the reference words with explicit semantics. To conduct the empirical analysis with our framework, we used the dataset from the central bank in the united states (FRB), where the federal law requires them to publish the policy documents regularly to keep their policy's transparency, and their policy behavior is observable qualitative by their policy rate (the federal funds rate). Our simulation results with the estimated time series model well used for finance (VAR model) revealed that the policy authority (FRB) uses different documents to explain their policy changes depending on the phase of their policy. We also conducted the prediction analysis of the policy behavior to study the performance of the different time series models and language models. Even for the prediction, our proposed framework showed a better performance than the others. Those results may suggest that the proposed framework provides not only interpretable results but also a better predictor.

While we found the policy explanation's semantics dynamics, some issues remain that further research needs to address. First, we need to expand our dataset and prove that our results are consistent. For example, we could conduct the same analysis for other central banks such as the Bank of England, European Central Bank, or the Bank of Japan. Such a comparative study is feasible because our embedding method do not depend on a specific language. Moreover, our idea does not depend on specific word embedding model. Our paper's central argument is that we should not rely on the language features that do not directly capture the policy explanation. Therefore, if there is a method that captures the semantic shift of a given set of words in more sophisticated or robust way, we could apply our idea to that method.

References

Federal Reserve Bank. 2020a. Board of governors of the federal reserve system, note = https://www.federalreserve.gov/monetarypolicy/fomc_historical.htm, last accessed May 10, 2020.

Federal Reserve Bank. 2020b. Fomc minute. https://stanford.edu/~rezab/useful/fomc_minutes.html, last accessed May 10, 2020.

Federal Reserve Bank. 2020c. What economic goals does the federal reserve seek to achieve through its monetary policy? Https://www.federalreserve.gov/faqs/what-economic-goals-does-federal-reserve-seek-to-achieve-through-monetary-policy.htm.

Alan S Blinder, Michael Ehrmann, Marcel Fratzscher, Jakob De Haan, and David-Jan Jansen. 2008. Central bank communication and monetary policy: A survey of theory and evidence. *Journal of Economic Literature*, 46(4):910–45.

Valerio Di Carlo, Federico Bianchi, and Matteo Palmonari. 2019. Training temporal word embeddings with a compass. In *Proceedings of the AAAI Conference on Artificial Intelligence*, volume 33, pages 6326–6334.

Nikhil Garg, Londa Schiebinger, Dan Jurafsky, and James Zou. 2018. Word embeddings quantify 100 years of gender and ethnic stereotypes. *Proceedings of the National Academy of Sciences*, 115(16):E3635–E3644.

Petra M Geraats. 2002. Central bank transparency. *The Economic Journal*, 112(483):F532–F565.

William L Hamilton, Jure Leskovec, and Dan Jurafsky. 2016. Diachronic word embeddings reveal statistical laws of semantic change. *arXiv preprint arXiv:1605.09096*.

Spyros Makridakis, Evangelos Spiliotis, and Vassilios Assimakopoulos. 2018. Statistical and machine learning forecasting methods: Concerns and ways forward. *PloS one*, 13(3):e0194889.

James H Stock and Mark W Watson. 2001. Vector autoregressions. *Journal of Economic Perspectives*, 15(4):101–115.

James H Stock, Mark W Watson, et al. 2003. *Introduction to Econometrics*, volume 104. Addison Wesley Boston.

the Federal Reserve Bank of Chicago. 2020. The federal reserve's dual mandate. https://www.chicagofed.org/research/dual-mandate/dual-mandate, last accessed May 10, 2020.

Jason Welker. 2020. The economics classroom. https://econclassroom.com/glossary, last accessed May 10, 2020.

Theresa Wilson. 2005. Subjectivity lexicon. https://mpqa.cs.pitt.edu/lexicons/subj_lexicon/, last accessed May 10, 2020.

Theresa Wilson, Janyce Wiebe, and Paul Hoffmann. 2005. Recognizing contextual polarity in phrase-level sentiment analysis. In *Proceedings of human language technology conference and conference on empirical methods in natural language processing*, pages 347–354.

Michael Woodford. 2005. Central bank communication and policy effectiveness. Technical report, National Bureau of Economic Research.

To What Extent Can English-as-a-Second Language Learners Read Economic News Texts?

Yo Ehara
Tokyo Gakugei University
4-1-1 Nukuikita-machi, Koganei-shi, Tokyo 184-8501 Japan
ehara@u-gakugei.ac.jp

Abstract

In decision making in the economic field, an especially important requirement is to rapidly understand news to absorb ever-changing economic situations. Given that most economic news is written in English, the ability to read such information without waiting for a translation is particularly valuable in economics in contrast to other fields. In consideration of this issue, this research investigated the extent to which non-native English speakers are able to read economic news to make decisions accordingly – an issue that has been rarely addressed in previous studies. Using an existing standard dataset as training data, we created a classifier that automatically evaluates the readability of text with high accuracy for English learners. Our assessment of the readability of an economic news corpus revealed that most news texts can be read by intermediate English learners. We also found that in some cases, readability varies considerably depending on the knowledge of certain words specific to the economic field.

1 Introduction

In the economic field, it is important to read news as primary information to make decisions quickly. While the majority of economic news is written in English, the economic activities of non-native English speakers, or English-as-a-Second-Language (ESL) learners also have a strong influence. To what extent can ESL learners read economic news? If, for example, certain economic news is difficult for ESL learners to read, then the language gap may affect their economic activities. Although this question is important, it was rarely addressed in previous studies.

The importance of the aforementioned question is also related to the *efficient market hypothesis*. The hypothesis is one of the major propositions in financial economics that forms the basis of the Black–Scholes equation, which is a fundamental formula used for market modeling. It assumes that "asset prices reflect all available information" [1]. Intuitively, the hypothesis maintains that no information gap, including the gaps caused by language deficiencies, exists in the market. However, this proposition does not hold in cases wherein most second language learners cannot read economic news to make economic decisions in the market. We tackled the challenge of illuminating this issue.

To this end, we first sought to understand the difficulty that economic news poses for non-native speakers of English. We approached this problem in two ways. The first was based on the field of educational NLP (Vajjala and Lučić, 2018). Using a corpus that is standard in this field, we constructed a machine learning classifier that can determine the difficulty of a text with high accuracy using deep learning methods, such as Bidirectional Encoder Representations from Transformers (BERT) (Devlin et al., 2019).

The second approach was to conduct readability assessments on the basis of information about the vocabulary of English learners. These methods have been well studied in the field of applied linguistics, where considerable research has shown that English learners need to know more than 95% of words in a text to read and understand them (Nation, 2006; Laufer and Ravenhorst-Kalovski, 2010). The idea of assessing text readability via each learner's vocabulary knowledge is beneficial for interpreting readability assessment results. Therefore, we also constructed a classifier that ascertains how many words in a text an English learner knows using a data set of English learners' vocabulary tests (Ehara, 2018).

In experiments carried out on a standard data set for evaluating readability (Vajjala and Lučić, 2018) in educational NLP, the two approaches to assessing readability derived results that were in close

[1] https://en.wikipedia.org/wiki/Efficient-market_hypothesis

Proceedings of the Third Workshop on Economics and Natural Language Processing, pages 62–68
Punta Cana and online, November 11.

agreement. Next, the experiments involving a real economic news corpus uncovered that most of the texts in the economic news corpus were readable by intermediate English learners. The analysis for which the second approach was used indicated that readability can be substantially improved for English learners through knowledge of a few words that are frequently used in economics.

The contributions of this study are as follows:

1. We constructed a high-performance readability evaluator and examined the readability of economic news for English learners.

2. We showed that intermediate English learners can read economic news texts.

3. We demonstrated that the knowledge of a few economic domain-specific words may considerably improve the readability of some economic news for second language learners.

2 Automatic Readability Assessment

This section formalizes the problem of automatic readability assessment. Let us suppose that we have N texts to assess: we write the set of texts as $\{\mathcal{T}_i | i \in \{1, \ldots, N\}\}$. Let $\mathcal{Y}$ be the set of readability labels. Labels are typically ordered in the order of difficulty. For example, in the *OneStopEnglish* dataset (Vajjala and Lučić, 2018), we can set $\mathcal{Y} = \{0, 1, 2\}$, where 0 is elementary, 1 is intermediate, and 2 is advanced. The number of levels depends on the evaluation corpus. Using $\mathcal{Y}$, we write the label for $\mathcal{T}_i$ as $y_i \in \mathcal{Y}$.

Given each text $\mathcal{T}_i$, an *assessor* outputs its readability score s_i. In a supervised setting, the *assessor* knows the number of levels in the evaluation corpus from training examples. Hence, s_i ranges within $\mathcal{Y}$: $s_i \in \mathcal{Y}$. However, in an unsupervised setting, it is noteworthy that the assessor does not know $\mathcal{Y}$, or how many levels the evaluation corpus has, because no label is given. Hence, even if only integers are allowed for y_i, s_i can be a real value.

Throughout this paper, we write arrays using [and]. Given N texts $[\mathcal{T}_i | i \in \{1, \ldots, N\}]$, our goal is to make an assessor output arrays of readability scores $[s_i | i \in \{1, \ldots, N\}]$ that *correlate well* with the array of labels $[y_i | i \in \{1, \ldots, N\}]$. Here, there are multiple types of correlation coefficients between the array of scores and the array of labels, which we explain in the later sections. Typically, we should use *rank coefficients* such as Spearman's ρ, defined as the Pearson's ρ between rankings, when s_i is real-valued.

```
15. deficit:
The company <had a large deficit>.
a: spent a lot more money than it earned
b: went down a lot in value
c: had a plan for its spending
                 that used a lot of money
d: had a lot of money stored in the bank
```

Figure 1: Examples of the Vocabulary Size Test, one of the most widely accepted vocabulary tests to quickly assess language learners. They are asked to choose the option that paraphrases the part between “<” and “>” from a, b, c, and d.

3 Vocabulary Testing-based Readability

Fig. 1 shows example questions from the vocabulary size test, a widely used vocabulary test in applied linguistics (Beglar and Nation, 2007). Each question asks about a word in a multiple-choice question format. The test consists of 100 questions like those shown in Fig. 1. Ehara (2018) used this test to have 100 second-language learners take the test and to collect their responses. Their data were published and made publicly available. We used their dataset to train our classifiers.

We want to analyze vocabulary test results to obtain word difficulty values encoding learners' language knowledge. To this end, we employed the idea of *item response theory* (Baker, 2004), a statistical model that can estimate learners' abilities and test questions' difficulties from the learners' responses to the questions.

Let $\mathcal{V}$ be the set of vocabulary, and let $\mathcal{L}$ be the set of learners. Let $z_{v,l} \in \{0, 1\}$ be the result of whether learner $l \in \mathcal{L}$ correctly answered the question for word $v \in \mathcal{V}$: $z_{l,v} = 1$ if l answered correctly for word v; otherwise, $z_{l,v} = 0$. Correct answers usually imply that l knows word v.

Then, by using $\{z_{v,l}\}$ as the training data, we train the following model:

$$p(z = 1 | v, l) = \text{sigmoid}(a_l - d_v) \quad (1)$$

In Eq. 1, a_l is the ability parameter of learner l, d_v is the difficulty of word w, and sigmoid denotes the logistic sigmoid function, i.e., $\text{sigmoid}(x) = \frac{1}{1+\exp(-x)}$.

The logistic sigmoid function is the binary version of the softmax function, which is frequently used in neural classifiers. It is a monotonously increasing function ranging within $(0,1)$. As $\text{sigmoid}(0) = \frac{1}{1+1} = \frac{1}{2}$, when a learner's ability a_l is larger than the word difficulty d_v, the probability that learner l knows word v can be written as follows: $p(z = 1|v, l) > \frac{1}{2}$ in Eq. 1. Likewise, by using Eq. 1, we can compare a learner's ability and word difficulty in the same dimension.

To estimate learner ability and word difficulty, $z_{v,l}$ is given as z in Eq. 1 in the training phase. In this way, in *item response theory*, learner ability and word difficulty are comparable, and these parameters are estimated from the test result data.

In Eq. 1, d_v denotes the word difficulty estimated from the vocabulary tests. Here, in addition to the word difficulty for the words within the vocabulary test, we also want to obtain word difficulty values for all words that may appear in the target language. To this end, we calculate d_v by using the word frequency in large balanced corpora as features as follows:

$$d_v = -\sum_{k=1}^{K} w_k \log(\text{freq}_k(v) + 1) \quad (2)$$

Eq. 2 assumes that we have K corpora to use as features to calculate word difficulty d_v. In Eq. 2, K is the number of corpora to use, $\text{freq}_k(v)$ denotes the frequency of word v in the k-th corpus, and w_k is the weight parameter of the k-th corpus. In summary, given the vocabulary test results $\{z_{v,l}\}$ and corpus frequency features $\text{freq}_k(v)$, we can estimate the parameters: namely, the weight of the k-th corpus w_k and learner l's ability a_l. To implement the model, we used logistic regression, by following (Ehara, 2018). Note that this model does not use the valuable readability label $\{y_i\}$ in the training phase, so is unsupervised.

After estimating the parameters using the above-mentioned procedure, we use the following formula to obtain the readability of given $\mathcal{T}_i$. Here, l_{avg} denotes the test-taker whose estimated ability parameter is closest to the average of the estimated ability parameter values $\{a_l\}$. Intuitively, the following equation calculates the probability that the average learner knows all the words that appear in $\mathcal{T}_i$ and uses it as the readability score. The use of the $-\log$ here has two reasons. The reason of using log is to prevent problems in numerical calculations, since the probability values can be very close to 0. While we want to design d_v so that the more difficult the word v, the larger the value, whereas the higher the probability, the easier the word. Hence, we use negative of log to make the two scales meet.

$$s_i = score(\mathcal{T}_i) = -\log\left(\prod_{v \in \mathcal{T}_i} p(z = 1|v, l_{\text{avg}})\right) \quad (3)$$

4 Experimental Settings

4.1 Readability Dataset

We used the OneStopEnglish dataset (Vajjala and Lučić, 2018) for the source of readability for second language learners because it is one of the newest, publicly available, and reliable in the sense that no known trivial features are effective for predicting its labels such as average sentence length.

The dataset has three levels: elementary, intermediate, and advanced. The original articles were taken from the Guardian newspaper. The OneStopEnglish dataset is a parallel corpus, i.e, language teachers manually rewrote the original articles into the three aforementioned readability levels. Hence, the corpus is designed so that its readability labels are not easily estimated from the topic of texts. While a text is usually a single newspaper article in the OneStopEnglish dataset. However, during the building of the dataset, it can be edited to be a unit shorter than an article. Therefore, henceforth, we simply call it a text.

All three levels have 189 texts each, 567 texts in total. We split these texts into a *training set* consisting of 339 texts, a *validation* set consisting of 114 texts, and a *test* set consisting of 114 texts. The *training set* and *validation* sets were used to train solely supervised methods for comparison. Unsupervised methods did not use the training and validation sets; they used only the test set.

4.2 Compared Methods

As the BERT-based sequence classification has been reported to achieve excellent results (Devlin et al., 2019), we applied the standard BERT-based sequence classification approach involving pretraining and fine-tuning. For the pretrained model, we used **bert-large-cased-whole-word-masking** in the Huggingface models [2].

Then, we fine-tuned the model using the 339 training texts. We named this fine-tuned model **spvBERT**, in which "spv" denotes being supervised. For fine-tuning, we used the Adam optimizer

[2] `https://huggingface.co/models`

Method	Spearman's ρ	Pearson's ρ
Flesch-Kincaid	0.324	0.359
ARI	0.317	0.351
Coleman-Liau	0.373	0.372
FleschReadingEase	-0.387	-0.426
GunningFogIndex	0.331	0.362
LIX	0.348	0.383
SMOGIndex	0.456	0.479
RIX	0.437	0.462
DaleChallIndex	0.495	0.506
TCN RSRS-simple	-	0.615(*)
Vocabulary-based	**0.730**	**0.715**
spvBERT	0.866	0.864

Table 1: Predictive Performance of Readability. Only **spvBERT** is supervised: the others are unsupervised.

Year/Month	Elem.	Int.	Adv.
Jan.2007	0.001	0.970	0.029
Feb.2007	0.003	0.975	0.022
Mar.2007	0.006	0.965	0.029
Apr.2007	0.002	0.976	0.022
May 2007	0.001	0.978	0.021
Jun.2007	0.009	0.964	0.027
Jul.2007	0.002	0.964	0.034
Aug.2007	0.002	0.951	0.047
Sep.2007	0.001	0.953	0.046
Oct.2007	0.005	0.949	0.047
Nov.2007	0.001	0.955	0.044
Dec.2007	0.012	0.944	0.044

Table 2: Readability Assessment Results of Economic News Texts in 2007. "Elem." denotes "elementary", "Int." denotes "intermediate", and "Adv." denotes "advanced".

(Kingma and Ba, 2015) with a setting of 10 epochs and a 10^{-5} training rate.

For the implementation of conventional readability formulae, we used the **readability** PyPI package [3]. We used almost all readability formulae implemented in this package for our experiments: namely, **Flesch-Kincaid** (Flesch-Kincaid Grade Level, FKGL) (Kincaid et al., 1975), **ARI** (Automated Readability Index) (Senter and Smith, 1967), the **Coleman-Liau** Index (Coleman and Liau, 1975), **Flesch Reading Ease** (Flesch, 1948), the **Gunning Fog Index** (Gunning, 1952), **LIX** (Björnsson, 1968), the **SMOG Index** (Mc Laughlin, 1969), the RIX index (Anderson, 1983), and the **Dale-Chall Index** (Dale and Chall, 1948). More details of these formulae and their implementation are described on the project page. All of these readability formulae are *unsupervised* in the sense that they do not require any training data.

The **Vocabulary-based** model was trained on a publicly available vocabulary dataset (Ehara, 2018). For the corpus word frequency, we used the frequencies taken from the British National Corpus (BNC Consortium, 2007) and the Corpus of Contemporary American English (COCA) (Davies, 2008). Both corpora are balanced general corpora used extensively in English education (Nation, 2006). Especially, the word frequencies of these corpora are important resources for determining word difficulty in English education.

[3] `https://pypi.org/project/readability/`

4.3 Experimental Results

Tab. 1 shows the experimental results. First, in all unsupervised methods, **Vocabulary-based** achieved the best results in all rank correlation coefficients. **TCN RSRS-simple** is the best model on the OneStopEnglish dataset in Martinc et al. (2021). As they show only the performance measured by the Pearson correlation, we filled "-" for Spearman's ρ in the table. While a direct comparison is not possible as denoted by $(*)$, **Vocabulary-based** outperforms it.

Importantly, we can observe that both **Vocabulary-based** and **spvBERT** achieve high predictive performance. This result indicates that the two approaches to assessing readability derived results that were in close agreement.

5 Experiments with Economic News

We used an economic news article dataset (Ding et al., 2014, 2015) for our analysis because it is publicly available and easy to replicate. The dataset consisted of 109,110 Reuters news articles published in 2006–2007. Tab. 2 shows the readability assessment results for each month of 2007. Each month included approximately 1,000 articles. Few of the articles were elementary, whereas most were intermediate. Approximately 2%–4% of the texts were advanced. The results show that intermediate English learners could read most but not 2%–4% of economic news.

We also conducted a vocabulary-based analysis. Using (Ehara, 2018), we chose a learner who could successfully answer 75 vocabulary questions among the 100 questions in the Vocabulary Size Test (Beglar and Nation, 2007). This learner was estimated to know $15,000$ words. Knowledge of this number of words should be sufficient for reading typical newspaper texts (Nation, 2006). However, in the vocabulary-based readability assessor, some words, such as "annuity" and "veritable", were predicted to be unfamiliar to this learner. In one article, these words greatly reduced the probability that this learner could read the text from 0.62 to 0.38: these probability values represented the probability that this learner knew at least 95% of the words in this text. The probability of knowing each word was represented by Eq. 1. Ehara (2019) proposed an algorithm to calculate the probability of knowing 95% or more of the words in a text from the probability of knowing each word. We simply used their algorithm to calculate these probabilities.

6 Discussion

In Eq. 2, word frequencies in the corpora are used as features. In this study, we used multiple balanced corpora. Eq. 2 is applicable when preparing K corpora in advance. k denotes the index of the prepared corpora.

In NLP, the **Proposed** method is closely related to complex word identification (CWI) tasks (Yimam et al., 2018; Paetzold and Specia, 2016). CWI is a task that aims to discover difficult words in a text. The relationship between CWI and personalized text readability was previously studied in (Ehara, 2019). The task of obtaining the difficulty of an English word for each individual ESL learner, as we performed in this study, can be regarded as personalized CWI (Ehara et al., 2012, 2014) [4]. Personalized CWI has many downstream applications in NLP, such as lexical simplification (Lee and Yeung, 2018, 2019), text recommendation for language learners (Ehara et al., 2013; Yeung and Lee, 2018; Lee, 2021), and translator selection in crowdsourcing (Ehara et al., 2016). Some studies have focused on the relationship between word semantics and word difficulty (Ehara et al., 2014; Beinborn et al., 2016; Ehara, 2020b). Regarding the interpretability of CWI classifiers, Ehara (2020a) studied the relationship between CWI classifiers' weights and vocabulary sizes.

[4] The journal version of (Ehara et al., 2012) is (Ehara et al., 2018).

7 Conclusions

In this paper, we focused on the readability of economic news texts for ESL learners. We conducted two approaches for measuring readability: the BERT-based approach and the vocabulary-based approach. We found that although most texts were readable to intermediate learners, 2.4% of articles were not readable to them. Furthermore, some economic words greatly reduced the readability for ESL learners. Future work will include investigating for differences in the readability of different types of economic news for ESL learners.

Acknowledgment

This study was supported by JST ACT-X with Grant Number JPMJAX2006 and JSPS KAKENHI with Grant Number 18K18118. We used the ABCI infrastructure from AIST for the computational resources. We appreciate anonymous reviewers for their valuable comments.

References

Jonathan Anderson. 1983. Lix and rix: Variations on a little-known readability index. *Journal of Reading*, 26(6):490–496.

Frank B. Baker. 2004. *Item Response Theory : Parameter Estimation Techniques, Second Edition*. CRC Press.

David Beglar and Paul Nation. 2007. A vocabulary size test. *The Language Teacher*, 31(7):9–13.

Lisa Beinborn, Torsten Zesch, and Iryna Gurevych. 2016. Predicting the Spelling Difficulty of Words for Language Learners. In *Proceedings of the 11th Workshop on Innovative Use of NLP for Building Educational Applications*, pages 73–83, San Diego, CA. Association for Computational Linguistics.

C. H. Björnsson. 1968. Läsbarhet, Stockholm.

BNC Consortium. 2007. The british national corpus, version 3 (bnc xml edition). Distributed by Bodleian Libraries, University of Oxford, on behalf of the BNC Consortium `http://www.natcorp.ox.ac.uk/`.

Meri Coleman and Ta Lin Liau. 1975. A computer readability formula designed for machine scoring. *Journal of Applied Psychology*, 60(2):283.

Edgar Dale and Jeanne S Chall. 1948. A formula for predicting readability: Instructions. *Educational research bulletin*, pages 37–54.

Mark Davies. 2008. The corpus of contemporary american english (coca). Available online at `https://www.english-corpora.org/coca/`.

Jacob Devlin, Ming-Wei Chang, Kenton Lee, and Kristina Toutanova. 2019. BERT: Pre-training of Deep Bidirectional Transformers for Language Understanding. In *Proc. of NAACL*, pages 4171–4186, Minneapolis, Minnesota.

Xiao Ding, Yue Zhang, Ting Liu, and Junwen Duan. 2014. Using structured events to predict stock price movement: An empirical investigation. In *Proceedings of the 2014 Conference on Empirical Methods in Natural Language Processing (EMNLP)*, pages 1415–1425, Doha, Qatar. Association for Computational Linguistics.

Xiao Ding, Yue Zhang, Ting Liu, and Junwen Duan. 2015. Deep learning for event-driven stock prediction. In *Twenty-fourth international joint conference on artificial intelligence*.

Yo Ehara. 2018. Building an English Vocabulary Knowledge Dataset of Japanese English-as-a-Second-Language Learners Using Crowdsourcing. In *Proc. of LREC*.

Yo Ehara. 2019. Uncertainty-Aware Personalized Readability Assessments for Second Language Learners. In *2019 18th IEEE International Conference On Machine Learning And Applications (ICMLA)*, pages 1909–1916.

Yo Ehara. 2020a. Interpreting neural CWI classifiers' weights as vocabulary size. In *Proceedings of the Fifteenth Workshop on Innovative Use of NLP for Building Educational Applications*, pages 171–176, Seattle, WA, USA → Online. Association for Computational Linguistics.

Yo Ehara. 2020b. Neural rasch model: How do word embeddings adjust word difficulty? In *Computational Linguistics*, pages 88–96, Singapore. Springer Singapore.

Yo Ehara, Yukino Baba, Masao Utiyama, and Eiichiro Sumita. 2016. Assessing Translation Ability through Vocabulary Ability Assessment. In *Proc. of IJCAI*.

Yo Ehara, Yusuke Miyao, Hidekazu Oiwa, Issei Sato, and Hiroshi Nakagawa. 2014. Formalizing Word Sampling for Vocabulary Prediction as Graph-based Active Learning. In *Proc. of EMNLP*, pages 1374–1384.

Yo Ehara, Issei Sato, Hidekazu Oiwa, and Hiroshi Nakagawa. 2012. Mining Words in the Minds of Second Language Learners: Learner-Specific Word Difficulty. In *Proceedings of COLING 2012*, pages 799–814, Mumbai, India. The COLING 2012 Organizing Committee.

Yo Ehara, Issei Sato, Hidekazu Oiwa, and Hiroshi Nakagawa. 2018. Mining Words in the Minds of Second Language Learners for Learner-specific Word Difficulty. *Journal of Information Processing*, 26:267–275.

Yo Ehara, Nobuyuki Shimizu, Takashi Ninomiya, and Hiroshi Nakagawa. 2013. Personalized Reading Support for Second-language Web Documents. *ACM Trans. Intell. Syst. Technol.*, 4(2):31:1–31:19.

Rudolf Flesch. 1948. A new readability yardstick. *Journal of Applied Psychology*, 32(3):221–233.

Robert Gunning. 1952. *The Technique of Clear Writing*. McGraw-Hill.

J Peter Kincaid, Robert P Fishburne Jr, Richard L Rogers, and Brad S Chissom. 1975. Derivation of new readability formulas (automated readability index, fog count and flesch reading ease formula) for navy enlisted personnel. Technical report, Naval Technical Training Command Millington TN Research Branch.

Diederik P Kingma and Jimmy Ba. 2015. Adam: A method for stochastic optimization. In *Proc. of ICLR*.

Batia Laufer and Geke C. Ravenhorst-Kalovski. 2010. Lexical Threshold Revisited: Lexical Text Coverage, Learners' Vocabulary Size and Reading Comprehension. *Reading in a Foreign Language*, 22(1):15–30.

John Lee and Chak Yan Yeung. 2018. Personalizing Lexical Simplification. In *Proceedings of the 27th International Conference on Computational Linguistics*, pages 224–232, Santa Fe, New Mexico, USA. Association for Computational Linguistics.

John Lee and Chak Yan Yeung. 2019. Personalized Substitution Ranking for Lexical Simplification. In *Proceedings of the 12th International Conference on Natural Language Generation*, pages 258–267, Tokyo, Japan. Association for Computational Linguistics.

John SY Lee. 2021. An editable learner model for text recommendation for language learning. *ReCALL*, pages 1–15.

Matej Martinc, Senja Pollak, and Marko Robnik-Šikonja. 2021. Supervised and Unsupervised Neural Approaches to Text Readability. *Computational Linguistics*, 47(1):141–179.

G Harry Mc Laughlin. 1969. Smog grading-a new readability formula. *Journal of reading*, 12(8):639–646.

I. Nation. 2006. How Large a Vocabulary is Needed For Reading and Listening? *Canadian Modern Language Review*, 63(1):59–82.

Gustavo Paetzold and Lucia Specia. 2016. Collecting and Exploring Everyday Language for Predicting Psycholinguistic Properties of Words. In *Proceedings of COLING 2016, the 26th International Conference on Computational Linguistics: Technical Papers*, pages 1669–1679, Osaka, Japan. The COLING 2016 Organizing Committee.

RJ Senter and Edgar A Smith. 1967. Automated readability index. Technical report, CINCINNATI UNIV OH.

Sowmya Vajjala and Ivana Lučić. 2018. OneStopEnglish corpus: A new corpus for automatic readability assessment and text simplification. In *Proceedings of the Thirteenth Workshop on Innovative Use of NLP for Building Educational Applications*, pages 297–304, New Orleans, Louisiana. Association for Computational Linguistics.

Chak Yan Yeung and John Lee. 2018. Personalized Text Retrieval for Learners of Chinese as a Foreign Language. In *Proc. of COLING*, pages 3448–3455.

Seid Muhie Yimam, Chris Biemann, Shervin Malmasi, Gustavo H. Paetzold, Lucia Specia, Sanja Štajner, Anaïs Tack, and Marcos Zampieri. 2018. A Report on the Complex Word Identification Shared Task 2018. *arXiv:1804.09132 [cs]*. ArXiv: 1804.09132.

Effective Use of Graph Convolution Network and Contextual Sub-Tree for Commodity News Event Extraction

Meisin Lee, Lay-Ki Soon, Eu-Gene Siew
Monash University
{mei.lee, soon.layki, siew.eu-gene}@monash.edu

Abstract

Event extraction in commodity news is a less researched area as compared to generic event extraction. However, accurate event extraction from commodity news is useful in a broad range of applications such as understanding event chains and learning event-event relations, which can then be used for commodity price prediction. The events found in commodity news exhibit characteristics different from generic events, hence posing a unique challenge in event extraction using existing methods. This paper proposes an effective use of Graph Convolutional Networks (GCN) with a pruned dependency parse tree, termed contextual sub-tree, for better event extraction in commodity news. The event extraction model is trained using feature embeddings from ComBERT, a BERT-based masked language model that was produced through domain-adaptive pre-training on a commodity news corpus. Experimental results show the efficiency of the proposed solution, which outperforms existing methods with F1 scores as high as 0.90. Furthermore, our pre-trained language model outperforms GloVe by 23%, and BERT and RoBERTa by 7% in terms of argument roles classification. For the goal of reproducibility, the code and trained models are made publicly available [1].

1 Introduction

World events such as geo-political and macro-economic-related events have been shown to impact commodity prices in both short-term and long-term (Brandt and Gao, 2019). Generally, events found in commodity news articles can be categorized into geo-political, macro-economic, supply-demand related, and commodity price movements. Commodity news is a valuable source of information to extract and mine for such events. Accurate

U.S. crude stockpiles **soared** by 1.350 million barrels in December from a mere 200 million barrels to 438.9 million barrels, due to this **oversupply** crude oil prices **plunged** more than 50% on Tuesday.

Figure 1: An example of a sentence from a piece of commodity news[3], loaded with three events (trigger words are in bold): (1) Crude oil inventory increase, (2) Oversupply and (3) Crude Oil price decrease. Three event arguments that are of the same entity type are highlighted in color.

event extraction is useful for many important downstream tasks, such as understanding event chains and learning event sequence, also known as scripts in (Schank and Abelson, 2013), that can be used for accurate commodity price prediction ultimately.

As defined in ACE (Automatic Content Extraction) Program[2], the event extraction task is made up of two subtasks: (1) event trigger extraction (identifying and classifying event triggers) and (2) event argument extraction (identifying arguments of event triggers and labeling their roles). In this work, we perform event extraction on the Commodity News dataset introduced in (Lee et al., 2021). Figure 1 shows a sample sentence from this dataset.

To illustrate the task of event extraction, consider the example in Figure 1 and the corresponding information tabulated in Table 1. In the event trigger extraction sub-task, the model is trained to identify the trigger word: **soared** and classify the right event type: **movement_up_gain**, while in the event argument extraction sub-task, the model is trained to identify event arguments from a pool of entity mentions within the sentence and then label the argument roles each entity plays in relation to the identified event.

[1] https://github.com/meisin/Commodity-News-Event-Extraction

[2] https://www.ldc.upenn.edu/collaborations/past-projects/ace

[3] This example is used throughout this paper.

Proceedings of the Third Workshop on Economics and Natural Language Processing, pages 69–81
Punta Cana and online, November 11. ©2021 Association for Computational Linguistics

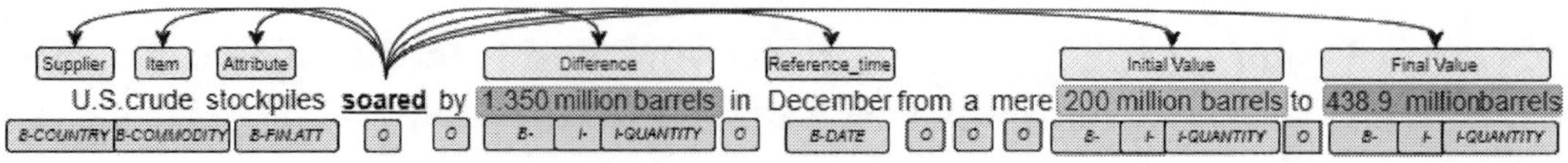

Figure 2: The example in Figure 1 is shown here with annotation provided in (Lee et al., 2021); trigger word is underlined and in bold, entity type for each entity mention is shown in blue below its respective word in BIO-tagging format while event argument role for each entity is shown in light yellow above the words; arches link argument to its trigger word.

Event	Entity Mention	Argument Role
Trigger:	U.S.	Supplier
soared	crude	Item
	stockpiles	Attribute
	1.350 million barrels	Difference
Event type:	December	Reference point
movement_	200 million barrels	Initial Value
up_gain	438.9 million barrels	Final Value
	more than 50%	NONE

Table 1: Event extraction of "crude oil inventory increase" event (first event in Figure 1).

The types of events found in commodity news are vastly different from generic events in ACE2005[4]. Below is a list of unique characteristics of these events:

1. **Number intensity** - Numbers (e.g., price, difference, percentage of change) and dates (including date of the opening price, dates of closing price) are abundant in commodity news. These numerical data is critical in expressing financial information. Generic information extraction methods may not work well for numeric data, as it is clearly seen in (Saha et al., 2017) where the authors introduced the first Open *numerical* relation extractor specifically to extract Open Information Extraction (IE) tuples that contain numbers or a quantity-unit phrase.
2. **Arguments homogeneity** - Many arguments of the same entity type plays distinct roles in an event. Figure 2 shows that *1.350 million barrels*, *200 million barrels*, *438.0 million barrels* are tagged as *QUANTITY* (see BIO-tagging at the bottom row). However, all three arguments play a different role in relation to the event (see Argument roles at the top row).
3. **Undifferentiated event types without its arguments** - Consider the event triggered by **"soared"** in Figure 1, it is incomplete to identify the event (movement-up-gain) without knowing "what" soared. In commodity news, possible events are 'price soared', 'supply soared', and 'demand soared'. To disambiguate events and represent them accurately, it is important to extract event arguments accurately as well.

With these challenges in mind, this paper proposes a solution applying Graph Convolutional Networks (GCN) over contextual sub-tree for the task of event extraction. The contextual sub-tree is a dependency parse tree uniquely pruned that provides not just dependency path information but also off-path information. The off-path information adds more context to the existing dependency path between two nodes; hence it is termed contextual sub-tree.

The contributions of this work are as follows: (1) We show that a domain-adaptive pre-trained Language Model, ComBERT, can yield promising performance over generic pre-trained language model when fine-tuned on event extraction tasks, and (2) we propose an effective usage of a graph neural network, in the form of a GCN with contextual sub-tree that outperforms other existing approaches. The usefulness is particularly apparent in the subtask of event argument classification.

2 Commodity News Dataset

The dataset introduced in (Lee et al., 2021) is a collection of annotated commodity news articles where its annotation is based on standards introduced by canonical programs such as ACE and TAC-KBP[5]. Figure 2 captures in graphical form, the annotatations found in the dataset: (1) Entity Mentions - both named and nominal (entity type shown in blue under the sentence in BIO-tagging format); (2) Event Trigger Words (word underlined and in bold); and (3) Argument roles (labels are in light yellow above the sentence) with arches linking each argument to the event it belongs. This dataset consists of 21 entity types, 18 event types, and 19 argument role types (each event type has

[4]ACE2005 is a multilingual Training Corpus developed under the ACE program

[5]https://tac.nist.gov/2015/KBP

its own set of argument roles. Event types are defined based on Ravenpack's[6] event taxonomy, out of which 18 event types are chosen. In terms of size, this dataset contains 8,850 entity mentions and 3,949 events. Table 2 shows the event type distribution. More information about the dataset, including argument roles, entity types, and example event types are found in Appendix A.

Event type	Type ratio	# sentence
1. Cause-movement-down-loss	13.35%	524
2. Cause-movement-up-gain	2.23%	88
3. Civil-unrest	2.53%	100
4. Crisis	0.76%	30
5. Embargo	3.75%	148
6. Geopolitical-tension	1.70%	67
7. Grow-strong	6.03%	238
8. Movement-down-loss	22.69%	896
9. Movement-flat	1.52%	60
10. Movement-up-gain	22.13%	874
11. Negative-sentiment	4.79%	189
12. Oversupply	2.63%	104
13. Position-high	3.82%	151
14. Position-low	3.11%	123
15. Prohibiting	1.06%	42
16. Shortage	1.04%	41
17. Slow-weak	5.47%	216
18. Trade-tensions	1.39%	55
Total		3949

Table 2: Event type distribution and sentence level counts

3 Related Work

Event Extraction in Finance/Economics. Generic event extraction-related work is covered in detail in the survey paper (Xiang and Wang, 2019) and in (Hogenboom et al., 2016). Here we focus specifically on event extraction within the domain of finance and economics. Most of the event extraction tasks in this domain focuses on extracting company-related events. Here is a summary of related methods in recent literature:

1. Rule-based approach: authors in (Malik et al., 2011) introduced statistical classifiers aided by rules, while authors in (Hogenboom et al., 2013) used rule-sets and domain ontology knowledge-bases together with other semantically-enabled components;
2. Usage of external resources: Semantic Frame was in (Xie et al., 2013) and Wikipedia for weak supervision in (Ein-Dor et al., 2019);
3. Open IE (Open Information Extraction): authors in (Ding et al., 2014) extracted events from news headline via Open IE; while in (Saha et al., 2017), authors introduced an extension of Open IE to extract numerical arguments in each Open IE tuple.
4. Deep learning approach: (Yang et al., 2018) proposed a deep learning approach to extract financial events from Chinese text.

Although company financial events and commodity news fall under the same domain, and both may involve numerical data as event arguments, existing methods for company financial event extractions are rather limited. For example, the solution in (Saha et al., 2017) caters for extracting only one numerical argument for each Open IE tuple. In comparison, the task of extracting company financial information in (Yang et al., 2018) is the closest match to this work in terms of extracting numerical data as event arguments. However, it is a solution for Chinese text and focuses on document-level event extraction.

Graph Convolutional Networks. The usage of Graph Convolutional Networks (GCN) coupled with syntactic information from dependency parse tree has been used for event extraction in (Nguyen and Grishman, 2018) and in (Liu et al., 2018). In (Nguyen and Grishman, 2018), the authors proposed using GCN over syntactic dependency graphs of sentences to produce non-consecutive k-grams as an effective mechanism to link words to their informative content directly for event detection. Authors in (Liu et al., 2018) on the other hand, used attention-based GCN to model graph information to extract multiple event triggers and arguments jointly. Their proposed solution, Joint Multiple Events Extraction (JMEE) framework, focuses on modeling the association between events to enhance the accuracy of event extraction. Both these solutions use the shortest dependency path.

Apart from event extraction, GCN has been used successfully for relation extraction in (Zhang et al., 2018). Instead of obtaining tokens strictly from the shortest dependency path, authors in (Zhang et al., 2018) made modifications to produce pruned a sub-dependency tree to include off-path information as well such as negation cue words. Among the related work listed here, the one that is closest to our work in terms of the task (event extraction) and scope (sentence level) is JMEE by (Liu et al., 2018).

[6]RavenPack is an analytics provider for financial services. Among their products are finance and economic data. More information can be found on their page: https://www.ravenpack.com/

4 Proposed Solution

In reference to the list of unique characteristics of events found in commodity news (listed in Section 1), this paper proposes a solution using Graph Convolutional Networks (GCN) with contextual sub-tree for effective event extraction in commodity news.

Syntactic dependency graphs represent sentences as directed trees with head-modifier dependency arcs between related words. Each word in such graphs is surrounded by its direct syntactic governor and dependent words (the neighbors), over which convolution operations can be performed on the most relevant words and avoid the modeling of unrelated words. Rather than using the full dependency parse tree, we propose to use a uniquely pruned dependency tree that is made up of the shortest path between two nodes (in our case - the **trigger candidate** and **entity mention**) and additional **off-path** nodes. The off-path nodes are included to provide additional contextual information. The resulting tree is termed **contextual sub-tree**.

4.1 Contextual Sub-tree

The dependency tree for the example sentence is shown in Figure 3 with one of the many candidate contextual sub-trees highlighted. Inspired by (Zhang et al., 2018), we prune the dependency tree to obtain the sub-tree rooted at the Least Common Ancestor (LCA) between the trigger candidate and the entity mention candidate while also contains off-path nodes. These off-path nodes provide additional and crucial contexts that enable better results in argument role classification. Off-path information is made up of tokens that are up to distance $DIST$ away from the dependency path. Algorithm 1 shows the steps of how to build the contextual sub-tree. As shown in (Zhang et al., 2018), $DIST = 1$ achieves the best balance between including contextual information and keeping irrelevant ones out of the resulting sub-tree as much as possible.

The usage of contextual sub-tree is targeted at **argument role classification**, the subtask within event extraction that classifies the argument role each entity plays in an event. Entity candidates are classified into one of the 19 argument roles. Figure 4 (Left) shows the sub-tree with the LCA path between event trigger and argument, while Figure 4 (Right) shows a slightly different sub-tree that not only contains the LCA path but also “off-path” information.

Algorithm 1: Build sub-parse tree from dependency head indexes

```
Result: sub-tree structure
convert head indexes to tree object;
if DIST < 0 then
    build the whole tree;
else
    find all ancestor nodes of trigger;
    find all ancestor nodes of entity;
    find lowest common ancestor;
    generate PathNodes (common nodes
      between trigger & entity);
    insert more nodes based on DIST away
      from PathNodes;
end
```

Below are three examples of contextual sub-trees (in words, without tree structure) between an event trigger and an entity mention. Off-path information are in *italics*. In these examples, the off-path words are prepositional words that help with the correct classification of the entity mention's argument role even though all the entities are of the same type, namely “quantity”:

1. **soared** *by* 1.350 million barrels
   argument role - difference
2. **soared** *from* a mere 200 million barrels:
   argument role - initial value
3. **soared** *to* 438.9 million barrels
   argument role - final value

4.2 Domain-Adaptive Pre-training: ComBERT

Pre-trained language models such as BERT have been shown to produce SOTA results in many NLP tasks, including event extraction in the ACE2005 corpus (Yang et al., 2019). Instead of using BERT, we have decided to further pre-train BERT on a commodity news corpus, adapting the model to the finance and economics domains. The resulting model is referred to here as ComBERT. In the commodity news corpus, there are some commodity-specific polysemous words that can be better represented with further pre-training with in-domain data. Apart from the famous 'bank' example where the word could mean (1) financial institution or (2) terrain that is part of the river, there are some commodity-specific polysemous words in the com-

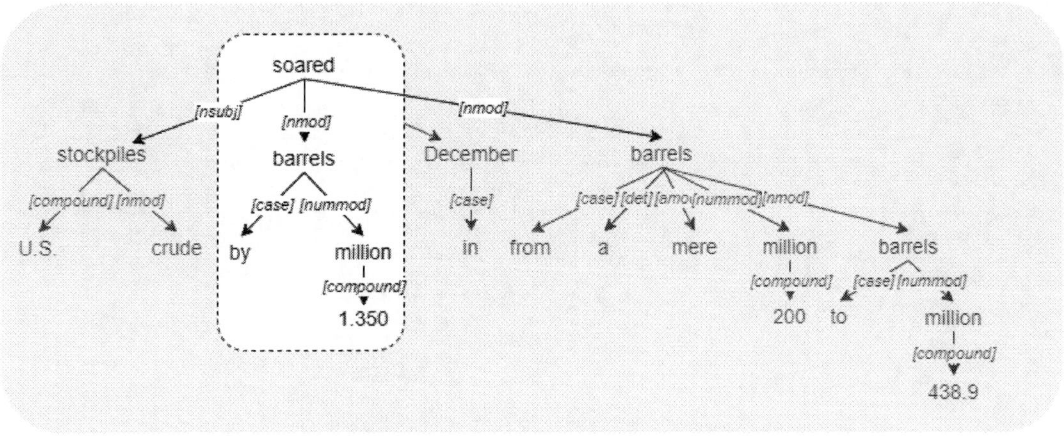

Figure 3: The dependency parse tree of the example sentence.

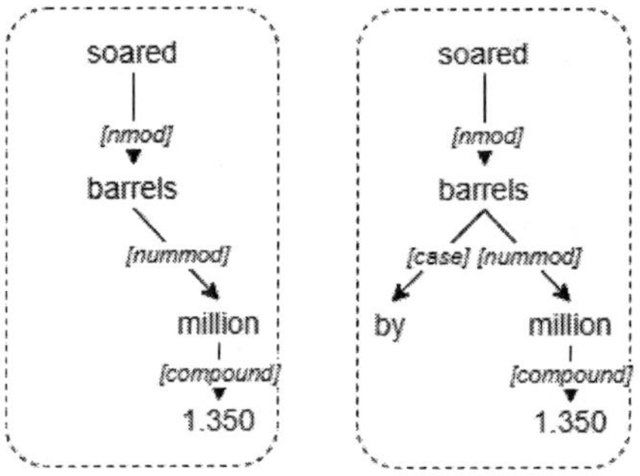

Figure 4: Left: Sub-tree with shortest path, Right: Contextual sub-tree with off-path information

modity news corpus that can be better represented with further pre-training with in-domain data, for example:

- **`stocks`**: (1) inventory and (2) shares
- **`tank`**: (1) storage vessel (noun), (2) market / price drop (verb)

The commodity news corpus is made up of about 20k news articles extracted from https://www.investing.com/commodities/crude-oil-news[7], with publishing dates ranging from 2013 to 2019. We initialized ComBERT with `bert-base-cased`, one of the pre-trained BERT models provided by (Devlin et al., 2019a) and have the same model settings of transformer and pre-training hyperparameters as BERT. We have decided to use cased vocabulary `bert-base-cased` instead of uncased because the event extraction task involves extracting event arguments that are made up of named entities and nominal entities. Examples of named entities are countries, organizations, and specific commodities-related terms such as WTI, ICE, NYMEX, Brent and etc. Having a case-sensitive model yielded slightly better performance for the downstream event extraction task.

The proposed solution is built on leveraging the power of a domain-adaptative pre-training model, ComBERT, to further fine-tune for event extraction with a smaller dataset and with fewer training steps.

4.3 Event Extraction

Both of the sub-tasks within event extraction: (1) event trigger extraction and (2) event argument extraction are conceived as sentence-level multi-label classification tasks. The overall architecture is shown in Figure 5.

4.4 Data Proprocessing

Input. The annotation files made public in (Lee et al., 2021) were first converted from Brat Annotation standoff format (*.ann* files) along with their corresponding news articles (*.txt* files) to *json* format. Each sentence in the dataset was parsed using Stanford CoreNLP toolkit, including sentence splitting, tokenization, POS-tagging, NER-tagging, and dependency parsing to generate dependency parse trees. For input to the model, we adopt the "multi-channel" strategy (shown in "1" in Figure 5) by concatenating three components listed below. Let $W = w_1, w_2, ...w_n$ be a sentence of length n where w_i is the *i*-th token:

1. The word embedding vector of w_i: this is the feature representation from a word embedding of ComBERT. It is made up of WordPiece

[7]the same source as the annotated dataset used here in event extraction.

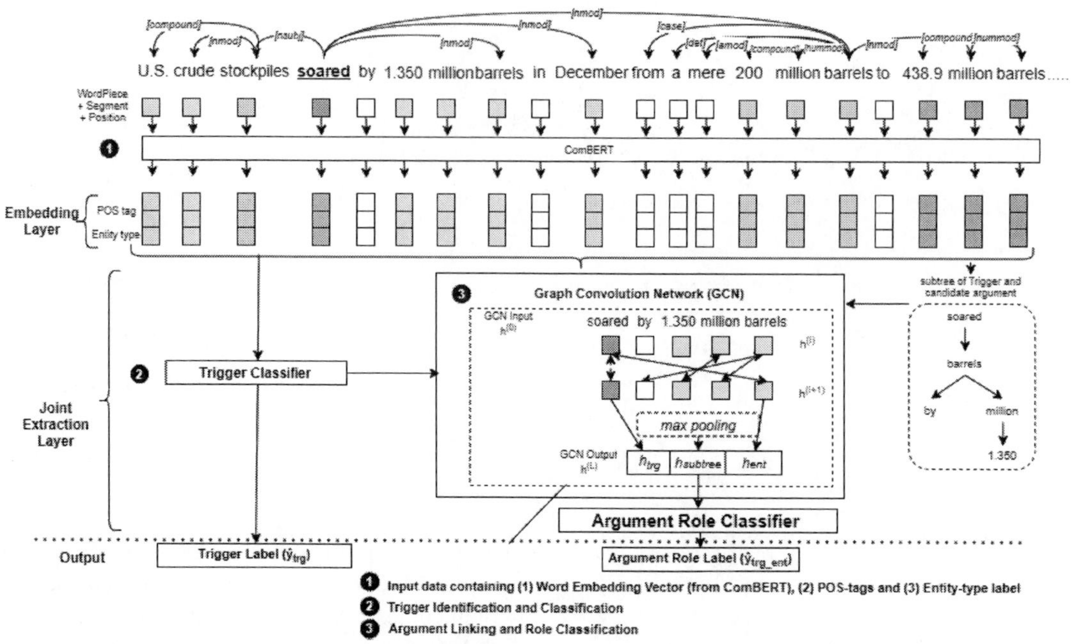

Figure 5: Architecture of the framework

tokenization (Wu et al., 2016) with [CLS] and [SEP][8] are placed at the start and end of the sentence.

2. The Part-of-Speech-tagging (POS-tagging) label embedding vector of w_i: This is generated by looking up the POS-tagging label embedding.
3. The entity type label embedding vector of w_i: Similar to the POS-tagging label embedding vector of w_i, entity mentions in a sentence were annotated using BIO annotation schema, and the entity type labels were transformed to real-valued vectors by looking up the entity label embedding.

4.4.1 Trigger Candidate and Argument Joint-Extraction

The experiments in this paper were conducted based on the joint-extraction approach where event trigger and arguments extraction are trained together.

Event Trigger Extraction. The event trigger extraction is setup as a token classification task, similar to that of Named Entity Recognition. The trigger classifier (shown as "2" in Figure 5) is a simple multi-layer perceptron (MLP) with a single hidden layer where each token within the input sentence is classified into one of 19 classes (18 event types and 'NONE' for non-event). All predicted event triggers are added to a list, $\widehat{y}_{trg}$ where $\widehat{y}_{trg} = t_1, t_2, ...t_j$.

Event argument extraction. For the second subtask, the event argument extraction task is setup as a sequence classification task. Candidate arguments are selected from the pool of entity mentions within the sentence. Each candidate argument will be paired with a candidate trigger for argument role classification. The classifier will classify each trigger-entity pair into one of 20 classes (19 argument roles and 'NONE' for entities with no links to the candidate trigger).

In the experiments, gold-standard entity mention E were used, $E = e_1, e_2, ...e_k$ where k is the number of the entity mentions in a sentence. With the list of predicted candidate triggers $\widehat{y}_{trg}$ with j number of triggers, and the list of golden entity mentions E with k number of entity mentions, we pair each candidate trigger with an entity, resulting in $j \times k$ number of pairs. For the pair $t_x e_y$, the task is to classify the argument roles entity e_y plays in event t_x.

[8][CLS], [SEP], [MASK] are special tokens of BERT. For experiments involving RoBERTa, Byte-Pair Encoding (BPE) tokenization and its special tokens are used.

4.4.2 Graph Convolutional Networks over Dependency Tree

A sentence's syntactic parse tree can be seen as a directed graph. Let $\mathcal{G} = \{\mathcal{V}, \mathcal{E}\}$ be the dependency parse tree for the sentence w with $\mathcal{V}$ and $\mathcal{E}$ as the sets of nodes and edges of $\mathcal{G}$ respectively. $\mathcal{V}$ contains n nodes corresponding to the n tokens $w_1, w_2, ..., w_n$ in w. Each edge $(v_i, v_j) \in \mathcal{E}$ is directed from the head word w_i to the dependent word w_j) with the Universal Dependency (UD) relation tags. Given a sentence's dependency parse tree with with n nodes, we convert each tree into its corresponding $n \times n$ adjacency matrix A with the following modifications:

1. Treating the dependency graph as undirected, i.e $\forall i, j, A_{i,j} = A_{j,i}$, where $A_{i,j} = A_{j,i} = 1$ if there is a dependency edge between tokens i and j;
2. Adding self-loops to the each node in the graph, following (Kipf and Welling, 2017): $\widetilde{A} = A + I$ with I being the $n \times n$ identity matrix

Stacking a GCN layer L times gives us a L-layer GCN where L is a hyperparameter of the model. During graph convolution at each layer l, each node gathers and summarizes information from its connected nodes ($\widetilde{A}_{i,j} = 1$) in the graph. We set $h^{(0)}$ as the input word vectors for an L-level GCN network and $h^{(L)}$ as the output word representations. The graph convolution operation of a single node, node i at level l of the GCN is as follows:

$$h_i^{(l)} = \sigma(\sum_{j=1}^{n} \widetilde{A}_{ij} W^{(l)} h_j^{l-1} / d_i + b^{(l)}) \quad (1)$$

where $h_i^{(l-1)}$ is the input vector, $h_i^{(l)}$ denotes the collective hidden representations, $W^{(l)}$ is the weight matrix, $b^{(l)}$ is a bias term, σ is the sigmoid activation function and $d_i = \sum_{j=1}^{n} \widetilde{A}_{ij}$, is the number of arches in the resulting graph.

4.4.3 Argument Role Classification with GCN

This section describes the operations shown as "3" in Figure 5.

Encoding Trigger-Entity Pair. Given a trigger-entity pair $t_x e_y$, we prune the dependency tree to obtain the contextual sub-tree between trigger t_x and entity e_y based on Algorithm 1. The nodes of this sub-tree form the input word vectors $h^{(0)}$ to the L-layer GCN network.

The subtree representation after L times of graph convolution is obtained as follows:

$$h_{subtree} = f(h^{(L)}) = f(GCN(h^{(0)})) \quad (2)$$

where $h^{(L)}$ is the output word representations produced by the L-layer GCN network and f is a max-pooling function that maps the input to the subtree vector, $h_{subtree}$. Besides the subtree representation, we also obtained a representation h_{trg} for trigger and h_{ent} for entity:

$$h_{trg} = f(h_t^{(L)}), h_{ent} = f(h_e^{(L)}) \quad (3)$$

Besides max-pooling, we have also experimented with average-pooling and sum-pooling to obtain the final vector for all three vectors (substree, trigger and entity). All three vectors are then concatenated into a vector which is then propagated through a fully-connected layer to classify the argument role:

$$\widehat{y}_{trg\_ent} = g(W_a[h_{subtree}; h_{trg}; h_{ent}] + b_a) \quad (4)$$

where g is the *softmax* operation to obtain a probability distribution over argument roles. $\widehat{y}_{trg\_ent}$ is the final output of the role the entity *ent* plays in the event triggered by the trigger candidate *trg*.

4.4.4 Loss Function for Joint-extraction

Event trigger and arguments extraction are jointly trained by minimizing the cross-entropy loss function.

$$\mathcal{L}_{joint} = \mathcal{L}_{trg} + \beta(\mathcal{L}_{arg}) \quad (5)$$

where β is the weightage placed on the loss of argument extraction task. In the experiment we use the value of 2, training the model with double the weightage on argument extraction.

5 Experiment Setup

Parameter settings. The data is split into 70% for training and 30% for testing. For all the experiments, the word embedding is of size 768 dimensions (same as `bert-base-cased`) while 50 dimensions for the other two embeddings - POS-tag embedding and entity-type embedding. For the GCN module, we use a two-layer GCN ($L = 2$) with a batch size of 4. The model is trained using the Cross-entropy loss function and Adam optimizer.

Method	Trigger Identification (%)			Trigger Classification (%)			Argument Identification (%)			Argument Role (%)		
	P	R	F1	P	R	F1	P	R	F1	P	R	F1
Sequence representation (**A**)	0.81	0.82	0.72	0.75	0.71	0.70	0.71	0.70	0.7	0.60	0.62	0.62
JMEE (**B**)	0.91	0.92	0.92	0.89	0.91	0.90	0.79	0.79	0.78	0.72	0.76	0.75
GCN with full tree (**C**)	0.92	0.97	0.95	0.92	0.94	0.92	0.80	0.81	0.81	0.74	0.75	0.73
GCN with LCA subtree (**D**)	0.92	0.96	0.94	0.93	0.95	0.94	0.89	0.90	0.89	0.87	0.86	0.85
GCN with contextual sub-tree (**E**)	0.93	0.98	0.95	0.91	0.97	0.93	**0.92**	**0.91**	**0.92**	**0.90**	**0.89**	**0.90**

Table 3: Comparing results (Precision, Recall, and F1 scores) across various methods with gold-standard entity mentions.

Models Settings. The architecture and setup for models listed in Table 3 are as follows:
(1) **Model A** - The embedding of trigger and candidate argument (from ComBERT) are concatenated and fed into a Bi-LSTM, which is then fed into a classifier with one fully connected (FC) layer.
(2) **Model B** - Jointly Multiple Events Extraction via Attention-based Graph Information Aggregation (JMEE) as presented in (Liu et al., 2018)[9].
(3) **Model C** - GCN with Full Tree uses the full dependency tree, $h_{fulltree}$. The same convolution operations are done on $h_{fulltree}$ in the place of $h_{subtree}$.
(4) **Model D** - GCN with LCA sub-tree with shortest dependency path between trigger candidate and entity candidate.
(5) **Model E** - GCN with contextual sub-tree, this setup is described in the Proposed Solution section.

6 Results and Analysis

6.1 Trigger Classification

As shown in Table 3, Trigger Identification and Trigger Classification achieve rather high F1 scores in all experiments regardless of whether full dependency tree or sub-tree, sequential or syntactic representation approach.

6.2 Argument Role Classification

From the results shown in Table 3, it can be concluded that syntactic representation (**Model C, D, E**) of a sentence yields better event extraction results. The results of Model B and C are not as good as using sub-tree because the full dependency tree contains unnecessary and noisy information that is not helpful in argument role classification. As for (Liu et al., 2018) (Model B), it did not produce the best results because it was designed for capturing the association between multiple events within a sentence via the attention mechanism. The events in the commodity news dataset do not exhibit the same strong association as the events in ACE2005 dataset. Model D uses the LCA subtree that has only the "bare minimum" information, while Model E contains additional crucial context information that has proved to be useful in argument role classification.

Table 4 presents the breakdown of Argument Classification by Argument Types to fully provide evidence to the effectiveness of the proposed solution on the corpus, which exhibits the characteristic of arguments homogeneity. It is shown clearly that arguments of the same entity type, for example, *Final_value*, *Initial_value* and *Difference* can be better differentiated and classified using a contextual sub-tree that contains the shortest path between an event trigger and its event argument as well as crucial off-path information. Symbols (♣, ◇, ♠) in Table 4 indicate the grouping of arguments by entity type.

As for the characteristic of having multiple events in a sentence, the proposed solution is able to detect and classify the events as well as link arguments to their rightful event, as shown in both Table 3 and Table 4.

6.3 Comparing Word Embedding and Pre-trained Language Models

Model E in Table 5 was further experimented using GloVe (Pennington et al., 2014) and other pre-trained language models namely BERT (Devlin et al., 2019b) and RoBERTa (Liu et al., 2019). These were compared against ComBERT.

[9]This was developed for the ACE2005 dataset.

Argument Roles	Entity Type	Argument Role Classification F1 Score				
		Model A	Model B	Model C	Model D	Model E
NONE	-	0.84	0.84	0.90	0.91	**0.94**
Attribute	Financial Attribute	0.40	0.65	0.79	0.75	**0.83**
Item	Economic Item	0.64	0.85	**0.88**	0.85	**0.88**
Final_value ♣	Money / Production unit / Price unit / Percentage / Quantity	0.43	0.39	0.71	0.75	**0.79**
Initial_value ♣	Money / Production unit / Price unit / Percentage / Quantity	0.56	0.56	0.73	0.69	**0.77**
Difference ♣	Money / Production unit / Price unit / Percentage / Quantity	0.58	0.69	0.84	**0.89**	**0.89**
Reference_point ♢	Date	0.54	0.69	**0.80**	0.71	**0.80**
Initial_reference_point ♢	Date	0.40	0.63	0.63	0.60	**0.66**
Contract_date ♢	Date	0.52	0.54	0.70	0.66	**0.80**
Duration	Duration	0.55	0.55	0.75	0.82	**0.84**
Type	Location	0.52	0.59	0.70	0.68	**0.76**
Imposer ♠	Country / State or province	0.71	0.69	**0.81**	0.79	**0.81**
Imposee ♠	Country / State or province	0.50	0.49	0.60	**0.68**	**0.68**
Place ♠	Country / State or province	0.58	0.69	**0.74**	0.60	**0.74**
Supplier_consumer ♠	Country / State or provience / Nationality / Group	0.49	0.71	0.73	0.73	**0.79**
Impacted_countries ♠	Country	0.42	0.69	0.72	0.70	**0.76**
Participating_countries ♠	Country	0.65	0.75	0.78	0.83	**0.89**
Forecaster	Organization / Group	0.62	0.75	0.78	0.80	**0.82**
Forecast	Forecast_Target	0.61	0.61	0.83	0.67	**0.91**
Situation	Phenomenon / Other acitivites	0.57	0.69	**0.73**	0.67	0.66

Table 4: F1-scores for each argument type.

Method	Trigger Classification (%)			Argument Role Class. (%)		
	P	R	F1	P	R	F1
GloVe	0.67	0.70	0.68	0.65	0.66	0.67
BERT	**0.93**	0.93	0.93	0.85	0.83	0.83
RoBERTa	0.89	0.96	0.93	0.86	0.85	0.83
ComBERT	0.91	**0.97**	**0.93**	**0.90**	**0.89**	**0.90**

Table 5: Comparing Word Embedding and Pre-trained Language Models for Model E

From the results in Table 5, it is shown that ComBERT produced the best result, further proving that a contextualized token representation helps boost the performance of event extraction. ComBERT is used in all models listed in Table 4.

7 Conclusion

This paper presents a graph-based deep learning framework to extract commodity-related events. This framework is tailored for the purpose of commodity news event extraction based on the new commodity news dataset introduced by (Lee et al., 2021). Our method addresses specific challenges exhibited by the characteristics of this dataset, in particular: (1) sentences containing lots of numerical information such as price, percentage of change, and dates, (2) entities of similar type playing distinctly different argument roles, and (3) the need for arguments extraction to disambiguate the identified events. The proposed solution uses a Graph Convolutional Network with a contextual sub-tree to extract events effectively. Experimental results demonstrate that the proposed solution outperforms existing solutions with higher F1 scores, particularly in argument role classification. With accurate event extraction from commodity news, the extracted information can be used for other downstream tasks such as learning event chains and event-event relations that can be further exploited for commodity price prediction.

References

Michael W Brandt and Lin Gao. 2019. Macro fundamentals or geopolitical events? a textual analysis of news events for crude oil. *Journal of Empirical Finance*, 51:64–94.

Jacob Devlin, Ming-Wei Chang, Kenton Lee, and Kristina Toutanova. 2019a. BERT: Pre-training of deep bidirectional transformers for language understanding. In *Proceedings of the 2019 Conference of the North American Chapter of the Association for Computational Linguistics: Human Language Technologies, Volume 1 (Long and Short Papers)*, pages 4171–4186, Minneapolis, Minnesota. Association for Computational Linguistics.

Jacob Devlin, Ming-Wei Chang, Kenton Lee, and Kristina Toutanova. 2019b. BERT: pre-training of deep bidirectional transformers for language understanding. In *Proceedings of the 2019 Conference of the North American Chapter of the Association for Computational Linguistics: Human Language Technologies, NAACL-HLT 2019, Minneapolis, MN, USA, June 2-7, 2019, Volume 1 (Long and Short Papers)*, pages 4171–4186.

Xiao Ding, Yue Zhang, Ting Liu, and Junwen Duan. 2014. Using structured events to predict stock price movement: An empirical investigation. In *Proceedings of the 2014 Conference on Empirical Methods in Natural Language Processing (EMNLP)*, pages 1415–1425.

Liat Ein-Dor, Ariel Gera, Orith Toledo-Ronen, Alon Halfon, Benjamin Sznajder, Lena Dankin, Yonatan Bilu, Yoav Katz, and Noam Slonim. 2019. Financial event extraction using Wikipedia-based weak supervision. In *Proceedings of the Second Workshop on Economics and Natural Language Processing*, pages 10–15, Hong Kong. Association for Computational Linguistics.

Alexander Hogenboom, Frederik Hogenboom, Flavius Frasincar, Kim Schouten, and Otto Van Der Meer. 2013. Semantics-based information extraction for detecting economic events. *Multimedia Tools and Applications*, 64(1):27–52.

Frederik Hogenboom, Flavius Frasincar, Uzay Kaymak, Franciska De Jong, and Emiel Caron. 2016. A survey of event extraction methods from text for decision support systems. *Decision Support Systems*, 85:12–22.

Thomas N. Kipf and Max Welling. 2017. Semi-supervised classification with graph convolutional networks. In *5th International Conference on Learning Representations, ICLR 2017, Toulon, France, April 24-26, 2017, Conference Track Proceedings*.

Meisin Lee, Lay-Ki Soon, Eu-Gene Siew, and Ly Fie Sugianto. 2021. An annotated commodity news corpus for event extraction.

Xiao Liu, Zhunchen Luo, and Heyan Huang. 2018. Jointly multiple events extraction via attention-based graph information aggregation. In *Proceedings of the 2018 Conference on Empirical Methods in Natural Language Processing*, pages 1247–1256, Brussels, Belgium. Association for Computational Linguistics.

Yinhan Liu, Myle Ott, Naman Goyal, Jingfei Du, Mandar Joshi, Danqi Chen, Omer Levy, Mike Lewis, Luke Zettlemoyer, and Veselin Stoyanov. 2019. Roberta: A robustly optimized bert pretraining approach. *arXiv preprint arXiv:1907.11692*.

Hassan H Malik, Vikas S Bhardwaj, and Huascar Fiorletta. 2011. Accurate information extraction for quantitative financial events. In *Proceedings of the 20th ACM international conference on information and knowledge management*, pages 2497–2500.

Thien Huu Nguyen and Ralph Grishman. 2018. Graph convolutional networks with argument-aware pooling for event detection. In *AAAI*, volume 18, pages 5900–5907.

Jeffrey Pennington, Richard Socher, and Christopher D Manning. 2014. Glove: Global vectors for word representation. In *Proceedings of the 2014 conference on empirical methods in natural language processing (EMNLP)*, pages 1532–1543.

Swarnadeep Saha, Harinder Pal, et al. 2017. Bootstrapping for numerical open ie. In *Proceedings of the 55th Annual Meeting of the Association for Computational Linguistics (Volume 2: Short Papers)*, pages 317–323.

Roger C Schank and Robert P Abelson. 2013. *Scripts, plans, goals, and understanding: An inquiry into human knowledge structures*. Psychology Press.

Yonghui Wu, Mike Schuster, Zhifeng Chen, Quoc V. Le, Mohammad Norouzi, Wolfgang Macherey, Maxim Krikun, Yuan Cao, Qin Gao, Klaus Macherey, Jeff Klingner, Apurva Shah, Melvin Johnson, Xiaobing Liu, Lukasz Kaiser, Stephan Gouws, Yoshikiyo Kato, Taku Kudo, Hideto Kazawa, Keith Stevens, George Kurian, Nishant Patil, Wei Wang, Cliff Young, Jason Smith, Jason Riesa, Alex Rudnick, Oriol Vinyals, Greg Corrado, Macduff Hughes, and Jeffrey Dean. 2016. Google's neural machine translation system: Bridging the gap between human and machine translation. *CoRR*, abs/1609.08144.

Wei Xiang and Bang Wang. 2019. A survey of event extraction from text. *IEEE Access*, 7:173111–173137.

Boyi Xie, Rebecca J. Passonneau, Leon Wu, and Germán G. Creamer. 2013. Semantic frames to predict stock price movement. In *Proceedings of the 51st Annual Meeting of the Association for Computational Linguistics (Volume 1: Long Papers)*, pages 873–883, Sofia, Bulgaria. Association for Computational Linguistics.

Hang Yang, Yubo Chen, Kang Liu, Yang Xiao, and Jun Zhao. 2018. DCFEE: A document-level Chinese financial event extraction system based on automatically labeled training data. In *Proceedings of ACL 2018, System Demonstrations*, pages 50–55, Melbourne, Australia. Association for Computational Linguistics.

Sen Yang, Dawei Feng, Linbo Qiao, Zhigang Kan, and Dongsheng Li. 2019. Exploring pre-trained language models for event extraction and generation. In *Proceedings of the 57th Conference of the Association for Computational Linguistics*, pages 5284–5294.

Yuhao Zhang, Peng Qi, and Christopher D. Manning. 2018. Graph convolution over pruned dependency trees improves relation extraction. In *Proceedings of the 2018 Conference on Empirical Methods in Natural Language Processing*, pages 2205–2215, Brussels, Belgium. Association for Computational Linguistics.

A Commodity News Dataset

A.1 Event Types

There are 18 event types that can be grouped into four main categories: (1) macro-economic, (2) geo-political, (3) supply-demand-related, and (4) commodity price movement events. In-depth details about the event types such as the categories they belong to, description, and as well as more example sentences are found in (Lee et al., 2021).

Event type	Examples
1. Cause-movement-down-loss	The pandemic has **zapped** demand to a level never seen before...
2. Cause-movement-up-gain	IEA tried to **boost** global oil demand by introducing.....
3. Civil-unrest	.....a fragile recovery in Libyan supply outweighed **fighting** in Iraq ......
4. Crisis	.....Ukraine declared an end to an oil **crisis** that has .....
5. Embargo	.....prepared to impose " strong and swift " economic **sanctions** on Venezuela...
6. Geopolitical-tension	....despite geopolitical **war** in Iraq , Libya and Ukraine.
7. Grow-strong	.....as **strong** U.S. employment data.....
8. Movement-down-loss	....further **decreases** in U.S. crude production.....
9. Movement-flat	U.S. crude is expected to **hold** around $105 per barrel.
10. Movement-up-gain	It expects consumption to **trend upward** by 1.05 million bpd.
11. Negative-sentiment	....due to **concern** about softening demand growth and awash in crude.
12. Oversupply	....the market is still working off the **gluts** built up.....
13. Position-high	Oil price remained close to four-year **highs**....
14. Position-low	Oil slipped more than 20% to its **lowest level** in two years on 1980s...
15. Prohibiting	U.S. has **prohibit** the sale of oil from Venezuela.
16. Shortage	......and there is no **shortfall** in supply , the minister added.
17. Slow-weak	U.S. employment data **contracts** with the euro zone....
18. Trade-tensions	... escalating global **trade wars**, especially between the US and China.

Table 6: Event types with examples.

A.2 Event Schema

Each event has its own set of event arguments. Below is the complete list of arguments for the event **movement_up_gain**. The argument text of this table is populated using the example sentence presented in Figure 1. For the complete list of event schemas refer to (Lee et al., 2021).

Argument Role	Entity Type	Argument Text
Type	Nationality, Location	
Supplier_consumer	Organization, Country, State_or_province, Group, Location	U.S.
Reference_point_time	Date	Tuesday
Initial_reference_point	Date	
Final_value	Percentage, Number, Money, Price_unit, Production_unit, Quantity	438.9 million barrels
Initial_value	Percentage, Number, Money, Price_unit, Production_unit, Quantity	200 million barrels
Item	Commodity, Economic_item	crude
Attribute	Financial_attribute	stockpiles
Difference	Percentage, Number, Money, Production_unit, Quantity	1.350 million barrels
Forecast	Forecast_target	
Duration	Duration	
Forecaster	Organization	

Table 7: Event Schema for the event **movement_up_gain**.

A.3 Argument Roles and Entity Types

Table 8 is a repeat of Table 4 showing the association of various entity types to each argument roles. The table below provides examples of entity mention for each argument roles.

Argument Roles	**Entity Type**	**Examples**
1. NONE	-	-
2. Attribute	Financial Attribute	*supply, demand, output, production, price, import, export*
3. Item	Economic Item	*economy, economic growth, market, economic outlook, employment data, currency, commodity-oil*
4. Final_value	Money / Production unit / Price unit / Percentage / Quantity	*$60, USD 50, 170,000 bpd, 400,000 barrels per day, 1 million barrels, $40 per barrel, USD58 per barrel, 0.5%*
5. Initial_value	Money / Production unit / Price unit / Percentage / Quantity	`-same as above-`
6. Difference	Money / Production unit / Price unit / Percentage / Quantity	`-same as above-`
7. Reference_point	Date	*1998, Wednesday, Jan. 30, the final quarter of 1991, the end of this year*
8. Initial_reference_point	Date	`-same as above-`
9. Contract_date	Date	`-same as above-`
10. Duration	Duration	*two years, three-week, 5-1/2-year, multiyear, another six months*
11. Type	Location	*global, world, domestic*
12. Imposer	Country / State or province	*China, Iran, Iraq, Washington, Moscow, Cushing, North America, Europe*
13. Imposee	Country / State or province	`-same as above-`
14. Place	Country / State or province	`-same as above-`
15. Supplier_consumer	Country / State or provience / Nationality / Group	`-same as above-` + *OPEC, non-OPEC countries, American, Russian*
16. Impacted_countries	Country	*China, U.S. Russia, Iran, Iraq*
17. Participating_countries	Country	`-same as above-`
18. Forecaster	Organization / Group	*OPEC, European Union, U.S. Energy Information Administration*
19. Forecast	Forecast_Target	*forecast, target, estimate, projection, bets*
20. Situation	Phenomenon / Other activities	`free text`

Table 8: List of Event Argument Roles and their corresponding entity types.

Cryptocurrency Day Trading and Framing Prediction in Microblog Discourse

Anna Paula Pawlicka Maule
Computer Science and Engineering
Michigan State University
East Lansing, MI 48824
apmaule@gmail.com

Kristen Marie Johnson
Computer Science and Engineering
Michigan State University
East Lansing, MI 48824
kristenj@msu.edu

Abstract

With 56 million people actively trading and investing in cryptocurrency online and globally in 2020, there is an increasing need for automatic social media analysis tools to help understand trading discourse and behavior. In this work, we present a dual natural language modeling pipeline which leverages language and social network behaviors for the prediction of cryptocurrency day trading actions and their associated framing patterns. This pipeline first predicts if tweets can be used to guide day trading behavior, specifically if a cryptocurrency investor should buy, sell, or hold their cryptocurrencies in order to make a profit. Next, tweets are input to an unsupervised deep clustering approach to automatically detect trading framing patterns. Our contributions include the modeling pipeline for this novel task, a new Cryptocurrency Tweets Dataset compiled from influential accounts, and a Historical Price Dataset. Our experiments show that our approach achieves an 88.78% accuracy for day trading behavior prediction and reveals framing fluctuations prior to and during the COVID-19 pandemic that could be used to guide investment actions.

1 Introduction

Beginning with the 2008 introduction of Bitcoin (BTC) (Nakamoto, 2008), a cryptocurrency for a Peer-to-Peer cash system, the use of cryptocurrencies and their corresponding blockchains have increasingly gained in popularity. In 2019, the number of Americans owning cryptocurrency doubled from 7% in 2018 to 14%, representing about 35 million people trading and investing with cryptocurrency (Partz, 2019).

This increase is largely due to the capability of cryptocurrency to improve various applications ranging from increased security of smart contracts to facilitating less expensive, faster cross-border international payments. Another contributing factor to this growth is that digital coins fulfill the property of storing value similar to other *fiat currencies*, which are government-issued currencies not backed by physical commodities, e.g., the American dollar or euro. Finally, cryptocurrency popularity can be associated with its high day trading volume. As of January 2021, the combined worth of all cryptocurrencies was $1 trillion [1], with Bitcoin accounting for $650 billion of this amount. To put this in perspective, the average trading volume of Amazon Inc. is $13 billion per day – less than one-fifth of the BTC daily volume of $70 billion. [2]

Cryptocurrencies were born on the internet, gained their visibility through online and social media coverage, and many investors follow the advice of well-known cryptocurrency experts on Twitter to guide their personal investment strategies (Mone, 2019). Because cryptocurrency prices can fluctuate quickly, resulting in real-life financial gains or losses, models that can rapidly analyze trending discourse on Twitter can be harnessed to guide and benefit investors.

Additionally, work in computational linguistics and the social sciences have shown the benefit of studying *framing*, which is how someone discusses a topic in order to influence or alter the opinion of the public, for understanding microblog discourse (Card et al., 2015; Johnson et al., 2017; Li and Goldwasser, 2019). Specifically, framing in Twitter can be used to understand social phenomena, such as political maneuvering or epidemiology coverage. However, few works exist which study the relationship between framing and cryptocurrency trading, especially during times of economic stress.

Currently, it is estimated that the COVID-19 pandemic has negatively impacted the global economy by hindering economic growth worldwide between 4.5% and 6.0%, with the potential for future global trade to fall up to 9.2% (CRS, 2020). Similar to

[1]https://coinmarketcap.com/charts/

[2]https://finance.yahoo.com/quote/AMZN

Proceedings of the Third Workshop on Economics and Natural Language Processing, pages 82–92
Punta Cana and online, November 11.

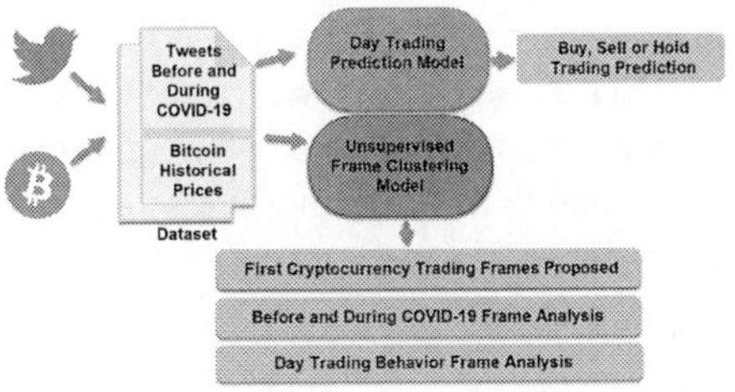

Figure 1: Cryptocurrency Day Trading Prediction and Framing Discovery Pipeline.

the pandemic's effect on Wall Street (i.e., the New York Stock Exchange and NASDAQ), the cryptocurrency market reflected a drastic 47.8% drop on March 12, 2020, one day after the World Health Organization (WHO) announced that COVID-19 could be characterized as a pandemic. Around the same time, a similar drop occurred in stocks worldwide. Therefore, we hypothesized that microblog discourse about day trading behaviors (i.e., buy, sell, hold) would be a useful predictive feature in understanding cryptocurrency trading and framing.

Our contributions include a cryptocurrency day trading behavior modeling pipeline (Figure 1) that leverages language and social network behavior extracted from tweets to implement: (1) a predictive model for investment actions, specifically, whether to buy, sell, or hold cryptocurrency based on daily discussions on Twitter, and (2) an unsupervised deep-learning clustering model to determine the underlying framing patterns used to discuss these investment actions. We have also compiled a Cryptocurrency Tweets Dataset (divided into Pre-COVID and during COVID portions) and Bitcoin Historical Price Dataset.[3] Lastly, we propose novel frames for economic and financial analysis. Our models are able to predict trading actions with 88.78% accuracy, while also revealing a distinction between how day trading behaviors are framed before and during the COVID-19 pandemic.

2 Related Work

Most relevant to this work are previous works that have studied public opinion, sentiment, stock market predictions, and framing using online discourse. Modeling social media microblogs, specifically Twitter, to show connections between online discourse and its effects on public opinion has been widely studied in NLP (Ritter et al., 2010; Walker et al., 2012; Abu-Jbara et al., 2013; Hasan and Ng, 2014; West et al., 2014; Sridhar et al., 2015) and the social sciences (Bollen et al., 2011; Harlow and Johnson, 2011; Meraz and Papacharissi, 2013; Burch et al., 2015; Jang and Hart, 2015). There are many works on Twitter sentiment analysis, but closest to our work are those concerning the use of Twitter sentiment for stock market predictions (Kouloumpis et al., 2011; Rao and Srivastava, 2012; Si et al., 2013; Derakhshan and Beigy, 2019).

There are relatively few works concerning cryptocurrency analysis and prediction. Of these, a majority use social media sentiment (Jain et al., 2018; Li et al., 2019), volume of tweets (Vidal, 2020), or both (Abraham et al., 2018) as the main feature for prediction. Furthermore, the prediction tasks are typically to predict prices or whether those prices will rise or fall. However, sentiment is known to be difficult to predict on Twitter. Furthermore, the volume of tweets can be falsely inflated by bots reporting currency prices, but not contributing to the discourse. Therefore, instead of sentiment or tweet volume, we aim to use the language directly extracted from tweets, their context, and features representing the social network behavior for a buy, sell, or hold investment action prediction.

Research has also shown that given an adequate amount of historical data, such as stock values and indices, it is possible to forecast future currency exchanges (Walczak, 2001). Different from this work, we focus on predicting cryptocurrency investment *actions*, instead of fiat currency prices, by extracting patterns from historical *tweets* rather than stock values and indices.

Previous works have shown the effectiveness of using frames to predict various social sciences phenomena, such as political framing of Twitter discourse, congressional speeches, and news coverage of current events (Boydstun et al., 2014; Baumer et al., 2015; Card et al., 2015; Tsur et al., 2015; Jang and Hart, 2015; Fulgoni et al., 2016; Johnson et al., 2017; Field et al., 2018). Framing has also been used to understand the role of Twitter discussions in influencing public opinion of events such as riots and protests (Harlow and Johnson, 2011; Meraz and Papacharissi, 2013; Burch et al., 2015). Despite this coverage, to the best of our knowledge we are the first to study the role of framing in economics, specifically concerning stocks or cryptocurrency day trading, or associated correlations with the current pandemic. This work presents a first step in understanding both cryptocurrency day

[3]https://github.com/MSU-NLP-CSS/crypto-framing

trading and how framing can reveal insights about cryptocurrency trading.

3 Data Annotation

This section describes the collection and preprocessing steps of the tweets and historical Bitcoin (BTC) transaction prices. Section 3.4 describes how tweets were annotated for use in the day trading behavior prediction model. The non-annotated version of these tweets were used in the framing clustering models.

3.1 Twitter Data Collection

For this work we collected tweets related to cryptocurrency, including BTC and other popular coin types such as Etheureum (ETH) and XRP, because prices of different cryptocurrencies are highly correlated (Magas, 2020). Rather than collect based on hashtags or keywords alone, we narrowed our search to specific time frames and user accounts.

Tweets were scraped from January 2017, when Bitcoin surpassed $1,000 per coin, until February 2020. This time range covers times of frequent changes in cryptocurrency trading and adheres to the finding that an optimal dataset for financial time series prediction consists of information from the past two years (Walczak, 2001). These tweets form our Pre-COVID Dataset.

Within these time frames, three types of user accounts were identified for tweet collection (details in A.1) to maximize the presence of discourse for analysis and minimize tweet noise. These include influential cryptocurrency Twitter accounts, or *influencers*, which are well known as sources for investment information and thus should provide features for message propagation. This category also includes users who frequently tweet about cryptocurrency and have at least ten thousand followers. Similarly, *media* accounts from traditional or online news sources, such as *@CNNBusiness* and *@BitcoinMagazine*, are used. Lastly, we include *company* accounts, e.g., *@IBMBlockchain* and *@BitPay*.

The majority of tweet activity comes from influencer accounts that have between 10,000 and 499,999 followers. There are fewer media accounts, however, these have a much broader reach, e.g., *@nytimes* potentially reaches 48.2 million people. More details of the number of tweets collected per account type are presented in Appendix A.1.

Using the same accounts, we then collected additional cryptocurrency tweets which occurred during the COVID-19 pandemic time frame: from March 2020 until June 2020. These tweets comprise our COVID Dataset. Table 1 summarizes the amount of unique tweets per account type in the two portions comprising the overall dataset.

3.2 BTC Historical Price Data Collection

In addition to cryptocurrency related tweets, we also collected the historical transaction prices of Bitcoin from CoinMarketCap. [4] This BTC Historical Price Dataset contains the following information: the opening price of Bitcoin (Open), the highest price (High), the lowest price (Low), and the closing price (Close) of Bitcoin on that particular day. This dataset also includes the date and the dollar volume of BTC traded that day.

3.3 Preprocessing

Before processing, a total of 484,025 tweets were scraped to collect text with meta-information, including number of replies, number of retweets, and date. Preprocessing consisted of three main steps. First, all tweets were standardized, i.e., we controlled for capitalization, applied stemming, and removed URLs, white space noise, and stop words. Second, we removed irrelevant tweets by filtering for the presence of cryptocurrency-based keywords or hashtags (e.g., bitcoin, btc, ethereum, crypto, cryptocurrency, blockchain, etc.) reducing the dataset to 64,685 tweets. Lastly, in order to create a balanced dataset for training and testing the models, we retained equal proportions of tweets that corresponded to each momentum-labeled group, as described in Section 3.4. After processing, a total of 18,900 Pre-COVID tweets were used in the day trading movement prediction experiments.

For the framing clustering experiments, an additional 123,515 tweets were collected during the beginning of the pandemic. Preprocessing for these tweets consisted of removing: duplicate tweets, English stop words, and references to other users, emails, or website links.

3.4 Annotation

Recall that we are first interested in predicting whether an investor should buy, sell, or hold their cryptocurrency based on tweets discussing cryptocurrency that day. However, such a trading prediction is a challenging task, requiring extensive

[4] https://coinmarketcap.com/

CRYPTOCURRENCY TWEETS DATASET	INFLUENCERS	MEDIA	COMPANY	TOTAL
PRE-COVID DATASET	136,637	128,041	110,846	375,524
COVID DATASET	48,254	24,014	36,233	108,501
TOTAL	184,891	152,055	147,079	484,025

Table 1: Quantity of Unique Tweets Per User Account Type.

domain knowledge, yet also susceptible to different investing strategies and conflicting knowledge from Twitter discussions.

Therefore, we used the price information in the BTC Historical Price Dataset (Section 3.2) to define a *momentum* metric that represents the fluctuation of cryptocurrency costs on a given day:

$$momentum = \frac{Price_{close} - Price_{open}}{Price_{open}} \quad (1)$$

If the momentum on a given day increases or decreases by 5% on the following day, then we label tweets of that given day as *buy* or *sell*, respectively. If there is less than a 5% change, these tweets are neutral in terms of buying or selling, and are therefore labeled as *hold*, to represent that an investor should take no action with their cryptocurrency. This 5% cutoff was chosen because BTC volatility during 2017 and 2018 was around 8% (Reiff, 2020), while between 2019 and 2020 it was 4.66% (Tuwiner, 2020). For comparison, the average day trading volatility of stocks is 3.3%, which is considered to be high (Kyröläinen, 2008). This annotation was automated with a Python script that cross referenced the date of the tweet with the BTC Historical Price Dataset and is dependent only on price data.

We then attempted manual annotation. One inexperienced investor and one long-term experienced investor were asked to label a randomly generated subset of the Pre-COVID dataset. They were instructed to label tweets as *buy*, *sell*, or *hold* based on the tweet content and BTC price percentage fluctuation from the previous day (details in A.2).

Table 2 reports the results of two different annotation approaches, where the true labels are those generated by the momentum equation (Eqn. 1). First, annotators were asked to label the tweets based on their content and give an overall label for that particular day based on all their individual tweet annotations (shown in the OVERALL DAY columns of Table 2). Both annotators performed significantly below random guessing, e.g., where the expected label was *sell*.

Second, they were asked to give another overall annotation for a particular day with the additional information about the BTC price percentage change from the previous day (shown in the TWEET + PRICE columns). This required annotators to take into consideration the price movement from the previous day to decide on what trading action, *buy*, *sell*, or *hold*, to take. The annotators have very contrasting results, with the inexperienced annotator outperforming random guessing by over 15%. This is likely because their strategy was to sell when prompted with a strongly worded tweet combined with big BTC price drops. By contrast, the experienced annotator did not perform well because a long term investing strategy, i.e., to invest with the goal of profiting in the next 20 years, was applied.

	OVERALL DAY		TWEET + PRICE	
LABEL	INEXP.	EXP.	INEXP.	EXP.
SELL	17%	20%	50%	0%
BUY	28%	36%	30%	0%
HOLD	36%	31%	34%	53%

Table 2: Annotation Precision Experiments.

The results of these annotation experiments illustrate that day trading is a non-trivial task for people with and without prior trading and investing experience. Given the high quantity of tweets and highly dynamic language of Twitter, the subjectivity of choosing to buy or sell under different investing strategies, and the large variance in labeling via human annotators, we used the momentum metric as a weak form of supervision to generate labels for investment actions in the day trading prediction.

4 Models & Features

This section describes the two models and their associated features, which represent social network aspects of Twitter and the actual language and context of tweets. Both models are incorporated into a pipeline (Figure 1) that enables us to make trading predictions and discover and analyze new frames.

4.1 Day Trading Behavior Prediction

Model. For the day trading prediction model, we experimented with a combination of features, models, and a balanced dataset where there is an equal number of *sell*, *buy*, and *hold* labels. Naive Bayes with Bag-of-Words (BOW) features was used for the baseline model. We then tested Random Forest, RNN, and LSTM models that resulted in final accuracies above 85%. We conclude in Section 5 that the best performing model for this task [5] is the RNN with three layers.

Features. Social network related features are extracted directly from the meta-information of the cryptocurrency tweets. This includes the number of retweets and the number of replies. In our experiments, we found that the number of retweets provided some information gain when weighting the tweet feature representation. The type of user account, either influencer, media, or company, that posted the tweet is also used as a feature.

In addition to social features, we also used features directly related to the language of the tweet. First, we implemented an LDA topic model (Jelodar et al., 2019) and used the presence of a top 10 topic in a given tweet as a feature. Next, the tweets were transformed into 768 language features using DistilBERT. [6] All of the tweets were concatenated according to their momentum label and for each group (buy, sell, or hold), DistilBERT was used to extract high-quality language features to represent each of the three tweet groups. Finally, we calculated the cosine similarity of each tweet to these three group representations. We selected the match between a tweet and group with the highest cosine similarity to be used as a feature for that tweet. More concretely, each tweet is compared to the DistilBERT representation of the buy, sell, and hold concatenated tweet groups and the highest similarity group is chosen to be used as a feature.

4.2 Discourse Framing Clustering

Model. From an NLP perspective, frames represent latent abstractions of a discussion and are *not* equivalent to topics. We hypothesized that *how* a topic is discussed, or framed, could be identified in an unsupervised manner by analyzing how the tweet content clusters together. In order to extract the clusters which represent such frames, we tried two modeling approaches. First, we used a basic k-means clustering. Second, we implemented the unsupervised Deep Embedded Clustering (DEC) approach of Xie et al.; Hadifar et al., which combines both an autoencoder and k-means clustering to achieve a more precise separation. DEC simultaneously learns feature representations and cluster assignments.

MODEL	BOW	ALL FEATURES
NAIVE BAYES	49.72%	61.58%
RANDOM FOREST	63.81%	86.61%
RNN	33.67%	**88.78%**
LSTM	31.57%	88.18%

Table 3: Experimental Results. The columns represent the accuracy of each model when using either a bag-of-words (BOW) or all features of Section 4.1 combined with a DistilBERT (Sanh et al., 2019) representation of the tweets as features.

Features. The features used for the basic k-means and DEC models were sparse representations of the word counts for each tweet. Both BOW and TF-IDF features were used as input to the k-means model and autoencoder of the DEC pipeline.

5 Experimental Results

In this section, we present our experimental setup and an analysis of our modeling results.

5.1 Day Trading Behavior Prediction

We conducted supervised experiments using five-fold cross-validation with random shuffling and an 80% training and 20% testing split. For the Neural Networks, we experimented with 50 epochs because the dropout after each layer was 0.001.

Table 3 shows the results of using the following models: Naive Bayes, Random Forest, Recurrent Neural Network, and an LSTM. Both the RNN and LSTM use three dense layers. The columns of Table 3 correspond to the tweet feature representations used with each model: a baseline where tweets are represented as BOW and the combination of all features described in Section 4.1.

From Table 3, we can see that using an RNN with all combined features has the highest accuracy of 88.78% across all three classes. Details of the label prediction distribution are shown in Table 8 in Appendix A.3. Predicting day trading behavior, i.e., whether to buy or sell stock, is a complicated task, especially in a volatile asset such as cryptocurrency. Ablation studies revealed that the most informative features for prediction were the

[5] Our task is classification for future use in downstream applications. Thus we do not perform regression or time-series analysis in this paper, but will use time-series in future work.

[6] DistilBERT had a 0.6% better performance than BERT.

language features, specifically the combination of DistilBERT representations with cosine similarity.

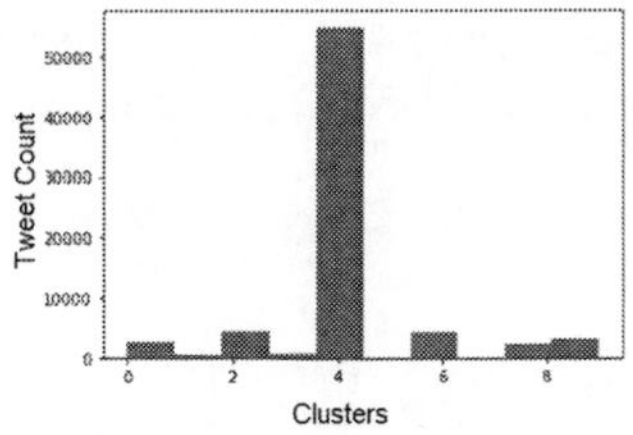

(a) Using k-means.

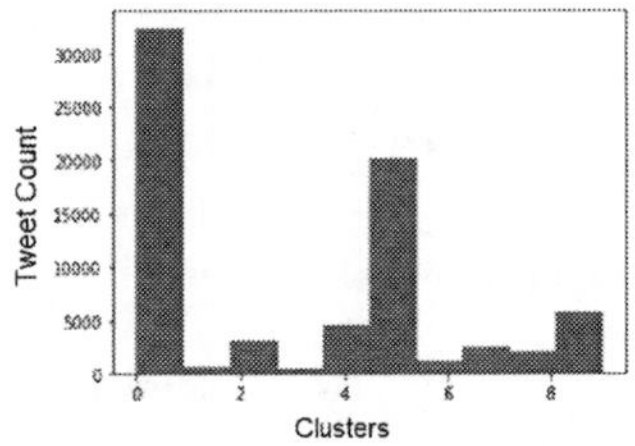

(b) Using DEC (Deep Clustering).

Figure 2: Number of Tweets Per Cluster. Both figures show the number of tweets per cluster using 10 initial clusters and BOW features for the Pre-COVID dataset.

5.2 Discourse Framing Prediction

We conducted unsupervised clustering experiments using (1) a basic k-means clustering and (2) deep clustering with autoenconders (DEC) as described in Section 4.2. The encoder outputs were used as inputs to the deep clustering layer, and similar to Hadifar et al., the k-means center clusters were used as initial weights for the deep clustering model. The tweets were randomly shuffled for training. The autoencoder ran for 100 epochs, achieving an accuracy of 99.99% with both training and validation loss on the order of 5.5453e-04 and without overfitting.

We initially experimented with 32 clusters because 32 is the default number of features that get compressed by the autoencoder. However, we observed that several clusters had similar, overlapping themes and keywords. Therefore, we conducted the rest of our experiments with 10 clusters. Figure 2 shows the number of tweets that fall into each of the 10 initial clusters for each modeling approach.

Figure 2a shows six clusters identified in our Pre-COVID Dataset by k-means clustering. Using Singular Value Decomposition (SVD) (Figure 3a) and an analysis of the most frequent words appearing in each cluster, we were able to extract three main clusters: the first cluster included tweets discussing

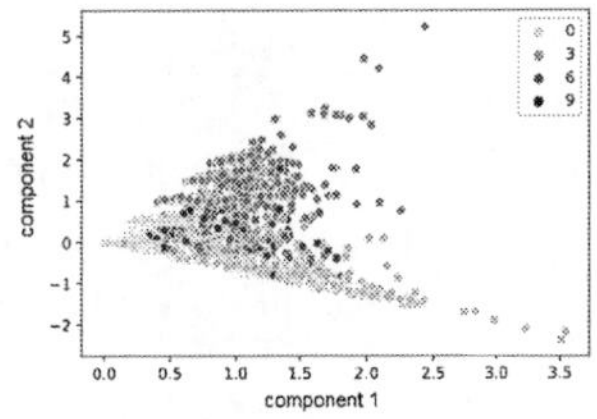

(a) Using k-means.

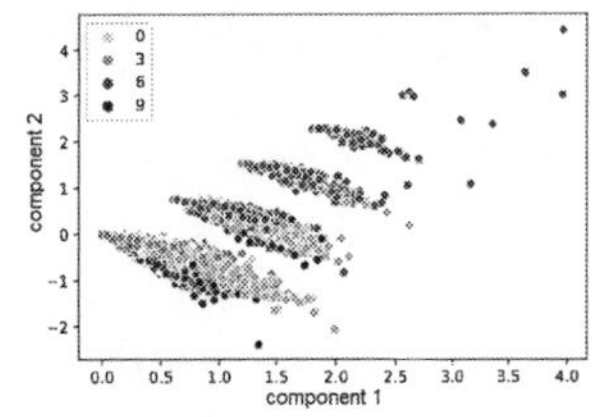

(b) Using DEC (Deep Clustering).

Figure 3: Pre-COVID Dataset Cluster Visualization on Reduced Dimensions Using SVD. SVD is used to reduce the clusters (0 to 9) to two dimensions to better visualize the frame groupings.

Bitcoin halving [7], the second concerns trading and investing cryptocurrency, and the third discussed how trading is affected by politics.

The DEC clustering of the Pre-COVID dataset (Figure 3b) also identified four main clusters: one discussing halving but with more emphasis on long term store value, one discussing political effects, and two discussing cryptocurrency trading and applications. This latter cluster splits the *cryptocurrency trading and investing* cluster identified as one large cluster by k-means into two clusters. Section 6 provides more analysis of the frames these clusters represent, how they are associated with trading behaviors, and how these associations change during the pandemic.

Cluster Verification. Given the novel aspect of this task, the difficulty of determining frames within tweets, and that both clustering approaches operate in an unsupervised setting, we conducted three cluster verification experiments. First, we asked an evaluator to determine how well the clusters represent how cryptocurrency discussions are framed. Given a subset of tweets, the evaluator was asked to "label" if cryptocurrency was discussed in the tweet with one of the DEC-identified frames using the following guidelines:

- *Trading Frame*: Does the tweet discuss how

[7] About every 4 years or so, the amount of BTC that can be mined (mining capacity) decreases by half.

TOPIC	TOP WORDS
KNOWLEDGE	know, bitcoin, time, blockchain, market, world, buy, change, people, point, today
BUSINESS	year, thank, start, problem, business, write, stop, plan, risk, reason, check
SUPPORT	make, think, work, want, day, people, need, use, year, week, support, happen, read
HOLD	look, price, money, try, build, econ, think, end, tell, idea, people, term, win, hold

Table 4: Pre-COVID Dataset Top 4 LDA Topics and Most Frequent Keywords.

or why to buy or sell cryptocurrency?

- *Application Frame*: Does the tweet emphasize the uses of cryptocurrency?
- *Store Value Frame*: Does the tweet discuss cryptocurrency in terms of long term value?
- *Political Frame*: Does the tweet put a political spin on cryptocurrency trading actions?

The evaluator's manual annotation was compared to the actual cluster (or frame) the tweet was assigned to by the DEC model. With this evaluation approach, we found the clustering to be 69.23% accurate. Given the lack of previous work on cryptocurrency framing, we compared this result to a previous work which found an annotator agreement of 73.4% on a tweet dataset labeled for political frames (Johnson et al., 2017).

Next, a chi-square test was performed to verify the hypothesis that the frames, represented by clusters, were independent of each other. In order to perform the test, the top word count was collected for each cluster, as well as their count in every other cluster. The resulting *p-value* was less than 0.05, indicating that the clusters are independent.

Lastly, to justify that these clusters represent how tweets are framed, we also performed an LDA topic analysis to ensure that clusters were not finding topics. Table 4 shows the top 4 LDA topics which are different from those extracted for frames (more details in Section 6). Topics represent the content of the tweet, e.g., the topic *Hold* represents holding cryptocurrency. Frames, however, are fundamentally different and represent *how* someone discusses a topic, e.g., how or why to hold.

6 Qualitative Results

In this section, we explore how cryptocurrency frames change over time and their correlation with cryptocurrency day trading behavior. Section 6.1 shows the effects of the pandemic on day trading discussions and behaviors. Section 6.2 discusses how day trading behaviors are framed.

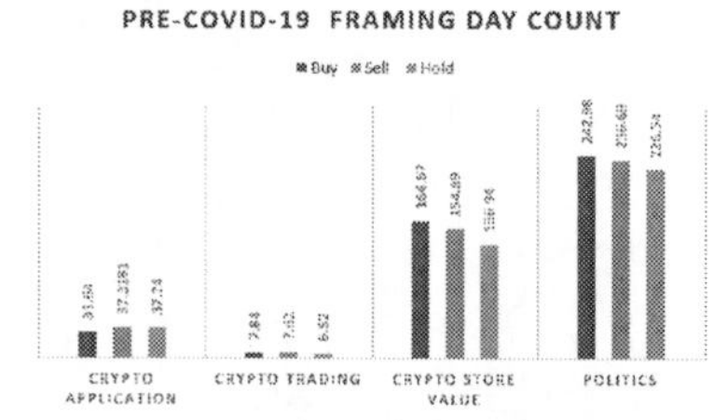

(a) Pre-COVID Frames with Actions.

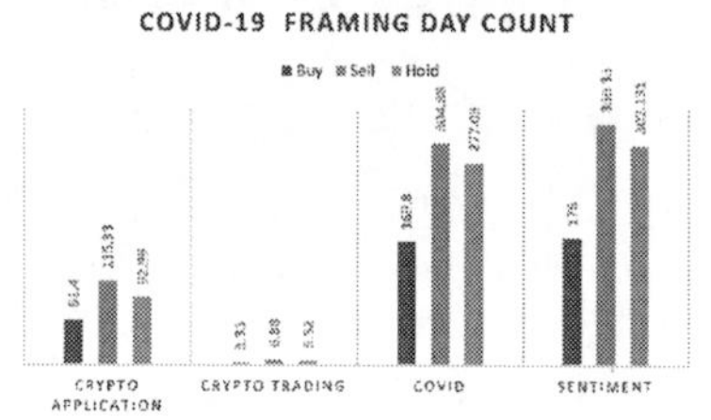

(b) COVID-19 Frames with Actions.

Figure 4: Predicted Frames and Investment Actions. Each figure shows the quantity of tweets using a certain frame (separated by a grey line) associated with each investment movement action: buy, sell, or hold.

6.1 Frames Before and During the Pandemic

Tables 5 and 6 show the most frequent words appearing in each of the four clusters extracted from the Pre-COVID or COVID Dataset, respectively. Prior to the pandemic, Table 5 shows that the cryptocurrency tweets were framed in terms of aspects important to cryptocurrency itself, i.e., trading actions, applications or uses, and long term store value. Table 6 shows that once the pandemic was occurring, the discussion shifted. People still discussed cryptocurrency in terms of trading and applications, however, there was a shift from focusing on long term value and political effects on cryptocurrency to sentiment concerning cryptocurrency and the pandemic.

One interesting event captured by the *Trading* frame in the COVID-19 Dataset was the BTC halving event on May 11, 2020. This halving marks the first quarter of the year as a historical event in the cryptocurrency world because this is the third halv-

Frame	Most Frequent Words
CRYPTO TRADING	price, bitcoin, usd, market, trading, value, action
CRYPTO APPLICATION	blockchain, btc, business, use, tech, crypto
CRYPTO STORE VALUE	bitcoin, people, need, want, use, market, value, years
POLITICS	world, man, president, america, china, work, government, time

Table 5: Most Frequent Words Per Cluster Prior to COVID-19 (Pre-COVID Dataset).

Frame	Most Frequent Words
CRYPTO TRADING	money, crypto, btc, trading, finance, investment, halving
CRYPTO APPLICATION	btc, crypto, time, right, know
SENTIMENT	like, look, things, dont, good, time, feel
COVID	people, coronavirus, covid, pandemic, bitcoin, world, dont

Table 6: Most Frequent Words Per Cluster During COVID-19 (COVID Dataset).

ing to take place. The past two times that halving occurred, Bitcoin later experienced an all-time high price jump. In future work, we aim to track this frame and use it to predict potential price jumps.

6.2 Frames and Momentum Patterns

From observing the frames and momentum patterns prior to the pandemic shown in Figure 4a, we can see that *Store Value* frames have a higher frequency when the momentum pattern suggests a *Buy* movement. This correlation makes sense because if there is a belief that some asset will store value it creates more confidence in buying and holding the cryptocurrency. It is also not surprising that there is an increase in *Political* frames associated with the *Buy* movement. Countries and economies often cited as being politically unstable, such as Botswana, Ghana, Venezuela, and India, have seen an increase in BTC interest because it is more stable than fiat currencies from those countries [8]. Another potential association with the slight increase in *Political* frames during a *Buy* movement is the increase of government adoption and additional regulation of cryptocurrencies. These patterns suggest that prior to the pandemic, if Twitter cryptocurrency discussions were framed in terms of store value or politics, an investor might consider buying more cryptocurrency.

During the COVID-19 time span (Figure 4b), all frames decrease during an indicated *Buy* movement. However, the opposite occurs, i.e., all frames increase, when the indicated movement is to *Sell.* Regarding both *Trading* and *Application* frames, it makes sense to purchase cryptocurrency when nobody is talking about it, and sell it when the interest in those topics rises. The *COVID* frame having a lower frequency during a *Buy* movement could indicate that investors feel less threatened by the market instability introduced by the pandemic, which is the opposite of the general sentiment of investors dealing with physical stock exchange markets.

7 Conclusion

We have presented a dual modeling pipeline to understand how the way influential people and news sources frame cryptocurrency discussions on Twitter affects cryptocurrency day trading. Using classic NLP techniques and cosine similarity between the DistilBERT representations of tweet features and cryptocurrency tweets, we provide a day trading prediction model that is capable of distinguishing between day trading actions such as buy, sell, or hold. Using our features and modeling approach we are able to achieve an accuracy of 88.78% over a 49.72% traditional baseline. Furthermore, we are first to present an unsupervised deep clustering approach to reveal the latent frames used to discuss these day trading behaviors. Our work shows interesting relationships between investment actions and how cryptocurrency discussions are framed on Twitter, as well as how these framing patterns change in response to a pandemic.

8 Acknowledgments

We thank Zachary Yarost and Kasper Standio for annotating the dataset, and the anonymous reviewers for their thoughtful comments and suggestions.

[8]https://news.coinsquare.com/government/government-instability-bitcoin/; https://www.un.org/africarenewal/magazine/april-2018-july-2018/africa-could-be-next-frontier-cryptocurrency

References

Jethin Abraham, Daniel Higdon, John Nelson, and Juan Ibarra. 2018. Cryptocurrency price prediction using tweet volumes and sentiment analysis. In *SMU Data Science Review: Vol. 1: No. 3, Article 1.*

Amjad Abu-Jbara, Ben King, Mona Diab, and Dragomir Radev. 2013. Identifying opinion subgroups in arabic online discussions. In *Proc. of ACL.*

Abderrahim Ait Azzi, Houda Bouamor, and Sira Ferradans. 2019. The FinSBD-2019 shared task: Sentence boundary detection in PDF noisy text in the financial domain. In *Proceedings of the First Workshop on Financial Technology and Natural Language Processing*, pages 74–80, Macao, China.

Eric Baumer, Elisha Elovic, Ying Qin, Francesca Polletta, and Geri Gay. 2015. Testing and comparing computational approaches for identifying the language of framing in political news. In *In Proc. of NAACL.*

Johan Bollen, Huina Mao, and Alberto Pepe. 2011. Modeling public mood and emotion: Twitter sentiment and socio-economic phenomena. In *Proc. of AAAI Conference on Weblogs and Social Media.*

Amber Boydstun, Dallas Card, Justin H. Gross, Philip Resnik, and Noah A. Smith. 2014. Tracking the development of media frames within and across policy issues.

Lauren M. Burch, Evan L. Frederick, and Ann Pegoraro. 2015. Kissing in the carnage: An examination of framing on twitter during the vancouver riots. *Journal of Broadcasting & Electronic Media*, 59(3):399–415.

Dallas Card, Amber E. Boydstun, Justin H. Gross, Philip Resnik, and Noah A. Smith. 2015. The media frames corpus: Annotations of frames across issues. In *Proc. of ACL.*

Congressional Research Service CRS. 2020. Global economic effects of covid-19.

Ali Derakhshan and Hamid Beigy. 2019. Sentiment analysis on stock social media for stock price movement prediction. In *Engineering Applications of Artificial Intelligence.*

Anjalie Field, Doron Kliger, Shuly Wintner, Jennifer Pan, Dan Jurafsky, and Yulia Tsvetkov. 2018. Framing and agenda-setting in Russian news: a computational analysis of intricate political strategies. In *Proceedings of the 2018 Conference on Empirical Methods in Natural Language Processing*, pages 3570–3580, Brussels, Belgium. Association for Computational Linguistics.

Dean Fulgoni, Jordan Carpenter, Lyle Ungar, and Daniel Preotiuc-Pietro. 2016. An empirical exploration of moral foundations theory in partisan news sources. In *Proc. of LREC.*

Amir Hadifar, Lucas Sterckx, Thomas Demeester, and Chris Develder. 2019. A self-training approach for short text clustering. In *Proceedings of the 4th Workshop on Representation Learning for NLP (RepL4NLP-2019)*, pages 194–199, Florence, Italy. Association for Computational Linguistics.

Summer Harlow and Thomas Johnson. 2011. The arab springl overthrowing the protest paradigm? how the new york times, global voices and twitter covered the egyptian revolution. *International Journal of Communication*, 5(0).

Kazi Saidul Hasan and Vincent Ng. 2014. Why are you taking this stance? identifying and classifying reasons in ideological debates. In *Proc. of EMNLP.*

Arti Jain, Shashank Tripathi, Harsh Dhardwivedi, and Pranav Saxena. 2018. Forecasting price of cryptocurrencies using tweets sentiment analysis.

S. Mo Jang and P. Sol Hart. 2015. Polarized frames on "climate change" and "global warming" across countries and states: Evidence from twitter big data. *Global Environmental Change*, 32:11–17.

Hamed Jelodar, Yongli Wang, Chi Yuan, Xia Feng, Xiahui Jiang, Yanchao Li, and Liang Zhao. 2019. Latent dirichlet allocation (lda) and topic modeling: models, applications, a survey. *Multimedia Tools and Applications*, 78(11):15169–15211.

Kristen Johnson, Di Jin, and Dan Goldwasser. 2017. Leveraging behavioral and social information for weakly supervised collective classification of political discourse on twitter. In *Proc. of ACL.*

Katherine Keith and Amanda Stent. 2019. Modeling financial analysts' decision making via the pragmatics and semantics of earnings calls. In *Proceedings of the 57th Annual Meeting of the Association for Computational Linguistics*, pages 493–503, Florence, Italy. Association for Computational Linguistics.

Efthymios Kouloumpis, Theresa Wilson, and Johanna Moore. 2011. Twitter sentiment analysis: The good the bad and the omg! In *Proc. of AAAI Conference on Weblogs and Social Media.*

Petri Kyröläinen. 2008. Day trading and stock price volatility. *Journal of Economics and Finance*, 32:75–89.

Chang Li and Dan Goldwasser. 2019. Social information with graph convolutional networks for political perspective detection in news media. In *Association for Computational Linguistics (ACL).*

Tianyu Ray Li, Anup S. Chamrajnagar, Xander R. Fong, Nicholas R. Rizik, and Feng Fu. 2019. Sentiment-based prediction of alternative cryptocurrency price fluctuations using gradient boosting tree model. *Frontiers in Physics*, 7:98.

Julia Magas. 2020. Truth about crypto price correlation: How closely does eth follow btc?

Sharon Meraz and Zizi Papacharissi. 2013. Networked gatekeeping and networked framing on #egypt. *The International Journal of Press/Politics*, 18(2):138–166.

Lesa Mone. 2019. I read crypto twitter for hours daily — here are the 40 accounts that really matter. In *ConsenSys Blog*.

Satoshi Nakamoto. 2008. Bitcoin: A peer-to-peer electronic cash system.

Helen Partz. 2019. Number of americans owning crypto doubled in 2019: Finder. In *Coin Telegraph*.

Tushar Rao and Saket Srivastava. 2012. Analyzing stock market movements using twitter sentiment analysis. In *Proc. of International Conference on Advances in Social Networks Analysis and Mining*.

Nathan Reiff. 2020. Why bitcoin has a volatile value.

Alan Ritter, Colin Cherry, and Bill Dolan. 2010. Unsupervised modeling of twitter conversations. In *Proc. of NAACL*.

Victor Sanh, Lysandre Debut, Julien Chaumond, and Thomas Wolf. 2019. Distilbert, a distilled version of bert: smaller, faster, cheaper and lighter.

Ramit Sawhney, Puneet Mathur, Ayush Mangal, Piyush Khanna, Rajiv Ratn Shah, and Roger Zimmermann. 2020. *Multimodal Multi-Task Financial Risk Forecasting*, page 456–465. Association for Computing Machinery, New York, NY, USA.

Jianfeng Si, Arjun Mukherjee, Bing Liu, Qing Li, Huayi Li, and Xiaotie Deng. 2013. Exploiting topic based twitter sentiment for stock prediction. In *Proc. of 51st Annual Meeting of the Association for Computational Linguistics*.

Dhanya Sridhar, James Foulds, Bert Huang, Lise Getoor, and Marilyn Walker. 2015. Joint models of disagreement and stance in online debate. In *Proc. of ACL*.

Oren Tsur, Dan Calacci, and David Lazer. 2015. A frame of mind: Using statistical models for detection of framing and agenda setting campaigns. In *Proc. of ACL*.

Austin Tuwiner. 2020. The bitcoin volatility index price and more.

Tiago Vidal. 2020. How traders can use twitter to anticipate bitcoin price moves, volume.

Steven Walczak. 2001. An empirical analysis of data requirements for financial forecasting with neural networks. *Journal of management information systems*, 17(4):203–222.

Marilyn A. Walker, Pranav Anand, Robert Abbott, and Ricky Grant. 2012. Stance classification using dialogic properties of persuasion. In *Proc. of NAACL*.

Robert West, Hristo S Paskov, Jure Leskovec, and Christopher Potts. 2014. Exploiting social network structure for person-to-person sentiment analysis. *TACL*.

Junyuan Xie, Ross Girshick, and Ali Farhadi. 2015. Unsupervised deep embedding for clustering analysis.

QUANTITY	INFL.	MEDIA	CO.
$10,000 - 99,999$	45	-	13
$100,000 - 499,999$	24	2	5
$500,000 - 999,999$	2	2	1
$\geq 1,000,000$	-	5	-

Table 7: Quantity of Followers Per User Account Type. Each row represents the number of user account types (columns: influencers, media, company) that have that quantity of followers who are actively tweeting about cryptocurrency.

MODEL	BUY	SELL	HOLD
NAIVE BAYES	57 %	62 %	65 %
RANDOM FOREST	82%	87 %	90%
RNN	85%	88 %	89%

Table 8: Label Distribution Results. The columns represent the accuracy of each label based on models using all the features of Section 4.1 combined.

A Appendix

A.1 Twitter Data Collection

In order to determine our Twitter accounts subset we narrowed it down to accounts that were associated with *crypto*, *cryptocurrency*, *bitcoin* and *blockchain* keywords. We only considered accounts that had more than *10,000* followers. Further, we segregated the accounts into three distinct groups *influencers*, *media*, and *companies*.

Table 7 presents the distribution of followers for accounts collected from the different types of accounts: influencers, media, or company. Column one lists the quantity of followers, divided into four groups. The remaining columns indicate how many of the influencer, media, and company accounts have the different number of followers. From this table, we can see that the majority of tweet activity comes from influencer accounts that have between 10,000 and 499,999 followers. There are fewer media accounts, however, these accounts have much broader reach. For example, *@nytimes* reaches up to 48.2 million people when tweeting about cryptocurrencies.

A.2 Annotations

For the annotation experiments, both annotators had different levels of experience in both investing and trading stocks and cryptocurrencies. One of the annotators was an inexperienced investor, who has never bought or sold cryptocurrencies or stocks. The second annotator is an experienced investor that has been investing and following the stock market for the past 5 years, and in the past 2 years has been investing in cryptocurrencies. Annotators were given a randomly selected subset of the Pre-COVID Dataset to label for supervised experiments for the day trading actions prediction. The reduced dataset for manual annotation has 798 unique tweets, covering approximately 1% of the total dataset. There are 114 different days represented, with 7 distinct tweets per day.

A.3 Day Trading Prediction Results

Table 8 shows the prediction accuracy for each label (buy, sell, or hold) for the three different models when using all features. We have also performed ablation studies for the features, which can be included with the final draft of the paper.

A.4 Somewhat Related Work

The combination of NLP and financial applications has been gaining interest in recent years. There have been three recent somewhat related publications working in an economics or financial domain. However, these papers are not *directly* related to this work and due to page constraints, we have moved them to the Appendix for now. Azzi et al. report shared task findings for sentence boundary detection of noisy financial PDFs in the First Workshop on Financial Technology and Natural Language Processing (FinNLP). Keith and Stent compare financial analysts' decision making with fiscal quarter earning calls. Finally, Sawhney et al. uses a multimodal text and audio attention model to predict stock market prices.

Extracting Economic Signals from Central Bank Speeches

Maximilian Ahrens
University of Oxford
mahrens@robots.ox.ac.uk

Michael McMahon
University of Oxford
michael.mcmahon@economics.ox.ac.uk

Abstract

Estimating the effects of monetary policy is one of the fundamental research questions in monetary economics. Many economies are facing ultra-low interest rate environments ever since the global financial crisis of 2007-9. The Covid pandemic recently reinforced this situation. In the US and Europe, interest rates are close to (or even below) zero, which limits the scope of traditional monetary policy measures for central banks. Dedicated central bank communication has hence become an increasingly important tool to steer and control market expectations these days. However, incorporating central bank language directly as features into economic models is still a very nascent research area. In particular, the content and effect of central bank speeches has been mostly neglected from monetary policy modelling so far. With our paper, we aim to provide to the research community a novel, monetary policy shock series based on central bank speeches. We use a supervised topic modeling approach that can deal with text as well as numeric covariates to estimate a monetary policy signal dispersion index along three key economic dimensions: GDP, CPI and unemployment. This "dispersion shock" series is not only more frequent than series that classically focus on policy announcement dates, it also opens up the possibility of answering new questions that have up until now been difficult to analyse. For example, do markets form different expectations when facing a "cacophony of policy voices"? Our initial findings for the US point towards the fact that more dispersed or incongruent monetary policy stance communication in the build up to Federal Open Market Committee (FOMC) meetings might be associated with stronger subsequent market surprises at FOMC policy announcement time.

1 Introduction

Understanding the causal effect of monetary policy on economic and financial variables is one of the most fundamental empirical questions in monetary economics. An extensive branch of literature focuses on this question; a key empirical reference is Christiano et al. (2005). In this theme, we address this pivotal monetary economics question, and in particular, the effect of central bank communication. Our research question is whether we can extract and measure policy signals, uncertainty, or shocks from central bank speeches.

Monetary policy shock identification: The starting point of any attempt to understand the causal macroeconomic effects of monetary policy is to identify the unanticipated, exogenous element in monetary actions to avoid endogeneity concerns. The literature on constructing these monetary shocks is vast. Some use VAR analysis (Christiano et al., 2005), others focus on the narrative approach (Romer and Romer, 2004), and, most recently, the emphasis has been on high-frequency identification (Gürkaynak et al., 2005; Gertler and Karadi, 2015; Nakamura and Steinsson, 2018; Gertler and Horvath, 2018). These are not all the same thing. Monetary shocks from the narrative approach, such as the Romer and Romer (2004) shocks, are exogenous to macroeconomic conditions but are not immediately observed outside the Federal Open Market Committee (FOMC); high-frequency surprise measures, such as in Gertler and Karadi (2015) represent the surprise for markets but may be endogenous to macroeconomics. As Ramey (2016) stresses, the focus on deviations from the systematic response of policy, or shocks, is "a search for instruments rather than for primitive macroeconomic shocks". However, essentially all approaches use changes in actual policy rates as part of the identification strategy. Empirically, though, there is very little surprise in monetary policy announcements: the average change in the Fed Fund futures market around announcements since the 1990s is only 2.7 basis points. To the extent that central bank communication between meetings

Proceedings of the Third Workshop on Economics and Natural Language Processing, pages 93–114
Punta Cana and online, November 11.

shapes expectations of subsequent policy decisions, it contains the true surprises. What is more, a pure focus on central bank meetings only provides a rather infrequent updating cycle.

NLP-based central bank speech analysis: In contrast to the 6-8 week frequency of FOMC meeting announcements, central bankers give speeches frequently throughout inter-meeting periods, oftentimes commenting on the economic and financial conditions as well as on monetary policy considerations. We therefore create a novel series of monetary policy shocks based on central bankers' public speeches; our key innovation is to use supervised natural language modelling approaches to map speeches into implied exogenous policy shocks. These implied shocks can then be used as instruments to identify the impact of monetary policy decisions on economic outcomes, or to explore the interaction of monetary transmission with communication.The main challenge to using inter-meeting communication is empirical; we need to map speeches, which are text documents, into implied policy signals.

Motivation - economic modelling approach: Our empirical strategy loosely extends on the seminal work of the monetary policy shock series by Romer and Romer (2004), who use the residual of a regression of the change in the Fed Funds Rate in each FOMC meeting on forecasts of future economic conditions as measured by the Greenbooks. The Greenbooks do not only contain numerical forecasts, as used by Romer and Romer, they also contain extensive text sections explaining and describing the respective forecasting exercises. We pair the Greenbook text sections with their respective numerical forecasts - focusing on three key dimensions: GDP, inflation (CPI) and unemployment. Using supervised text representation learning that jointly considers both text features as well as numerical features, we obtain text representations that map from Greenbook language to forecasts. This is where our setup substantially differs from the Romer and Romer approach or from a pure prediction exercise. We try to learn domain specific text features that have strong explanatory power over the target variables (the Greenbook forecasts), whilst controlling for the influence of other numerical covariates. The assumption here is that if there is any economic meaning captured in those text representations, they should be transferable to other related datasets. In our case, this would be the central bank speeches, for which we have the speeches' text but obviously no forecast figures, as their next update will only be disclosed at the next FOMC meeting. For each speech, we can then estimate a) the implied monetary policy signal on changes in GDP, CPI and unemployment forecasts and b) establish a measurement for the information dispersion across central bank speeches, which is an interesting economic measure in itself when it comes to assessing the effectiveness of central bank communication and guidance and its effect on market expectations.

Motivation - topic modelling approach: To construct the mapping from central bank texts to forecasts, we use supervised learning methods in form of topic models that can incorporate both numerical covariates as well as labels (Card et al., 2018; Ahrens et al., 2021). The key reasons why we opted for a topic modelling approach to represent the text features are that such models yield a reasonably high level of interpretability whilst working reliably even in research settings with relatively "small" datasets compared to more mainstream NLP applications with millions of datapoints. Supervised topic models, such as Card et al. (2018); Ahrens et al. (2021), allow us to learn the domain specific text representation whilst controlling for other numeric covariates such as macroeconomic and financial market conditions, which also potentially affect the textual content of central bank reports. The use of generative topic models can further be motivated from the economic modelling side. Generative models are akin to structural models in economics, and provide a complete description of the joint distribution of text, covariates, and dependent variables (policy signals in our case).

Our contribution: With this paper, we aim to provide to the research community a novel, monetary policy shock series based on central bank speeches.[1] We construct a monetary policy signal dispersion index along three key economic dimensions: GDP, CPI and unemployment. This shock series is not only more frequent than series that focus on FOMC meetings, it also opens up the possibility of answering new questions that have up until now been difficult to analyse. For example, do markets form different expectations when facing a "cacophony of policy voices". Our initial estimates suggest there might be evidence for it.

[1] available at: github.com/MaximilianAhrens/data/tree/main/central_bank_speech_signals

Finally, we further advance the empirical use of machine learning and data-science methodologies in economics.

2 Related Work

2.1 Economics - Monetary Policy and Central Bank Communication

In the introduction, we already outlined the different mainstream approaches on identifying monetary policy shocks (Romer and Romer, 2004; Gürkaynak et al., 2005; Gertler and Karadi, 2015; Nakamura and Steinsson, 2018; Gertler and Horvath, 2018). The monetary policy literature suggests there is evidence that central bank communication can have an impact on an array of different financial market instruments, for example see Gürkaynak et al. (2005); Boukus and Rosenberg (2006); Blinder et al. (2008); Carvalho et al. (2016). However, whilst some papers on monetary policy shocks consider the timings of central bank meetings and announcements, they tend not to look into the actual language content of the central bank communication. With the onset of more accessible natural language processing models for the wider research community, this has recently started to change. Bholat et al. (2015) introduced initial text mining and language modelling approaches for central bank communication. Shiller (2017) brought forward the notion of *Narrative Economics*, suggesting the importance of language-based narrative in forming public beliefs and emphasizing more systematic incorporation of information conveyed through language into economic modelling. For monetary policy in particular, Haldane and McMahon (2018) outline the importance of central banks' roles in shaping public narrative on economic conditions and uncertainties. Hansen and McMahon (2016) use dictionary methods and topic models analysing the content of central banks' forward guidance and find that it has larger effects on financial markets than announced views of current economic conditions. Ahrens (2018) extends the Romer and Romer (2004) shock series with topic features based on FED Beigebook to extract a more exogenously driven monetary policy shock series that reconciles recent empirical data with monetary policy theory. Ochs (2021) builds on this text analysis framework for monetary policy shocks as well and comes to similar conclusions. Hansen et al. (2019) analyse the Bank of England's Inflation Reports via topic modelling and find that communication plays an important role in shaping perceptions of uncertainty in long-run interest rates.

Some former monetary policy makers believe that monetary policy decisions hold greater weight with markets when the committee communicates a single message (Schonhardt-Bailey, 2013) . The open question is how should a central bank "communicate effectively and honestly" (Blinder, 2018) when the central bank has multiple decision makers who, naturally given the complex nature and uncertainty of the decisions, often disagree. While many worry about the effects of a cacophony of voices, there is no hard evidence on the exact extent or nature of it in practice. Compared with using the policy shocks associated with the announcements, our shock series is uniquely placed to address this cacophony of voices problem. Firstly, the cacophony arises most generally through speeches and interviews (individual member communications) rather than through the statements or even minutes; while the existing literature typically ignores the signals in individual member communications, they are the focus of our analysis. Yellen (2017) suggests that one of the main disruptive effects of policymakers' public speeches is the transmission of disagreement regarding individual short-run policy goals. Our shocks capture exactly this. We can use their range and variance as a measure of cacophony.

2.2 NLP - Modelling with Numeric and Text Data

We use a supervised topic modelling approach that learns a domain specific text representation that is optimized to predict the target variable together with other numerical covariates.

Topic models are a popular choice when it comes to incorporating text features into, for example, social and data science models (Gentzkow et al., 2019). Many topic models have built on the seminal work by Blei et al. (2003). Supervised topic models such as (Blei and McAuliffe, 2008; Zhu et al., 2012; Chen et al., 2015) allow to infer topics that are relevant for predicting a domain specific label. Topic models such as (Eisenstein et al., 2011) and (Roberts et al., 2014) take into account the effect of numeric covariates on the topic distributions but do not explicitly use labels to guide the topic discovery process. However, recent supervised topic models such as (Card et al., 2018; Magnusson et al., 2020; Ahrens et al., 2021), have combined those previous two approaches, which allow for jointly learning text representations and prediction parameters based on both labels and numeric covariates. Such topic model class is the most suitable for our research setup, where our labels are the numeric forecasts in the Greenbook section, which we want to predict based on their associated text sections as well as other relevant economic and financial indicators at that time. Card et al. (2018) have proposed such model (SCHOLAR) for classification tasks. Ahrens et al. (2021) propose a Gibbs-sampled alternative to SCHOLAR, BTR, as well as a regression extension of SCHOLAR, rSCHOLAR. We use rSCHOLAR for our work.[2]

3 Data

Our empirical dataset consists of two distinct yet related data subsets - the FED's *Greenbook* data and the *public speeches* of its central bankers. The first one comprises all numerical and text data captured in the 145 Greenbooks released from 1990 to 2013. [3] The Fed drafts a new Greenbook report about every 6-8 weeks in the run-up to the FOMC meetings. The Greenbook data contains numerical estimates on a multitude of contemporary economic figures as well as forecasts for several time horizons. Those numbers are accompanied by paragraphs which, for instance, put the forecasts into context and explain the rationale behind them. Different sections in the Greenbook focus on different economic and financial indicators. We use the provided separation by headlines and sections to obtain a granular mapping about which text passages pertain to which numerical figures. Our second data subset comprises textual transcripts of over 3000 speeches given by different central bank officials over the time-span from 1993-2013.

4 Topic Model

SCHOLAR (Card et al., 2018) is a supervised topic model that generalises both sLDA (Blei and McAuliffe, 2008) as it allows for predicting labels, and SAGE (Eisenstein et al., 2011) which handles jointly modelling covariates via 'factorising' its topic-word distributions into deviations from the background log-frequency of words and deviations based on covariates. SCHOLAR is solved via neural variational inference (Kingma and Welling, 2014; Rezende et al., 2014). However, it was not primarily designed for regression tasks. We therefore use rSCHOLAR, an extension by Ahrens et al. (2021), which incorporates linear and non-linear regression layer options in the prediction network of the model. As we don't further modify this model, we outline the generative process here and refer to Card et al. (2018) for more details on the model:

for each document $i = 1, \ldots, D$:

1. $\boldsymbol{\zeta}_i \sim \mathcal{N}\left(\boldsymbol{\zeta}|\boldsymbol{\mu}_0(\alpha), diag(\boldsymbol{\sigma}_0^2(\alpha))\right)$
2. $\boldsymbol{\theta}_i = softmax(\boldsymbol{\zeta}_i)$
3. $\boldsymbol{\eta}_i = f_{\text{gen}}(\boldsymbol{\theta}_i, \boldsymbol{c}_i)$
4. **for** each word $n = 1, \ldots, N_d$ in document i:
   (a) $w_{i,n} \sim Multi(w|softmax(\boldsymbol{\eta}_i))$
5. $\boldsymbol{y}_i \sim p(\boldsymbol{y}|f_y(\boldsymbol{\theta}_i, \boldsymbol{c}_i))$

where $\boldsymbol{\zeta}$ is the reparametrisation variable (Kingma and Welling, 2014), and $\boldsymbol{\mu}$ and $\boldsymbol{\sigma}^2$ are the mean and diagonal-variance parameters of the logistic normal prior for document-topic distribution $\boldsymbol{\theta}$ (Srivastava and Sutton, 2017). α is a Dirichlet hyperparameter for $\boldsymbol{\zeta}$. $\boldsymbol{\eta}$ are the topic assignments, $\boldsymbol{c}$ are the numeric covariates, w the words and $\boldsymbol{y}$ the label (or target variable). f_{gen} is a neural network for the generative topic modelling part. f_y is the prediction layer part of the model, which can be chosen to be virtually any form of adequate neural network structure. In our case, we focus on i) the special case where it is just a linear regression and ii) when topics and covariates are allowed to interact with each other through feed-forward layers. Regression network f_y and generative network f_{gen} are jointly optimized via backpropagation using Adam (Kingma and Ba, 2015).

5 Economic NLP Model

As described earlier, the model estimation process is broken down into two stages: 1) learning the mapping from central bank language to economic conditions, 2) applying the learned mapping to central bank speeches. This section will outline the estimation equations at each stage and for the three economic signals: GDP, CPI, and unemployment.

5.1 Stage 1 - Learn Mapping from Central Bank Language to Economic Conditions

In the first stage, we learn text representations that map from the FED's Greenbook texts to its forecasts. We categorize the Greenbook sections according to which forecast they pertain to. Subsequently, we estimate a separate mapping equation for each of the three distinct economic signals. For each of these equations respectively, the left hand

[2] https://github.com/MaximilianAhrens/scholar4regression

[3] Greenbook data is released to the public with a 5 year delay

side is the FED's Greenbook forecast for GDP, CPI or unemployment over the next year. We control for both the latest contemporary values of GDP, CPI and unemployment as well as the forecast values in the previous Greenbook report. The respective Greenbook text sections serve as the text features for which we want to learn their association with the corresponding Greenbook forecasts, controlling for the influence of the numeric covariates.

As an example, we show below the mapping equation for CPI, where the target variable is denoted as $\Delta\phi_{4:0,m}$. It represents the change in the CPI forecast π over the next year at FOMC meeting timestamp m. The target variable for GDP is $\Delta g_{4:0,m}$ and $\Delta u_{4:0,m}$ for unemployment. Otherwise, the equations for GDP and unemployment have the same RHS variables except that the text corpus is each time specific for the respective Greenbook forecast section, i.e. θ_π represents the topic mixtures for the CPI corpus. Similarly we have θ_g for GDP and θ_u for unemployment. $\theta_{\{\pi,g,u\},k}$ represents the kth topic feature for the respective corpus. In the linear case, we can write out the entire explicit regression equation for $\boldsymbol{y}_i \sim p(\boldsymbol{y}|f_y(\boldsymbol{\theta}_i, \boldsymbol{c}_i))$ from above quite easily as

$$\begin{aligned}\Delta\phi_{4:0,m} &= \rho_u u_{0,m-1} + \rho_\pi \pi_{0,m-1} + \rho_g g_{0,m-1} \\ &+ \rho_{\Delta u}\Delta u_{4:0,m-1} + \rho_{\Delta\pi}\Delta\pi_{4:0,m-1} \\ &+ \rho_{\Delta g}\Delta g_{4:0,m-1} + \sum_{k=1}^{K}\omega_k\theta_{\phi,k} + \epsilon_m. \qquad (1)\end{aligned}$$

The ρs and ωs represent the regression weights and ϵ is the measurement error. If we thought in the spirit of the narrative approach in Romer and Romer (2004), we could now divide the RHS of this equation into two economically meaningful parts - the 'policy preference' component and the 'policy shock' component. The regression parameters ω serve as the policy mapping from numerical (u, π, g) and text $(\boldsymbol{\theta})$ data features to the related central bank forecast. They represent the estimated 'policy preference' function of the equation. Under the assumption that the numerical and text features cover the relevant information space for the central bank to form its forecasts, the regression residual can be seen as the part of the forecast or policy decision that cannot be explained by the information accessible to the central bankers and therefore would be considered as some sort of an exogenous monetary policy shock to an observer. Our primary focus lies on identifying the policy mapping function rather than the classical Romer and Romer policy shock component. We want to identify this mapping and then subsequently apply it to central bank speeches. Equation (1) is being estimated with rSCHOLAR, which jointly estimates the topic mixtures and regression parameters in order to best explain the target variable.

5.2 Stage 2 - Apply Mapping to Central Bank Speeches

In the second stage, we take the estimated mapping from stage 1 and apply it to our central bank speeches dataset. We take the estimated regression parameters from stage 1, $\hat{\rho}$ and $\hat{\omega}$ as well as the estimated domain specific topic features $\hat{\boldsymbol{\theta}}$ and apply it to each speech. The numerical features will be the last Greenbook forecasts that a central banker will have had access to at a given point in time $(m-1)$, which is in line with the regression setup in equation (1). We then obtain (i) an implied monetary policy signal for the respective target variable, and (ii) a measure of signal dispersion by assessing the range of signals that central bankers convey during any inter-meeting period.

6 Results

The results section is divided into three main steps that build upon each other. In the first step, we assess the quality of our mapping from Greenbook texts to forecasts and the implied predictive signal for the different policy dimensions that we estimate out of sample in the speeches. In the next step, we then derive policy signal dispersion measures from those implied predictive signals. Finally, we use the calculated dispersion indices to estimate some initial market and policy transmission effects.

6.1 Estimating Implied Signals in Speeches

In the first stage of our model, we aim to identify meaningful text representation in the Greenbook dataset. The training has been done by splitting the Greenbook dataset into a training and a validation set.[4] We trained the models for 2000 epochs, however the validation set optimum was virtually always achieved significantly earlier. The K=20 model with interaction terms yielded the best validation set results across topic size (range 3-50 topics[5]) when evaluated according to minimizing mean-squared error in the regression part and

[4]Training-validation randomly split 80-20

[5]larger topic models (K>50) did not yield better MSE results and were therefore dropped from further analyses.

minimizing perplexity in the topic modelling part (topic compositions shown in Appendix A, validation set performance Appendix B). Table 1 shows the training set (on Greenbook data) and test set (on speech data) predictive R^2, which is defined as $R^2 = 1 - \frac{mse(data)}{var(data)}$. It reflects the percentage of explained variance of the respective target variable. The bottom part of the table shows that the model with numeric and text features fits the Greenbook validation /training data a lot more accurately than the purely numeric baseline model. Those results might be an indicator that our NLP model learned relevant text representations. However, purely judging on the training results does not yet give us much insight into whether these results might be a mere artefact of potential overfitting. When looking at the upper half of Table 1, we get assurance that our model did not just fit noise in the training data. The supervised mapping from Greenbook language to forecasts has been applied to the speeches dataset which had not been used at all as part of the training process. The NLP model substantially outperforms the purely numeric model. It explains 66% more out-of-sample variance in the speech data for the CPI target, 10% more variance on the GDP target, and 8% more variance on the unemployment target. All results are based on mean outcomes over 50 model runs per target. Figure 1 visualizes the actual FED forecast series (blue) and the predicted forecast values based on the speech dataset.

predictive R^2	numeric	numeric + text
Speeches - GDP signal	0.524	**0.577 (0.016)**
Speeches - CPI signal	0.346	**0.575 (0.039)**
Speeches - Unempl. signal	0.630	**0.681 (0.019)**
Greenbook - GDP training	0.502	**0.766 (0.080)**
Greenbook - CPI training	0.295	**0.790 (0.147)**
Greenbook - Unempl. training	0.458	**0.657 (0.011)**

Table 1: Predictive R^2. Models trained on Greenbook dataset, tested on speeches dataset. Best model in bold. Reported means across 50 model runs, standard errors in brackets. Numeric (OLS) has analytical solution.

6.2 Estimating Speech Dispersion

We can now construct economic signal dispersion measures, based on the estimated implied signals on future FED forecast changes on GDP, CPI and unemployment, which we derived from the speeches. For each of the three dimensions, we calculate the range of the implied signal for each inter-meeting period of the FOMC. This is simply done by taking the distance between the most positive and most negative speech signal. There are further ways to refine this measure that we are currently exploring, for instance, by weighting the signal according to an author-relevance metric. The FED chairperson's speeches might intuitively carry higher weight than other FED officials' announcements. Figure 2 visualizes all inferred CPI signals across speeches of all central bankers who spoke during the period of our data sample. Equivalent dispersion figures for GDP and unemployment are in Appendix C. Intuitively, higher dispersion in the signal conveyed by central bank officials could be perceived as a less united policy stance and therefore a higher degree of uncertainty about future policy guidance and decision making. In a next step, we compare our policy signal dispersion measures against two common market and policy uncertainty measures - the VIX and the Economic Policy Uncertainty (Baker et al., 2016) (EPU) index. Figure 3 shows how these indices compare over time. Our dispersion indices tend to increase in similar periods when also VIX and the EPU indicate higher market uncertainty. Furthermore, our dispersion measures seem to provide a more granular insight into specific monetary policy uncertainties. As an example, before and at the onset of the global financial crisis in 2007-9, there seems to have been a relatively high degree of dispersion in terms of the CPI and GDP stance. During the crisis however, the FED appears to have communicated with a much more united and aligned voice. In the aftermath of the crisis then, as some pundits feared a threat of inflationary pressures due to ultra-low interest rates, the CPI dispersion score jumps up whilst the signals for GDP and unemployment remain more united.

If we go back and look into the raw texts of the speeches at the top and bottom end of this CPI dispersion peak around end of 2008, we find that the speech that signalled the strongest "likelihood for higher future inflation/more dovish monetary policy stance on inflation" was given on 19th of November 2008 by Donald Kohn [6] who is generally considered a moderate dove in terms of monetary policy. In this speech, he quite clearly expresses his inflation policy view (full transcript of speech in Appendix D). He sums up his speech with the words:

"[...]In sum, I am not convinced that the events of the

[6] Former Vice Chair of the Federal Reserve.

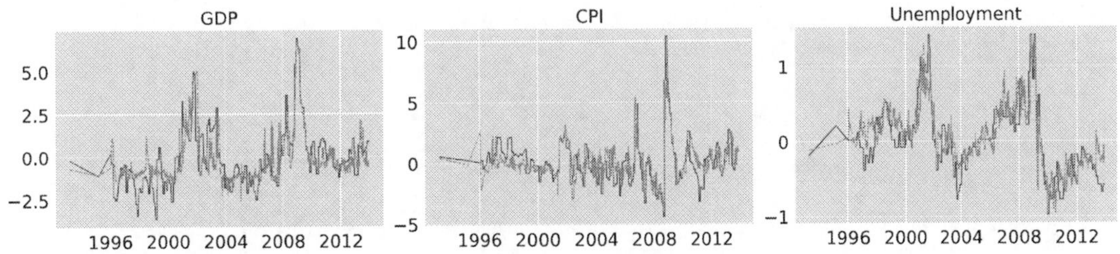

Figure 1: Out of sample implied policy signals: realised value (blue), topic model K=20 (orange)

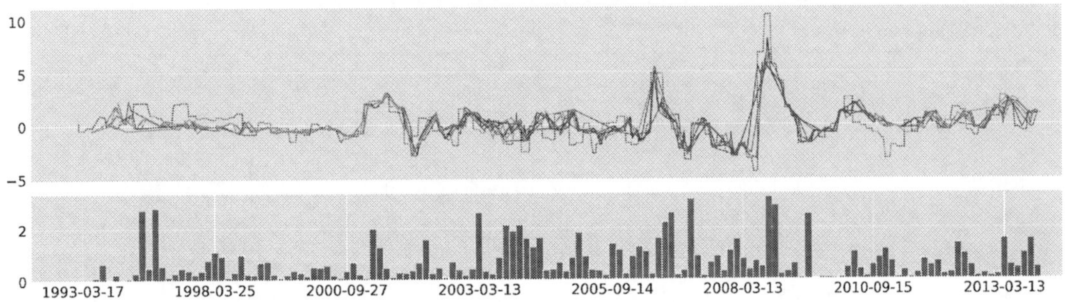

Figure 2: Out of sample estimation of monetary policy signals on CPI. Top figure: signal by individual central banker speaker. Bottom figure: derived dispersion measure (grouping window: inter-FOMC-meeting periods).

past few years and the current crisis demonstrate that central banks should switch to trying to check speculative activity through tighter monetary policy whenever they perceive a bubble forming. [...] For these reasons, the case for extra action still remains questionable, despite our having learned that the aftermath of a bubble can be far more painful than we imagined.[...] ".

On the flip side, one of the speeches perceived as the most "hawkish" during the same time window was given by Jeffrey M. Lacker [7], where he expressed his policy stance on inflation in his speech on 3rd of December 2008 with:

"[...]Since 2004, overall inflation has trended upward, and has been higher than I would like, over the last few years. [...]Many economists are forecasting relatively low inflation in the months ahead, on the grounds that widening economic slack is generally associated with declining price pressures. [...]I would be cautious about relying on it as a causal relationship. And while it may seem premature to be worrying about how inflation behaves after the recession is over, we need to be sure our policy remains consistent with a strategy that does not allow inflation to ratchet up over the business cycle.[...]."

6.3 Estimating Dispersion Effects

In order to examine the effect of FOMC members singing, or not, from the same hymn sheet, we use the three dispersion indices to create a variable indicating inter-meeting periods as characterised either by Cacophony or One Voice. There are many ways to define such an indicator but for simplicity, and to protect against outliers which would affect the standard deviation or range of the signal distribution, we use the interquartile range (IQR) for each of the GDP, CPI and unemployment series. We then average these dispersion series to get a single composite dispersion index; as an alternative, we average the two most-dispersed series, recognising that cacophony could be driven by different signals on only a subset of the three indicators. We then define a period as one of *Cacophony* when the series is above the median, and *One Voice* when below.

Figure 4 plots the Kernel Density of market surprises at the FOMC policy announcement after the inter-meeting period in which the speeches are measured. These market surprises are calculated using a narrow, 30-minute window around the FOMC announcement and, therefore, should reflect all market information priced into asset prices right before the meeting. The left figure is constructed using the average of all three signal series, and the right figure is based on the series using the two most dispersed signal series each period. Our estimates suggest that the periods in the run-up to FOMC meetings that carried a higher degree of

[7] Former President, Federal Reserve Bank of Richmond

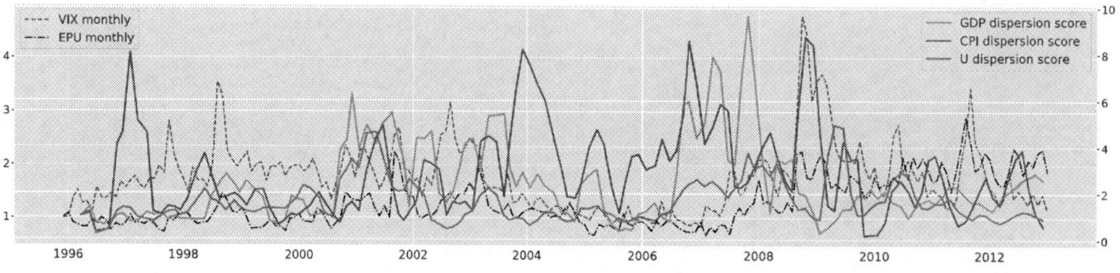

Figure 3: Dispersion scores for GDP, CPI and unemployment compared to VIX and Economic Policy Uncertainty (EPU) index. All indices re-indexed to beginning of displayed time-series.

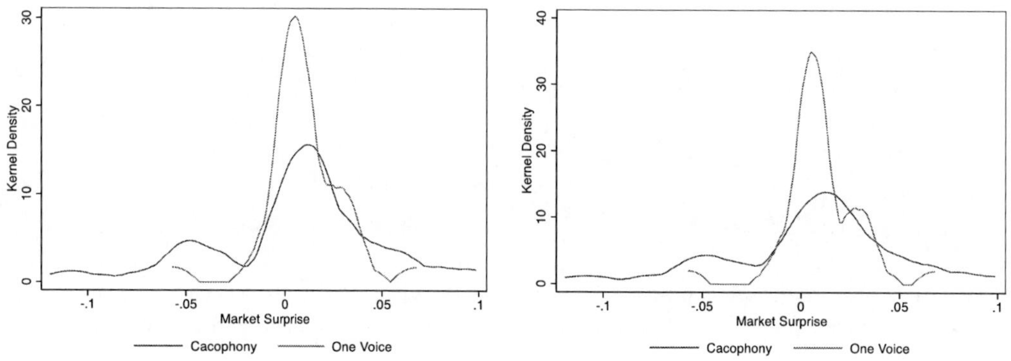

Figure 4: Kernel Density of Market Surprises when preceded by Cacophony (blue) and One Voice (red) for two different measures of the Cacophony Indicator - the left figure shows a measure based on above median values of the average of all three signal series and the right figure looks at just the two most dispersed signal series each period.

cacophony, are associated with larger market surprises at FOMC announcement time.

More formally, we run a simple OLS specification to see if our dispersion series can predict the market news. The specification involves regressing the absolute value of the market surprise on a number of controls, including an NBER recession indicator, the count of the number of speeches, as well as measures of market volatility (VIX) and uncertainty (BBD). The average signal for each indicator is also included. Table 2 reports the main findings using our two composite dispersion indices described above.

Cacophonous periods predict market surprises even when controlling for economic conditions, suggesting that our policy dispersion signals capture an important dimension of central bank communication.

7 Further Work

Further work on language modelling: We are currently extending our research work on the language modelling part to cover a larger range of NLP methods. This includes simpler sentiment analyses and word regressions as well as more complex fine-tuned general language models. By doing so, we aim to further refine and strengthen the central bank language mapping results.

Further work on prediction: Our current analysis focuses primarily on an approach driven by monetary economic theory modelling and interpretability in light of policy communication. We are currently extending our work into additional more prediction-focused applications such as mar-

Regressors	(1) Mkt News	(2) Mkt News	(3) Mkt News
Lagged Dispersion Index		0.019*** [0.002]	
Lagged Dispersion Index (alt)			0.014*** [0.004]
Controls	YES	YES	YES
R-squared	0.180	0.262	0.261

Table 2: Estimates of the effect of Cacophony on subsequent market surprise (Mkt News). Higher dispersion index implies more cacophony.

ket news analyses. For such exercises, we not only strictly divide the training and test by informational source but ensure that speeches in the test set do not predate Greenbooks in the training set, to counteract risks of information leakage. We will apply this approach across all applications in further versions of this work.

8 Conclusion

With our paper, we aim to provide to the research community a novel, monetary policy shock series based on central bank speeches. Based on a supervised topic modelling approach, we construct a monetary policy signal dispersion index along three key economic dimensions: GDP, CPI and unemployment. This "dispersion shock" series is not only more frequent than series that focus purely on FOMC meetings, it also opens up the possibility of answering new questions that have up until now been difficult to analyse. For example, is monetary policy communication more effective when communicated with "one united voice" to the markets and likewise do markets form different expectations when facing a "cacophony of policy voices". Our initial findings point towards the fact that more "cacophonous" policy communication in the build-up to FOMC meetings might be associated with stronger subsequent market surprises at FOMC policy announcement time. With our work, we hope to encourage and facilitate further research in this area.

Acknowledgements

Maximilian Ahrens is grateful for support by the Economic and Social Research Council of the UK (grant number ES/P000649/1) and the Oxford-Man-Institute. McMahon gratefully acknowledges financial support from the European Research Council (Consolidator Grant Agreement 819131).

References

Maximilian Ahrens. 2018. Natural language processing and monetary policy. *MPhil Thesis, Oxford University.*

Maximilian Ahrens, Julian Ashwin, Jan-Peter Calliess, and Vu Nguyen. 2021. Bayesian topic regression for causal inference. In *Proceedings of the 2021 Conference on Empirical Methods in Natural Language Processing (EMNLP) (forthcoming).*

Scott R Baker, Nicholas Bloom, and Steven J Davis. 2016. Measuring economic policy uncertainty. *The quarterly journal of economics*, 131(4):1593–1636.

David Bholat, Stephen Hansen, Pedro Santos, and Cheryl Schonhardt-Bailey. 2015. *Text mining for central banks.* Number 33 in Handbooks. Centre for Central Banking Studies, Bank of England.

David M Blei and Jon D McAuliffe. 2008. Supervised topic models. In *Advances in Neural Information Processing Systems*, pages 121–128.

David M Blei, Andrew Y Ng, and Michael I Jordan. 2003. Latent dirichlet allocation. *Journal of Machine Learning Research*, 3(Jan):993–1022.

Alan S Blinder. 2018. Through a crystal ball darkly: The future of monetary policy communication. In *AEA Papers and Proceedings*, volume 108, pages 567–71.

Alan S. Blinder, Michael Ehrmann, Marcel Fratzscher, Jakob De Haan, and David-Jan Jansen. 2008. Central Bank Communication and Monetary Policy: A Survey of Theory and Evidence. *Journal of Economic Literature, American Economic Association*, 46(4):910–45.

Ellyn Boukus and Joshua Rosenberg. 2006. The information content of FOMC minutes. Technical report, Federal Reserve Bank of New York.

Dallas Card, Chenhao Tan, and Noah A. Smith. 2018. Neural models for documents with metadata. In *Proceedings of the 56th Annual Meeting of the Association for Computational Linguistics (Volume 1: Long Papers)*, pages 2031–2040. Association for Computational Linguistics.

Carlos Carvalho, Eric Hsu, and Fernanda Nechio. 2016. Measuring the effect of the zero lower bound on monetary policy. Working Paper Series 2016-6, Federal Reserve Bank of San Francisco.

Jianshu Chen, Ji He, Yelong Shen, Lin Xiao, Xiaodong He, Jianfeng Gao, Xinying Song, and Li Deng. 2015. End-to-end learning of lda by mirror-descent back propagation over a deep architecture. In *Advances in Neural Information Processing Systems*, volume 28. Curran Associates, Inc.

Lawrence J. Christiano, Martin Eichenbaum, and Charles L. Evans. 2005. Nominal Rigidities and the Dynamic Effects of a Shock to Monetary Policy. *Journal of Political Economy*, 113(1):1–45.

Jacob Eisenstein, Amr Ahmed, and Eric P Xing. 2011. Sparse additive generative models of text. In *Proceedings of the 28th international conference on machine learning (ICML-11)*, pages 1041–1048. Citeseer.

Matthew Gentzkow, Bryan Kelly, and Matt Taddy. 2019. Text as data. *Journal of Economic Literature*, 57(3):535–74.

Mark Gertler and Peter Karadi. 2015. Monetary policy surprises, credit costs, and economic activity. *American Economic Journal: Macroeconomics*, 7(1):44–76.

Pavel Gertler and Roman Horvath. 2018. Central bank communication and financial markets: New high-frequency evidence. *Journal of Financial Stability*, 36(C):336–345.

Refet S Gürkaynak, Brian Sack, and Eric Swanson. 2005. Do Actions Speak Louder Than Words? The Response of Asset Prices to Monetary Policy Actions and Statements. *International Journal of Central Banking*, 1(1).

Andrew Haldane and Michael McMahon. 2018. Central bank communications and the general public. In *AEA papers and proceedings*, volume 108, pages 578–83.

Stephen Hansen and Michael McMahon. 2016. Shocking language: Understanding the macroeconomic effects of central bank communication. *Journal of International Economics*, 99:S114–S133.

Stephen Hansen, Michael McMahon, and Matthew Tong. 2019. The long-run information effect of central bank communication. *Journal of Monetary Economics*, 108:185–202.

Diederik P. Kingma and Jimmy Ba. 2015. Adam: A method for stochastic optimization. In *3rd International Conference on Learning Representations, ICLR 2015, San Diego, CA, USA, May 7-9, 2015, Conference Track Proceedings*.

Diederik P. Kingma and Max Welling. 2014. Auto-encoding variational bayes. In *2nd International Conference on Learning Representations, ICLR 2014, Banff, AB, Canada, April 14-16, 2014, Conference Track Proceedings*.

Måns Magnusson, Leif Jonsson, and Mattias Villani. 2020. Dolda: a regularized supervised topic model for high-dimensional multi-class regression. *Computational Statistics*, 35(1):175–201.

Emi Nakamura and Jón Steinsson. 2018. High-frequency identification of monetary non-neutrality: the information effect. *The Quarterly Journal of Economics*, 133(3):1283–1330.

A. C.R. Ochs. 2021. A New Monetary Policy Shock with Text Analysis. Cambridge working papers in economics, Faculty of Economics, University of Cambridge.

Valerie A. Ramey. 2016. *Macroeconomic Shocks and Their Propagation*, volume 2 of *Handbook of Macroeconomics*, pages 71–162. Elsevier.

Danilo Jimenez Rezende, Shakir Mohamed, and Daan Wierstra. 2014. Stochastic backpropagation and approximate inference in deep generative models. In *Proceedings of the 31st International Conference on Machine Learning*, volume 32 of *Proceedings of Machine Learning Research*, pages 1278–1286, Bejing, China. PMLR.

Margaret E Roberts, Brandon M Stewart, Dustin Tingley, Christopher Lucas, Jetson Leder-Luis, Shana Kushner Gadarian, Bethany Albertson, and David G Rand. 2014. Structural topic models for open-ended survey responses. *American Journal of Political Science*, 58(4):1064–1082.

Christina D. Romer and David H. Romer. 2004. A new measure of monetary shocks: Derivation and implications. *American Economic Review*, 94(4):1055–1084.

Cheryl Schonhardt-Bailey. 2013. *Deliberating Monetary Policy*. MIT Press, Cambridge.

Robert J. Shiller. 2017. Narrative Economics. *American Economic Review*, 107(4):967–1004.

Akash Srivastava and Charles Sutton. 2017. Autoencoding variational inference for topic models. *arXiv preprint arXiv:1703.01488*.

Janet Yellen. 2017. Remarks at central bank communications conference, ecb, 14 november 2017. `https://www.youtube.com/watch?v=DI7p-g5108g`.

Jun Zhu, Amr Ahmed, and Eric P Xing. 2012. Medlda: maximum margin supervised topic models. *Journal of Machine Learning Research*, 13(Aug):2237–2278.

A Appendix - Topic Compositions

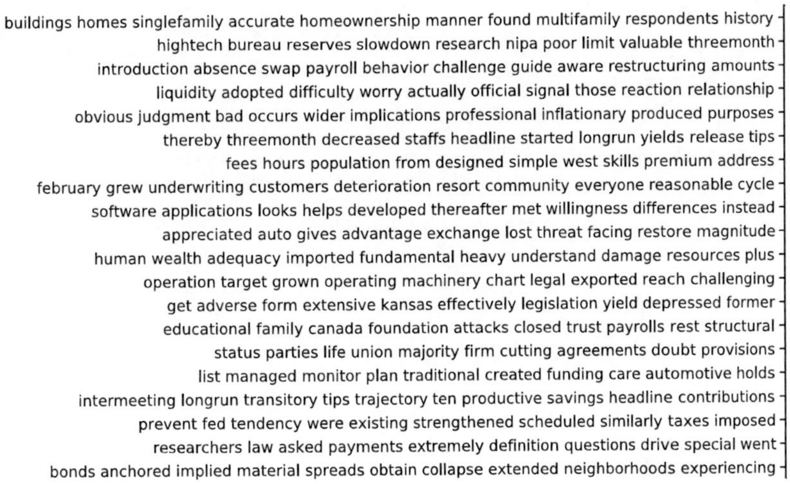

Figure 5: Top words for CPI model with interaction terms between topics and numerical covariates (K=20)

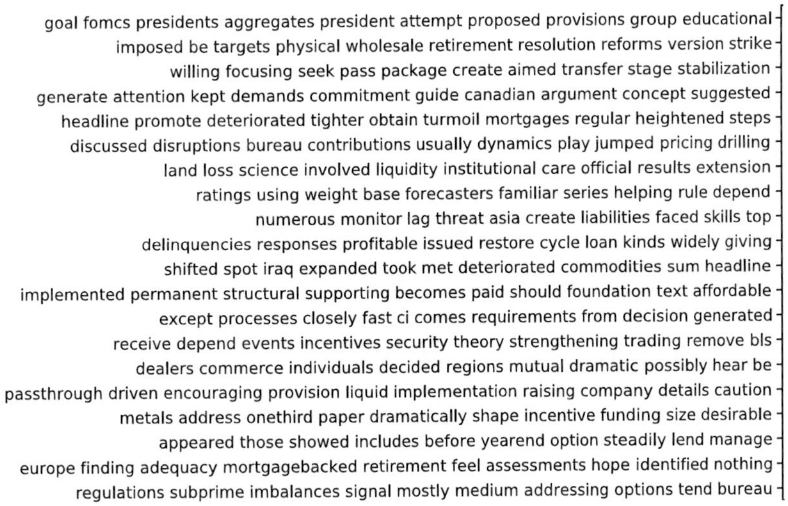

Figure 6: Top words for GDP model with interaction terms between topics and numerical covariates (K=20)

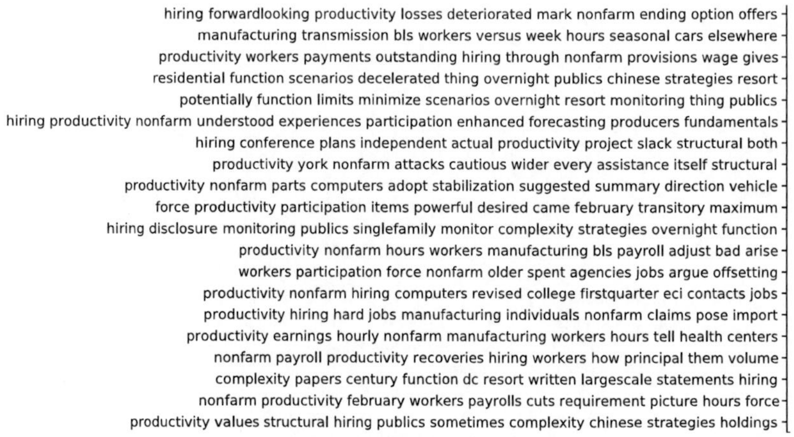

Figure 7: Top words for Unemployment model with interaction terms between topics and numerical covariates (K=20)

B Appendix - Validation set performance

Exemplary validation set performances for model estimation runs on targets: (1) GDP, (2) CPI, and (3) unemployment. MSE and perplexity reported. Optimal parameters correspond to epoch that yielded lowest validation set MSE. Max. epochs = 2000.

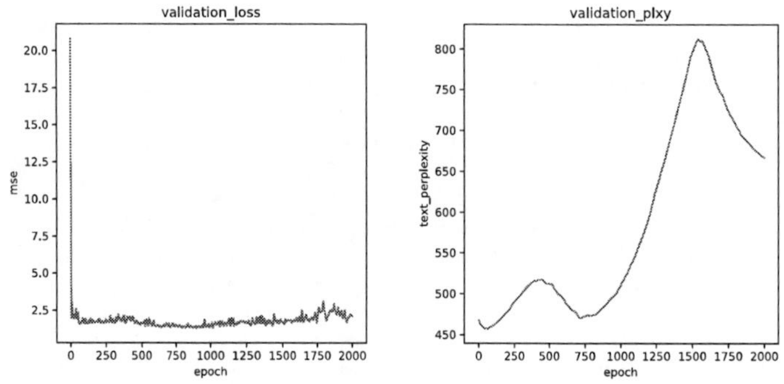

Figure 8: GDP

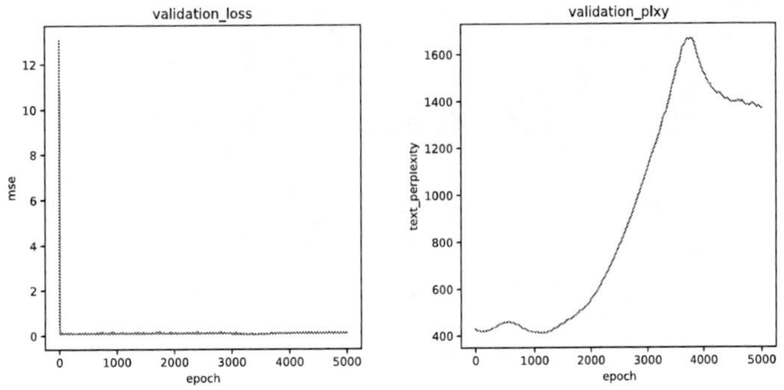

Figure 9: GDP

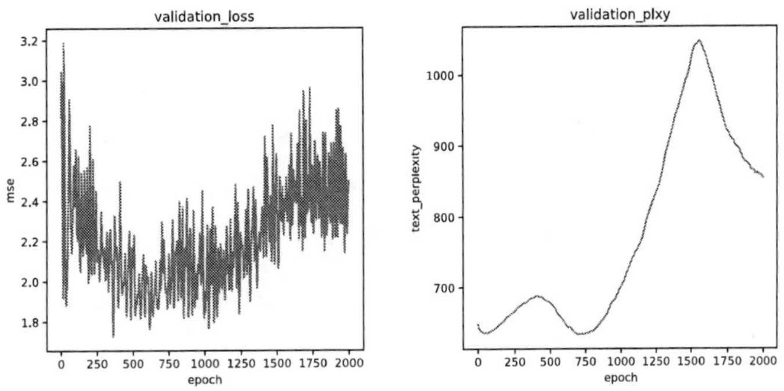

Figure 10: GDP

C Appendix - Implied Signal Dispersions

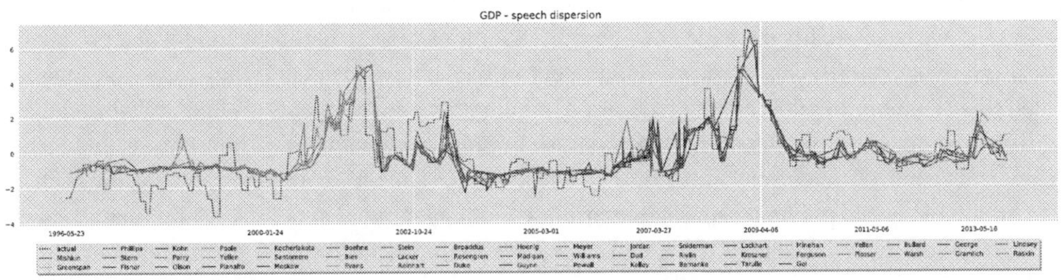

Figure 11: GDP speech signal by central banker

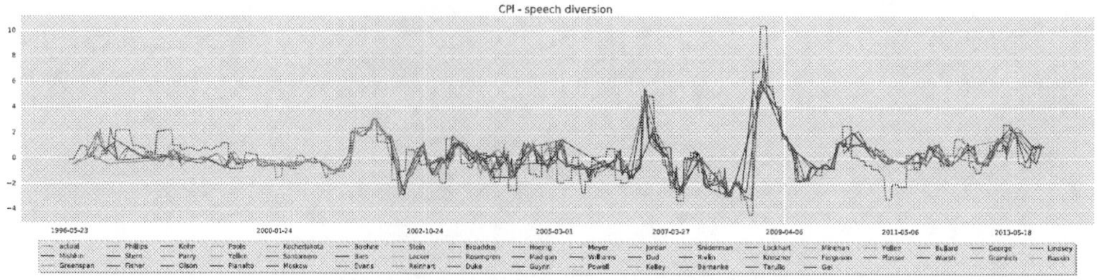

Figure 12: CPI speech signal by central banker

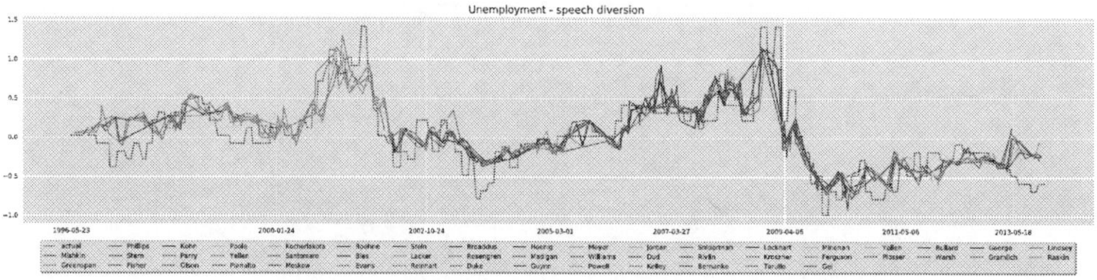

Figure 13: Unemployment speech signal by central banker

D Appendix - Central Bank Speech Examples

Speech by Donald Kohn, 19th of November 2008. Estimated as indicating a very dovish stance on CPI,given all other economic indicators at that time:

Vice Chairman Donald L. Kohn At the Cato Institute's 26th Annual Monetary Policy Conference, Washington, D.C. November 19, 2008 Monetary Policy and Asset Prices Revisited As you know, we are in the midst of a global financial crisis that is now weighing heavily on economies around the world. Although the outlook remains extremely uncertain, both the fragility of the financial system and the weakness in real activity seem likely to persist for a while. To promote maximum sustainable economic growth and price stability, the Federal Reserve has responded to this crisis by easing monetary policy markedly, and we have greatly expanded our liquidity facilities to keep credit flowing when private lenders have become reluctant or unable to do so. Other central banks have also cut policy rates significantly and expanded their lending. In addition, the federal government and governments around the world have taken extraordinary actions to strengthen financial systems to preserve the ability of households and businesses to borrow and spend.1 The current situation is so severe that it calls for careful review of how such a crisis evolved and how we can prevent a similar situation from happening again. This conference is a welcome step in that review, as it asks about the lessons we have learned, particularly for monetary policy, from the collapse of subprime lending and the preceding house-price bubble–developments that contributed importantly to the present financial crisis. This morning I would like to reflect on some of what I, in my role as a monetary policy maker, have learned from recent developments in the housing sector and, more broadly, in financial markets as a whole. In doing so, I will revisit the remarks I made in 2006 in Frankfurt at a festschrift for Otmar Issing.2 There I argued that a central bank facing a possible asset bubble would have to surmount some high hurdles before it would be justified in tightening policy beyond what the outlook for output and inflation would require, after taking into account past and projected asset price developments. In the aftermath of the collapse of the housing market and in the midst of the ensuing financial and economic turmoil, does that conclusion still hold? More time and study will be needed before we can be confident about the lessons of the current crisis. But to foreshadow the remainder of these remarks, based on what we know today, I still have serious questions about whether trying to use monetary policy to check speculative activity on a regular, systematic basis would yield benefits that outweigh its costs. I hasten to add that it is evident from the current crisis that much has to change on the regulatory

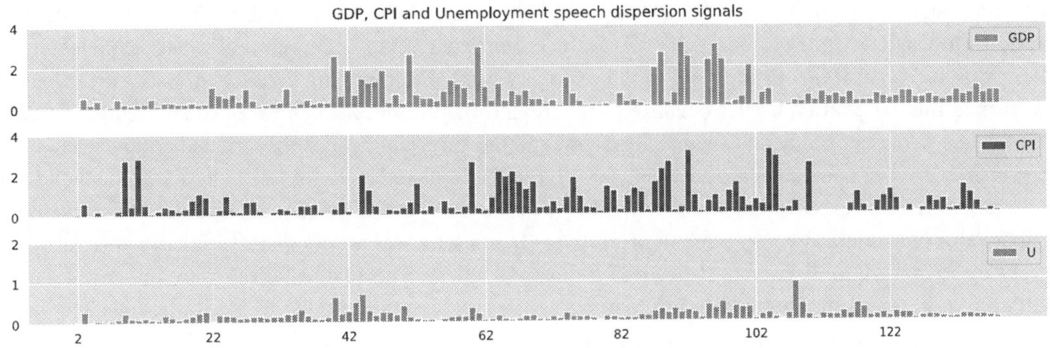

Figure 14: Signal dispersion across speakers (grouping window: inter-FOMC-meeting periods)

front. Governments around the world face the challenge of revamping the regulatory structure governing financial markets. And changes in this area, I believe, will prove to be the most necessary and effective at reducing the odds on another severe financial crisis. Today, however, I will focus on some of the lessons of the current crisis for monetary policy. Alternative Strategies for Addressing Asset Price Bubbles In my 2006 speech, I discussed two different strategies for monetary policy to deal with a possible asset price bubble–the "conventional strategy" and "extra action." A central bank following the conventional strategy does not attempt to use monetary policy to influence the speculative component of asset prices, on the assumption that it has little ability to do so and that any attempt will only result in sub-optimal economic performance in the medium run. Instead, the central bank responds to asset price movements, whether driven by fundamentals or not, only to the degree that those movements have implications for future output and inflation. This conventional strategy conforms to the Federal Reserve's dual mandate under the law and it has been our policy strategy; it also has been consistent with the practices of most inflation-targeting central banks. However, some observers have argued for a more activist policy than this one. Specifically, they have urged central banks, upon perceiving the development of an asset bubble, to take extra action by tightening policy beyond what the conventional strategy would suggest, with the hope of limiting the size of the bubble and thus the fallout from its deflation. Such a strategy, if successful, could deliver substantial benefits, and a number of central bankers have talked about the need to consider a policy of extra action on occasion, and perhaps have even implemented such a strategy. However, taking extra action also would entail some costs, such as creating, for a time, higher unemployment and lower inflation than would otherwise be desired. In assessing these two alternatives for monetary policy, in the 2006 speech I concluded that a strategy of extra action might be justified if three tough conditions were met. First, policymakers must be able to identify bubbles in a timely fashion with reasonable confidence. Second, a somewhat tighter monetary policy must have a high probability that it will help to check at least some of the speculative activity. And third, the expected improvement in future economic performance that would result from the curtailment of the bubble must be sufficiently great. Of course, we live in an uncertain world, and accordingly policymakers should always be open to the possibility that these conditions might be satisfied and that extra action would be appropriate. But my thought at the time was that, in practice, the likelihood of ever meeting the three conditions seemed remote. In the aftermath of the bursting of the housing bubble, however, the severity of the fallout might seem to call this judgment into question. So let's re-examine each of the three conditions and see what the current crisis has taught us. Potential Gain from Limiting Bubbles Let me start with my third condition, the potential gain from limiting bubbles, because this is where my views have changed the most. Although I was concerned about the potential fallout from a collapse of the housing market, I think it is fair to say that these costs have turned out to be much greater than I and many other observers imagined. In particular, I and other observers underestimated the potential for house prices to decline substantially, the degree to which such a decline would create difficulties for homeowners, and, most important, the vulnerability of the broader financial system to these events. In retrospect, I may have been unduly comforted by the resilience of the

U.S. economy to the collapse of the high-tech bubble, to the earlier Russian debt default and failure of Long-Term Capital Management, and even to the commercial and residential real estate debacles of the late 1980s and early 1990s (as difficult as that recovery was). But mopping up after this asset price bubble has turned out to be much harder because of its greater magnitude, the centrality of residential housing and finance to our economy and financial system, and the surprising ways obscure and complex financial transactions have exposed banks and other financial institutions to heavy losses. In addition, financial and economic linkages across countries have made this crisis truly global in scope, affecting both developed and developing economies. As a result of all these factors, the economic disruption here and abroad is likely to be considerably more severe than in past episodes. The severe fallout may indicate a larger potential gain than I had anticipated to leaning against excess exuberance in asset markets. However, realizing that potential rests on meeting my two other conditions as well–the timely identification of the bubble, and the ability of a central bank to materially influence the trajectory of the speculative component of asset prices. Identifying Bubbles in a Timely Manner As for the first of the three conditions, events of the past few years, coupled with advances in our understanding of how bubbles form and persist, have made me a little less dubious that policymakers can reliably identify a serious bubble before it bursts. However, I am still skeptical about our ability to detect bubbles early enough to make a general policy of leaning against them successful on average. The identification of bubbles in real time is tricky because not all the fundamental factors driving asset prices are directly observable; thus, any judgment by a central bank that an asset is overpriced is by nature uncertain. My views on this aspect of the identification problem have been reinforced by my experience during the inflation of the housing bubble. Over the first half of the decade, we saw a sustained, rapid rise in both home values and mortgage debt. As this process continued, concern about its sustainability grew and many observers started speculating that a bubble was in place. During this period, staff throughout the Federal Reserve System examined whether house prices were overvalued and arrived at a wide range of answers. For example, one set of models that linked rental rates and house prices indicated as early as the start of 2004 that the market was significantly overvalued, while another set of models suggested, even as late as December 2005, that house prices could be justified by fundamentals.3 Thus, controversy over the existence of a bubble persisted almost right up to the actual peak in the housing market. Because the economic consequences of mistakenly responding to a misidentified bubble are substantial, central bankers may be reluctant to take extra action in the face of such uncertainty, especially if they are risk-averse. Policymakers may also be reluctant to act because a bubble "call" might seem to require them to be more knowledgeable than market participants. After all, if at least some market participants perceive the emergence of a bubble, wouldn't they arbitrage that mispricing away? Recent research, however, suggests reasons for why market participants who think they know that a bubble exists still may not trade to eliminate it. For example, if some market participants recognize the presence of a bubble but do not know how common their knowledge is, they might reasonably expect to make the most profits by riding the bubble for as long as possible, with the goal of trying to sell the asset just before it collapses.4 Other research emphasizes that certain institutional structures–such as secured lending and delegated portfolio management–can create substantial costs in trading against an asset price bubble, so that even market participants who are conscious of the bubble will not find it profitable to trade against it.5 Together, these studies suggest that policymakers may be able to detect bubbles that will not be quickly arbitraged away, thus strengthening the argument for considering extra action.6 Nonetheless, even if policymakers are confident that a bubble has emerged, the question of the timeliness of the call remains. The essential problem is the timing of the detection of the bubble relative to the timing of its collapse. The risk is that the detection and subsequent policy response occur not long before the bubble collapses on its own. Given the lags associated with monetary policy, the resulting contractionary effects on the economy of the monetary tightening would occur just when the adverse effects of the bubble's collapse are being realized, worsening rather than mitigating the effects of the bubble's collapse. And the inevitable lags in detecting bubbles increase the likelihood that, by the time action is taken, speculative activity will have progressed to the point that its collapse is not far off. Thus, even if we could have known for sure that a housing bubble existed, and that tighter monetary policy would have significantly checked the unwarranted rise in home prices, policymakers would have had to make this call early on–at least a year and probably more before the peak in the real estate market in 2006–for such an action to have been beneficial. Ability of Monetary Policy to Influence Bubbles This brings me to the remaining condition–the requirement that monetary policy be able to materially check expansions in asset bubbles. Clearly, interest rates play an important role in determining the fundamental value of corporate equity, houses, and other assets. However, I noted in my earlier speech that the influence of interest rates on the speculative component of asset prices is unclear from both a theoretical and empirical standpoint. My views on this issue have not changed much, largely because of the still-murky role that monetary policy played in promoting the surge in house prices and the accompanying run-up in both conventional and subprime mortgage debt. Although tighter monetary policy might have succeeded in shifting down the path of house prices, it is still not clear to what extent small or even moderate policy actions would have discouraged the broader speculative developments that have characterized the current episode: overly optimistic expectations of price appreciation, excessive leveraging, and a marked increase in risk-taking by homeowners and investors. Of course, a substantial tightening of policy, leading to a significant slowing in the economy and rise in unemployment, might have had a marked effect on housing price gains. But undertaking such a policy course on a regular basis whenever asset price misalignments are detected would likely prove to be a relatively poor strategy on average, especially given the possibility of false positives in identifying these misalignments, and the existence of other potential remedies. In general, taking more-targeted steps–for example, regulatory changes intended to strengthen the financial system–would seem a better course of action under such circumstances. To be sure, some observers contend that the low level of the federal funds rate in 2003 and 2004 was clearly a primary cause of the housing bubble, and that a significantly tighter stance of monetary policy would have been warranted. As you know, the Federal Open Market Committee (FOMC), after having sharply lowered its policy rate during the 2001 recession, further lowered the federal funds rate in late 2002 and 2003 in response to an outlook for continued tepid real growth and a possible unwelcome disinflation. This accommodative stance helped set the stage for a more robust recovery, and as the expansion took hold in 2004, the FOMC began to tighten in a gradual manner that was publicly signaled in advance. How might these monetary policy actions have fueled speculation? Perhaps a low policy rate early in the decade, by stimulating housing demand and pushing up the level of home prices, incorrectly led households and lenders to extrapolate these price increases into the indefinite future. Overly optimistic expectations may have had an unusually stimulative effect on the housing market after 2003 because borrowing constraints were being eased by new financial developments, such as the growth of subprime lending and other nontraditional mortgages, fueled in part by investor demands for the higher yields on complex structured products.7 In addition, the increased use of adjustable-rate mortgages–which are more closely tied to short-term policy rates–may have initially boosted the stimulus from a lower federal funds rate. These stories have a certain plausibility, but a closer examination raises questions about monetary policy and the housing and credit bubbles. Although low short-term interest rates probably supported housing demand and home prices for a time–an effect that helped offset the negative effects on economic growth and employment of the steep decline in business investment–the role of monetary policy in fueling the speculation in real estate is still not clear. Studies that have tried to address how much monetary policy contributed to the increase in house prices during this period are inconclusive.8 And in general, the channel from interest rates to house prices has not been strongly established empirically, suggesting it might take a very large hike in the federal funds rate to have a substantial effect on real estate values.9 Moreover, if accommodative monetary policy engendered extrapolative expectations and speculation starting in 2003, why did it not restrain these factors after mid-2004 as the federal funds rate was increased? Tightening should have limited the extent to which households (especially those using variable-rate mortgages) were able to borrow, thereby slowing the pace of house price appreciation. Furthermore, many of the worst subprime loans were made after the federal funds rate had normalized, and reflected a wide array of deficiencies in the financial markets. The contrasting movement of short-run and long-term interest rates over this period further complicates any assessment of the link between monetary policy and the housing market. Housing demand and home prices are, presumably, most closely linked to the 30-year fixed mortgage rate and the expected average borrowing rate to be paid over the life of adjustable-rate mortgages. That these actual and expected loan rates moved sideways even as the federal funds rate rose suggests that other factors besides monetary policy were at work, especially since the FOMC clearly signaled that it would be returning the funds rate to a normal level over time (albeit at a "measured pace"). A good portion of the appreciation in house prices probably is due to the structural changes that were taking place in mortgage financing–specifically, the opening up of subprime lending and the expansion in associated securitization markets with its strong demand for mortgages from investors. Gauging the effects of expanded subprime lending on house prices is complicated by two-way causality–more lending can drive up house prices, but expected house price increases can also induce more lending. Undoubtedly, causality did indeed run both directions. But studies do indicate that an expansion in credit leads to increased house prices, and suggest that structural changes in mortgage finance likely boosted the rate of house price appreciation.10 Another key observation that must be reconciled with any explanation of recent events is that the run-up and subsequent decline in house prices was not limited to the United States; indeed, some countries have experienced even larger swings in house prices.11 In most countries during this period, long-term interest rates were low despite the fact that their central banks did not ease monetary policy as markedly as the Federal Reserve. A common factor behind these low rates, and perhaps in part behind the shared increase in house prices as well, is the "global saving glut" identified by Chairman Bernanke–the large amounts of savings, both official and private, from Asian and oil-exporting nations that tended to lower neutral interest rates globally.12 In a broader sense, perhaps the underlying cause of the current crisis was complacency. With the onset of the "Great Moderation" back in the mid-1980s, households and firms in the United States and elsewhere have enjoyed a long period of reduced output volatility and low and stable inflation. These calm conditions may have led many private agents to become less prudent and to underestimate the risks associated with their actions. While we cannot be sure about the ultimate sources of the moderation, many observers believe better monetary policy here and abroad was one factor; if so, central banks may have accidentally contributed to the current crisis. But would a somewhat tighter stance of policy in recent years have reversed this complacency? It seems doubtful. Central banks would likely have needed to produce recessions of some consequence in order to force agents to reevaluate the costs of taking on risk–an outcome unlikely to improve societal welfare. Rather than using the blunt tool of monetary policy to induce prudence, we should examine more closely the possibility of using regulation and prudential supervision to address concerns about overleveraging and other risk-taking behavior. In short, we still do not fully know what caused the run-up in house prices and over-building. Short-term rates were low in 2002-04 as the Federal Reserve countered the risks it saw to good economic performance, and these low rates probably had some effect on housing markets at the time. But the problems largely built up after policy rates were well on their way to neutral, and other factors appear to have played major roles. We have learned little about the likely effect that a somewhat higher funds rate would have had on the speculative element of prices. Of course, it is important to keep an open mind about the relationship of short-term interest rates and speculative activity. If it becomes clear that monetary policy can predictably influence the evolution of bubbles, central banks should take that ability into account when crafting policies intended to keep output rising in line with its potential and inflation low and stable. Conclusion In sum, I am not convinced that the events of the past few years and the current crisis demonstrate that central banks should switch to trying to check speculative activity through tighter monetary policy whenever they perceive a bubble forming. The recent experience may have made us a bit more confident about detecting bubbles, but it has not resolved the problem of doing so in a timely manner. Nor has it shown that small-to-modest policy actions will reliably and materially damp speculation. For these reasons, the case for extra action still remains questionable, despite our having learned that the aftermath of a bubble can be far more painful than we imagined. Some may object to this assessment, arguing that the current crisis is so bad that, in retrospect, monetary policy should have been appreciably tighter to deflate or forestall the housing boom earlier in the decade, even if that meant a substantially weaker economy. This argument has two defects. First, monetary policy is made in real time, not with the benefit of hindsight, and any evaluation of competing strategies for the systematic conduct of policy must be grounded in that fact. Although we must learn from history, we cannot implement policy strategies that assume more information about the future than we can ever have. Second, even if we ignore the fact that policymakers at the time could not have known what the future held in store if the funds rate followed the path it actually did, we also need to recognize that we cannot be sure what would have happened if policy had taken a different course. If policy had tightened appreciably at an early stage of the housing boom, say in mid-2003, it would have done so when the unemployment rate was still rising and inflation seemed poised to move to an undesirably low level. Such a course of action might well have created its own unforeseen consequences that we might now be ruing. This assessment aside, recent events would seem to have some implications for the conduct of monetary policy. For example, in light of the demonstrated importance to the real economy of speculative booms and busts (which can take years to play out), central banks probably should always try to look out over a long horizon when evaluating the economic outlook and deliberating about the appropriate accompanying path of the policy rate. The Federal Reserve staff has for sometime regularly provided the FOMC with this sort of extended-horizon analysis. In particular, the staff regularly generates likely paths for the economy over the next five years or so under different economic and policy assumptions; these scenarios often highlight different possibilities for the evolution of prices for homes and other assets. Note that the focus here is not a single baseline outlook; rather, the emphasis is on exploring the various ways events could play out and the implications for monetary policy. Another lesson of the current crisis is that central banks need to improve their understanding of the workings of the financial system, its vulnerabilities, and its links to the real economy. We must try to find ways to discern more quickly if financial innovation and other factors are leading to a buildup of destabilizing forces, such as rapidly rising asset prices or excessive leverage. Moreover, the unexpectedly rapid resonance of financial turmoil through global markets signals a need for further study of the complex cross-country linkages among lenders and borrowers, and the ways in which those linkages are influenced by such factors as leverage, interdependent counterparty relationships, and backup liquidity agreements. Finally, more effort needs to be spent on further investigation of the financial accelerator and other credit-channel effects, given the accumulating evidence that such effects can give rise to an adverse feedback loop between financial markets and the real economy. Overcoming these deficiencies in our knowledge will not be easy, but the potential benefits could be great. Finally, as I emphasized at the outset, we must thoroughly review the regulatory structure of the U.S. and global financial systems, with the objective of both identifying and implementing the comprehensive changes needed to reduce the odds of future bubbles arising, and improving the ability of banks and other financial institutions to weather the fallout from unexpected adverse changes in asset prices. Ultimately, this process should prove our best line of defense against the problems of the sort we now face.

Speech by Jeffrey M. Lacker, 3rd of December 2008. Estimated as indicating a very hawkish stance on CPI, given all other economic indicators at that time:

These are economically trying times. In my remarks, I would like to discuss the factors I see affecting the outlook for the U.S. economy and monetary policy. As always, I speak only for myself, and not for my Federal Reserve System colleagues.1 Financial market conditions loom large in any discussion of the economy these days. The heart of the problem, of course, is the home mortgages made from late 2005 through early 2007, near the end of the long U.S. housing boom that began in 1995. Since the peak in activity in 2005, housing investment has fallen by more than 40 percent. Average housing prices, as measured by the FHFA repeat sales index, have fallen 6 percent since their peak in April 2007. Some markets have experienced more dramatic declines; the home price index for California fell 18 percent, for example. The resulting erosion in home equity for many borrowers has meant that mortgages made near the peak of the boom, especially the subprime and non-traditional categories, are experiencing much larger losses than expected. It will take years of research to untangle the quantitative contribution of various causal factors to the rise in subprime mortgage lending and the increase in subprime losses, so I wont attempt such an analysis here. Let me simply offer a list of plausible suspects. One candidate is the wave of technological innovation in retail credit delivery, which contributed to an expansion of consumer credit, including unsecured and mortgage credit. As in any industry in the midst of innovation, this expansion may have involved overshooting and retrenchment. A second suspect is the regulatory and supervisory framework surrounding U.S. housing finance, which may have been insufficiently prepared for the possibility of a swing in housing demand of the magnitude and geographic extent that we have seen. Private sector incentives to foresee and protect against such shocks were to some extent dampened by the presence of the federal financial safety net, and perhaps by official policies aimed at increasing homeownership. In addition, the unscrupulous and fraudulent practices of some mortgage brokers outside of the banking sector may have contributed to the problem. I would also cite relatively low interest rates after the recession earlier this decade, especially in 2003 and 2004. Some economists have argued, with the benefit of hindsight, that tighter monetary policy during that period would have led to better outcomes by preventing core inflation from rising, thus limiting the housing boom and mitigating the subsequent bust.2 While I find this view plausible, again, further research will be required to substantiate this hypothesis. That's all prologue, however, to the turmoil that has plagued financial markets since the middle of last year, when the potential scale of the home mortgage problem became more widely appreciated. The turmoil intensified in mid-September this year, and volatility has been elevated since. Financial market participants have faced three major categories of uncertainty. The first concerns the aggregate amount of losses on mortgage lending. For mortgages made in 2006 and early 2007 the vintages in which losses are concentrated significant uncertainty still remains regarding total losses. Second, financial market participants face uncertainty about where the losses will turn up. Mortgage risks were split up and spread widely, both within the United States and in Europe, through securitization and use of the insurance capabilities provided by credit derivative contracts. As a result, financial market participants are understandably apprehensive about whether a particular counterpartys mortgage-related losses will erode their capital buffer enough to threaten their viability. This has led to elevated risk premia in interbank credit markets for institutions with at least some presumed mortgage-related exposure. Third, market participants have at times faced uncertainty about prospective public sector intervention.3 The disparate responses to potential failures at several high-profile organizations this year may have made it difficult for market participants to forecast whether and in what form official support would be forthcoming for a given counterparty. Shifts in expectations regarding official intervention may have added volatility to financial asset markets that already were roiled by an increasingly uncertain growth outlook. The striking feature of central bank lending during the recent turmoil is the extent to which it has extended well beyond the boundaries that previously were understood to constrain such lending, both in the range of institutions and the contractual terms on which credit has been provided. Intervention has been driven by a desire to prevent damaging disruptions to financial markets, and thus reduce the overall costs of the turmoil. While this objective is clearly understandable, central bank lending can create the expectation that similar support will be forthcoming when market disruptions occur in the future. Such expectations can themselves be very costly, because they can distort the incentives faced by, and as a result, the choices made by private-sector participants. The critical policy question of our time is where to establish the boundaries around the public-sector safety net provided to financial market participants, now that the old boundaries are gone. In doing so, the prime directive should be that the extent of regulatory and supervisory oversight should be commensurate with the extent of access to central bank credit in order to contain moral hazard effectively. The dramatic recent expansion in Federal Reserve lending, and government support more broadly, has extended public sector support beyond existing supervisory reach, and thus could destabilize the financial system, if no corrective action is taken. Restoring consistency between the scope of government support and the scope of government supervision is essential to a healthy and sustainable financial system. One option is simply to adapt our regulatory and supervisory regime to the new wider implied reach of government lending support. This strikes me as an unattractive option, if for no other reason than the current uncertainty about the outer bounds of that support. Constraining moral hazard in such a regime would be an immense and daunting task. I take it as given, therefore, that the scope of financial safety net ultimately must be rolled back. Note that it will not be sufficient simply to roll back the current lending programs when the economy recovers. The precedents that have been set during this episode will influence how market participants expect policymakers to react during the next episode of financial market turmoil. Establishing a coherent and stable financial regulatory regime will require rolling back expectations about how the policymakers will respond to the next financial market disturbance. Rolling back those expectations will be impossible if moral hazard concerns are always set aside in the exigencies of a crisis.4 Assessing the effects of financial market turmoil on real economic spending is not as straightforward as it might seem. One popular notion is that the credit market disruptions weve seen over the last year or so impede the financial sectors ability and willingness to extend credit to households and business firms, thereby creating an additional drag on spending. But causation can flow in the opposite direction as well. When overall economic activity seems poised to contract, the outlook for household income and business revenues deteriorates as well, and such borrowers become less creditworthy, all else constant. My reading of current conditions is that bank lending is constrained more now by the supply of creditworthy borrowers than by the supply of bank capital. The decline in U.S. housing activity since early 2006 has affected not only credit markets it has had a significant impact on broader economic activity as well. For a time, the weakness was isolated in the housing market, as the rest of the economy continued to expand at a relatively healthy rate. But late last year, consumer spending began to slow. Household net worth has declined as home prices have fallen virtually nationwide over the last year-and-a-half, and, more recently, equity prices have slumped. Increases in energy prices up through the middle of this year took a substantial bite out of real incomes. Moreover, payroll employment peaked last December, and has since shed 1.2 million jobs. As the labor market has weakened, wage growth has tapered off. Except for the temporary bulge due to the stimulus payments earlier this year, real personal income has steadily decelerated, and is now below where it was a year ago. Given this catalog of adverse developments for U.S. households, it should be no surprise that consumer spending was sluggish in the first half of the year and has fallen significantly in recent months. When household spending slows substantially, business capital investment is usually not far behind. Business spending on equipment and software fell in the first half of 2008, and the near-term outlook is not favorable. Many firms are facing dimmer sales prospects, higher funding costs, and more restrictive borrowing terms. The other segment of business fixed investment, spending on new structures, has been booming recently. In 2007 and the first half of 2008, real nonresidential fixed investment a segment that includes office buildings, hotels, malls and the like grew at a 14 percent annual rate. That category seems to have topped out over the summer, and is certain to decline in coming months. Foreign trade has added significantly to GDP growth last year and the first half of this year. Unfortunately, the trade contribution to U.S. growth is likely to decline in the near term in response to diminishing world growth prospects and the recent strength in the dollar. Two days ago, the National Bureau of Economic Research officially confirmed what virtually all economists already knew namely, that a recession began last December when payroll employment peaked. For a time, the decline was fairly mild in fact milder than the last two recessions, both of which were themselves mild by historic standards. But conditions downshifted dramatically sometime in September, just as financial market turmoil was accelerating. Since then, according to reports, many households and firms are taking a wait and see attitude, reducing or postponing nonessential outlays in response to a general sense of uncertainty about the potential meaning of these dramatic events for their own economic circumstances. A wide array of economic indicators has deteriorated markedly since then as well. Looking ahead, uncertainty about the outlook is greater than usual, though probably not greater than is typical for this phase of a business slowdown. It strikes me as reasonable to expect the U.S. economy to regain positive momentum sometime in 2009, for several reasons. First, monetary policy is now quite stimulative. Second, the energy and commodity price shocks that dampened economic activity earlier this year have subsided already or are in the process of doing so. And as Ive mentioned, the drag from housing seems likely to lessen in the next year, and in fact, I would be surprised if we dont see a bottom in housing construction sometime in 2009. This is the third straight year, however, that Ive been expecting a bottom in the housing market in the middle of next year, so my outlook is tempered by more than the usual amount of humility. While the downturn in real economic activity is going to pose challenges for monetary policy in the period ahead, its essential that we not let inflation drift from view. Since 2004, overall inflation has trended upward, and has been higher than I would like, over the last few years. Much of the acceleration we saw earlier this year reflected energy prices, however, and with oil prices down we have seen overall inflation subside in recent months. Many economists are forecasting relatively low inflation in the months ahead, on the grounds that widening economic slack is generally associated with declining price pressures. While this correlation is detectable in many datasets, I would be cautious about relying on it as a causal relationship.5 And while it may seem premature to be worrying about how inflation behaves after the recession is over, we need to be sure our policy remains consistent with a strategy that does not allow inflation to ratchet up over the business cycle. As I said at the outset, these are not the best of economic times. We have weathered economic downturns before, however, both nationally and globally. And there is no sign that the fundamental creative process that drives innovation and improves well-being over time has been mortally wounded. What sets this episode apart is the nature of the turmoil plaguing the financial sector, and the array of unprecedented government lending programs. While navigating the slowdown in real economic growth is a challenge, the larger and more significant challenge will be to re-establish the boundaries around central bank lending and public sector support and reconstruct the relationship between the public sector and financial markets. How well we meet this challenge will determine the extent to which innovation, despite the associated volatility, will continue to contribute to the effectiveness of our financial system and to overall economic growth.

Association for Computational Linguistics
209 N. Eighth Street
Stroudsburg, Pennsylvania 18360

ISBN 978-1-7138-9180-2